WELFARE TO WORK HANDBOOK

CENTRE FOR ECONOMIC & SOCIAL INCLUSION AND NEIL BATEMAN

FOURTH EDITION

Financial support and help towards
work for adults of working age

The Centre for Economic & Social Inclusion

This book has been produced by the Centre for Economic & Social Inclusion, an independent not-for-profit organisation dedicated to tackling disadvantage and promoting social justice. *Inclusion* offers research and policy services, tailored consultancy, bespoke and in-house training, and event management services.

Inclusion also produces the **Young Person's Handbook**. More information about this publication, and our other products and services, is available on our website at www.cesi.org.uk.

Neil Bateman

Neil Bateman is a nationally acclaimed author, trainer and consultant who specialises in welfare rights and social policy issues. He provides services to a wide range of organisations in the third sector. More details are at www.neilbateman.co.uk.

WELFARE TO WORK HANDBOOK

Financial support and help towards work for adults of working age

ISBN: 9781870563772
© 2010 Centre for Economic & Social Inclusion

First edition published in 2003
Second edition published in 2004
Third edition published in 2007
Centre for Economic & Social Inclusion
3rd floor, 89 Albert Embankment, London SE1 7TP

Design: www.origin8creative.co.uk
Printing: Cromwell Press Group

Disclaimer

Every effort has been taken to ensure the accuracy of the advice in this handbook. However, we cannot guarantee the information is completely accurate. This is because guidance is constantly changing. Furthermore, partners can only endorse the contents of their own chapter(s). As far as the authors are aware, all chapters contain correct information at the time of writing.

WELFARE TO WORK HANDBOOK

About this book

The Welfare to Work Handbook draws on the authors' expertise in benefits and welfare to work programmes to provide a reference guide for anyone involved in the welfare to work agenda or seeking information on the financial support and provisions currently available to those moving towards work.

This handbook is aimed at adults of working age. For information on financial support and welfare to work programmes available to young people aged 14 to 19, *Inclusion* also publishes the **Young Person's Handbook**. For further information on this publication, please visit our website at www.cesi.org.uk.

Acknowledgements

We are grateful for the contributions of the following people in producing this handbook:
Neil Bateman for expertise in welfare rights and social policy
Gary Vaux for advice on benefits
Kevin Ducksbury and **Michael Fothergill** for help with the Housing Benefit section
Chris Melvin for checking information on Employment Zones
Keith Povey of Keith Povey Editorial for copy-editing
Andy Mattock of origin8 creative for design and layout
Stuart King for indexing the handbook

We are also grateful for the contribution of the following *Inclusion* staff:
Erin Schwarz and **Rachel Fox** for researching and writing content, editing and proofreading
Polly Green for project management and proofreading
Paul Bivand for expertise on policy and programmes
Lorraine Sims and **Rosie Gloster** for expertise on policy
Rosanna Singler, Laurie Bell and **Lydia Finnegan** for researching and writing content
Dave Simmonds, Fran Parry, Jo Casebourne and **Craig Watt** for advice and quality control
Mike Stewart for advice on support for people with an offending background
Jade Onofrio for marketing, customer liaison and distribution

Thanks is due to former *Inclusion* employees **Liz Britton, James Holyfield, John Prosser, Beejal Parmar, Nicola Smith, Danielle Mason, Justine Roberts, Cait Weston, Ken Wan** and **Becky Shah**, who contributed to previous editions of this handbook.

Contents

3   Skills Health Check, Work Focused Interviews and Work Trials   146

4   Out of work and a parent   164

Foreword

The complexity of the current welfare system is partly owing to the myriad factors that cause people to be out of work, from redundancy to being a lone parent, from having a disability to being a problem drug user. Advisers and specialists may find that navigating the system is challenging and time-consuming, but this task is infinitely more difficult for individual claimants, many of whom are simply seeking financial help to make ends meet, and a pathway back to employment.

The Welfare to Work Handbook is intended as a reference guide for anyone involved in the advice and employment sector, or for any individual who is seeking information on the financial support and welfare-to-work programmes available to them in their situation. Unemployed jobseekers, lone parents, people with a disability or ill-health, carers, partners of benefit claimants, drug and alcohol misusers, homeless people and ex-offenders can all find useful guidance in this book, to help them on their journey from benefits to employment, or if they lose their employment. Plus, those who are about to embark on parenthood, are facing a crisis or bereavement, or require assistance with housing costs, will find relevant advice here about the financial help they can get in their circumstances. For people who successfully enter work, this book also covers the range of financial support and training available, such as Working Tax Credit, benefit run-ons and Train to Gain.

What's changed since the last edition of the handbook?

Since the third edition of The Welfare to Work Handbook was published in 2007, the health of the UK's economy has deteriorated substantially, and the welfare-to-work policy landscape has undergone major changes, some of which were introduced in response to the economic crisis. There have also been significant changes to the benefits system.

How to use this handbook

Information in the fourth edition of The Welfare to Work Handbook is generally arranged into customer groups, such as lone parents, people with a disability or ill-health, and people who are unemployed and seeking work. Some chapters of this book are therefore dedicated to the benefits and welfare-to-work programmes available to a specific customer group. Chapters for the three biggest customer groups (those claiming Jobseeker's Allowance, Employment and Support Allowance, or Income Support for lone parents) are written as a 'customer journey', complete with flow diagrams and tables to illustrate, to guide claimants along the path from welfare to work, starting at Day 1 of their claim.

Other chapters of this book contain general information that could be relevant to more than one type of customer. This includes information on in-work benefits and credits, the Skills Health Check, Work Focused Interviews, benefits for specific circumstances (such as maternity benefits and Housing Benefit), and appealing decisions about benefits and tax credits.

1 Introduction to welfare benefits and tax credits

This chapter is an introductory guide to the main benefits that are available to people not in work or working less than 16 hours per week. Some benefits are paid if you are out of work, others if you meet certain conditions (for example, if you have a child), and some also have a means test, which looks at your personal circumstances, income and capital. Some benefits can be paid when you are in paid work.

Most social security benefits are administered by the Department for Work and Pensions (DWP) through two separate services: Jobcentre Plus and the Pensions, Disability, and Carers Service. Two benefits are administered by local authorities (LAs): Housing Benefit and Council Tax Benefit. Child Benefit, Child Tax Credit and Working Tax Credit are administered by Her Majesty's Revenue and Customs (HMRC). Each benefit and tax credit has its own rules of entitlement.

The information in this section gives a general overview of entitlement. It is a complex subject and there are many exceptions to rules, and your circumstances may not fit the rules precisely. It is therefore important to obtain advice from a reputable, independent advice agency.

If you are receiving benefits because you are not in work, and you are thinking of taking up a job, it is very important to obtain advice about what the effect of this will be on your overall finances. Sometimes, people can find that a job does not pay enough, especially if you have high housing or childcare costs, or if the costs of taking a job (such as travel) are high. Jobcentre Plus is testing a guarantee that you will be £20 per week better off in work after reasonable travel costs. You can ask a reputable advice agency or the Jobcentre to calculate how your benefits will be affected by taking a particular job but, to calculate this accurately, the adviser will need to know:

- the exact hourly rate of pay for the job and the number of hours you will be working
- the expenses associated with taking the job (for example, travel to work, work-related clothing and equipment, and childcare costs)
- accurate figures for your housing costs
- the precise amount of any other income and savings
- your household composition and the dates of birth of anyone in your household
- any special circumstances, such as whether you need a lot of prescriptions, or have children who get free school meals or other educational benefits, which may be lost if you start working.

If you are a newcomer to the United Kingdom (UK), you may find that you are refused benefits because:

- you need permission from the Home Office Immigration and Nationality Directorate to be in the UK (you are a 'Person Subject to Immigration Control'), or
- you have 'No Recourse to Public Funds' stamped in your passport, or
- even if you are allowed to enter and remain in the UK, benefit officials do not accept that you have a 'right to reside', or that you are 'habitually resident', in the UK.

There is normally a right to appeal to an independent tribunal if you are refused a benefit and you should get help from an independent advice agency if this happens to you. Appeals have a good chance of success, especially if you attend the hearing and also have someone to represent you.

If you are subject to immigration control and, as part of your permission to stay in the UK, you are not usually allowed to claim 'public funds', you must get independent advice before even enquiring about your benefits at a social security or LA office.

Outline of the benefits system

The UK's social security benefits system is a mix of different types of benefits, each with different rules. There are contributory benefits with entitlement based on National Insurance (NI) records, non-contributory benefits with entitlement based on meeting certain rules of eligibility. (Your income, capital, or your NI record do not matter, though sometimes your earnings can affect the rules of eligibility). There are also means-tested benefits with entitlement based on detailed eligibility criteria and rules about income and capital. There are also benefits for employees that are administered by employers (such as Statutory Sick Pay and Statutory Maternity, Paternity and Adoption Pay).

Tax Credits are a form of income maintenance based on a mix of social security and income tax rules. They are paid by HMRC.

Finally, there is a range of education benefits administered by local authorities, and there are health benefits that can help towards certain health-related costs such as prescriptions. In England, these health benefits are administered by the National Health Service. In Wales, Scotland and Northern Ireland, the administrative arrangements for these benefits are different.

Some benefits are designed to complement others, so it is best to view the social security system as a jigsaw with interlocking pieces – entitlement to one benefit can sometimes be based on entitlement to another benefit. This is done so that particular groups can receive additional help (for example, people with children or people with a disability) and it is commonly referred to as 'passporting'.

Benefits at a glance

Contributory benefits	Non-contributory benefits	Means-tested benefits and tax credits	Employee benefits
Retirement Pension ■ ● ▲	Disability Living Allowance	Income Support *or* Income-Based Jobseeker's Allowance ■ *or* Income-Related Employment and Support Allowance *or* State Pension Credit *and* Child Tax Credit *and/or* Working Tax Credit Housing Benefit Council Tax Benefit Health benefits Social Fund Education benefits	Statutory Sick Pay ▶
Employment and Support Allowance or Incapacity Benefit ■ ● ▲	Attendance Allowance		Statutory Maternity Pay ▶
Jobseeker's Allowance ■ ▲	Child Benefit		Statutory Paternity Pay ▶
Maternity Allowance ▲	Industrial injury benefits		Statutory Adoption Pay ▶
Bereavement Allowance ▲	War pensions		
Widowed Parent's Allowance ▲ ●	Carer's Allowance ▲ ●		
	Employment and Support Allowance or Incapacity Benefit (non-contributory)/ Severe Disablement Allowance ● ■ ▲		

■ There are both contributory and non-contributory versions of these.

● There are Child Dependency Additions to these benefits, but only for people receiving them before 7 April 2003. Claims made after this date will be treated as a claim for Child Tax Credit.

▲ These benefits are covered by the overlapping benefits rules. This means that you can only receive the highest of whichever benefit you qualify for.

▶ You can only receive one of these at any one time.

Who is entitled to which benefits?

The following list is a broad indication of the various benefits available to different groups of people. People often receive a combination of benefits and may be unclear about which benefits they receive. People must meet the conditions of entitlement for each benefit or tax credit, so you may not qualify for each benefit under the category you fit into on this chart.

Benefits and beneficiaries

Older people (aged 60+)	Sickness or disability	Carers
Retirement Pension	Statutory Sick Pay or Employment and Support Allowance	Carer's Allowance
Attendance Allowance		Income Support
and/or	*or*	Child Tax Credit
Disability Living Allowance	Incapacity Benefit	Housing Benefit
Pension Credit	Disability Living Allowance	Council Tax Benefit
Housing Benefit	Income Support	Health benefits
Council Tax Benefit	Housing Benefit	Education benefits
Carer's Allowance	Council Tax Benefit	
Bereavement Allowance	Industrial injury benefits	
Health benefits	War Pension or Armed Forces Compensation Scheme	
Education benefits		
Winter Fuel Payment	Child Tax Credit	
Jobseeker's Allowance (up to age 64)	Working Tax Credit	
	Health benefits	
	Education benefits	

Unemployed or part-time work (less than 16 hours per week)	Full-time work (more than 16 hours per week)	People with children	Bereavement
Jobseeker's Allowance	Working Tax Credit	Child Benefit	Bereavement Allowance/Widow's Pension
Income Support (if you're not required to be available for work and to sign on for work (for example, lone parents with a child under age 12)	Child Tax Credit	Child Tax Credit	Widowed Parent's Allowance/
	Housing Benefit	Working Tax Credit	Widowed Mother's Allowance
	Council Tax Benefit	Education benefits	Bereavement Payment
	Health benefits	Health benefits	Income Support
Child Tax Credit	Education benefits	All other benefits	Housing Benefit
Housing Benefit			Council Tax Benefit
Council Tax Benefit			Child Tax Credit
Health benefits			Working Tax Credit
Education benefits			

Making benefit claims

You can make claims for some benefits by using claims forms that are available from Jobcentre Plus offices or the DWP website: www.dwp.gov.uk/eservice/#. Tax credits can also be claimed by using the forms on the HMRC website: www.hmrc.gov.uk. Alternatively, you can start the claim by making a phone call to the relevant organisation.

For certain benefits – Jobseeker's Allowance (JSA), Income Support (IS), and Employment and Support Allowance (ESA) – you can start the claim by phoning Jobcentre Plus on 0800 055 6688 (between 8am and 6pm on Monday to Friday). A textphone service is available on 0800 023 4888 if you have a speech or hearing impairment. Make sure that your claim is dated from your first call.

If you cannot use the phone to make a claim, or if you would prefer not to use the phone, you can ask for a 'clerical claim' form to complete and send in, or you can use a form downloaded from the DWP website and send it in. Do not let the DWP staff put you off, if you prefer to claim on paper rather than by phone. The law does not stipulate that benefit claims must be made by phone.[1]

When you make a benefit claim, you are required to:

- provide your NI Number, or
- provide information to enable your NI Number to be located, or
- apply for an NI Number.[2]

There can be delays in obtaining an NI Number and, if this holds up your benefit claim, you should ask for an interim payment of the benefit you have claimed.[3] If this is refused, seek independent advice.

If there is a delay in processing your benefit claim, you can ask for an interim payment to be made. Jobcentre Plus has targets to process claims in 11.5 days for JSA and 10 days for IS. For DWP benefits, there is discretion to make an interim payment if your claim has been delayed,[4] but if you are a private tenant (including a Housing Association tenant), the LA must make an interim payment if they cannot process your claim, unless they have asked you for information or evidence that they reasonably require and you have failed 'without good cause' to supply this information.[5]

Most DWP benefits are paid weekly. However, from April 2009 people who make new claims for these benefits will be paid fortnightly and everyone else will gradually be moved onto fortnightly payments by 2011. The day of the week on which you are paid depends on the last two digits of your NI Number.

Housing Benefit is paid weekly unless you are a private tenant (including a Housing Association tenant), when it will be paid monthly, four-weekly, fortnightly or weekly, depending on your reasonable needs and convenience (consideration is given to when your rent is due). Many local authorities do not make it widely known that you can be paid at different intervals and only offer one payment arrangement.[6]

Endnotes

[1] Reg. 4(1) Social Security (Claims and Payments) Regulations 1987.

[2] S 1(1A) and (1B) Social Security Administration Act 1992, and Reg. 2A Income Support (General) Regulations 1987.

[3] Reg. 2(1) Social Security (Payments on Account, Overpayments and Recovery) Regulations 1988.

[4] Reg. 2 Social Security (Payments on Account, Overpayments and Recovery) Regulations 1988.

[5] Reg. 93 Housing Benefit Regulations 2006.

[6] Reg. 92 Housing Benefit Regulations 2006.

1

2 Unemployed and claiming Jobseeker's Allowance

Jobseeker's Allowance

What is Jobseeker's Allowance?

Jobseeker's Allowance (JSA) is a benefit for people who are either not working, or are working fewer than 16 hours per week on average. To claim JSA, you must be aged between 18 and 60 if you are a woman, or aged between 18 and 65 if you are a man. Young people aged 16 or 17 can only get JSA under certain conditions – see The Young Person's Handbook by the Centre for Economic and Social Inclusion for more details.

Customer journey chart for Jobseeker's Allowance

The following chart depicts the journey that JSA claimants can expect to take on their claim.

Customer journey chart for Jobseeker's Allowance

1. Call Jobcentre Plus

Call 0800 055 6688 to start your claim.

If you have speech or hearing difficulties, you can use textphone 0800 023 4888.

Or, you can start your claim online at www.dwp.gov.uk/eservice or by downloading a claim form.

Try to have at hand details of:

- your National Insurance number
- your rent or mortgage charges
- your past or present employer
- income and savings
- other adults who live in your house.

You will be given a date for your first interview and the person you speak to will tell you what to bring along (see page 29).

↓

2. Visit Jobcentre Plus

Within about two weeks of calling Jobcentre Plus, you will have your first face-to-face interview, where you will draw up a Jobseeker's Agreement with your adviser (see page 29).

You will be given a copy of your agreement and a log where you fill in your jobseeking actions (see page 49).

Try to take with you to your first interview:

- Your P45 and P46 from your last employer
- National Insurance Number
- a payslip
- any letters from Social Security
- anything else you have been told to bring.

You cannot get Jobseeker's Allowance if you have not signed a Jobseeker's Agreement.

↓

3. Signing on and jobsearch

For Weeks 2 to 13 of your claim, you will need to visit Jobcentre Plus once per fortnight to sign on and get your payment. You will keep a log of your jobseeking actions during the two weeks between each visit (see page 49), and this log will be reviewed when you sign on.

↓

4. Back to Work session

You may be asked to attend a Back to Work session about 6 weeks into claiming Jobseeker's Allowance (see page 31).

↓

5. Review meeting

Once you have been claiming for 13 weeks, you will attend a review meeting with your adviser, in addition to your regular fortnightly jobsearch reviews. Your adviser will go over your Jobseeker's Agreement with you (see page 31).

You should sign on once a week to get your payment (see page 32).

↓

6. Directed jobsearch

For six weeks after your review meeting, you will sign on weekly instead of fortnightly. This period is called 'directed jobsearch' (see page 32)

↓

7. Restart Interview

When you have been claiming JSA for 26 weeks, you will attend a Restart Interview with your personal adviser, in addition to your regular jobsearch reviews (see page 33).

↓

8. Frequent follow-up meetings

After your Restart Interview, you will attend weekly meetings with your adviser for 6 weeks. They will help you to draw up a personal action plan (see page 33).

↓

9. Months 6 to 12 – Supported Jobsearch

You will meet with your personal adviser regularly.

You will need to do more than two jobsearch actions per week during this time (see page 35). You will also take part in one to three mandatory employability activities (see page 35)

↓

10. Months 6 to 24 – Employment programmes

You will be required to take part in Flexible New Deal (after 12 months of claiming; see page 77), the Young Person's Guarantee (from 10 months; see page 82), jobs through the Future Jobs Fund (after 6 to 12 months; see page 64), New Deal for Young People (after 6 months of claiming; see page 85), New Deal for 25 Plus (after 18 months of claiming; see page 95), or Employment Zones (see page 103).

Day 1 of your Jobseeker's Allowance claim

If you want to claim JSA, your first step is to call Jobcentre Plus on 0800 055 6688 for a short initial interview. They should offer to phone you back – this is very important if you need to use a mobile phone because calls to 0800 number can be very expensive. If they do not offer to phone you back, you should ask them to do so. They will take initial details and give you a date for your first face-to-face interview. Alternatively, you can make a claim online at www.dwp.gov.uk/eservice or by completing a letter or a paper claim form – the law does not require that all claims must be done by phone. When you call Jobcentre Plus, you should have the following things at hand:[1]

- your National Insurance (NI) Number
- your rent or mortgage charges, and any service charges you pay for your accommodation
- details of your past or present employer
- details of your income and savings
- details of any other adults who live in your home.

For your claim to be successful, you will have to meet the JSA eligibility rules. There are two different kinds of JSA: Contribution-Based JSA (CJSA) and Income-Based JSA (IBJSA). Both types of JSA share some basic eligibility rules, but each type has its own specific rules that you will have to meet as well.

You will meet the basic eligibility rules if you are:

- aged under 60 (for women) or under 65 (for men)
- not working, or working for fewer than 16 hours per week
- capable of work
- available for work
- actively seeking work, and
- resident in the UK.

Being available for work does not only mean that you are willing immediately to accept any work that is offered to you, it also means you are able to work a certain number of days or hours each week. Usually, you must be able to work for 40 hours per week to be deemed 'available' and get your JSA payments, although this rule is not set in stone. 'Actively' seeking work means that you are taking at least two steps each week to find a job. These steps can include such things as oral or written job applications, drawing up a CV, searching for job vacancies, and making a list of employers to contact about the possibility of a job, among other things. For a more detailed explanation of these rules, and their exceptions, see page 40.

Keep in mind that you may not be eligible for JSA if you:

- are studying full-time (see page 55, for exceptions), or
- received pay in lieu of notice when your job ended.

Contribution-Based JSA is a short-term benefit, available for up to 28 weeks. Eligibility is based on your NI contribution record, so you can only get CJSA if you have paid (or have been treated as paying) NI contributions in the past. See page 58, for more information about CJSA.

Income-Based JSA is a means-tested benefit, so eligibility depends on your capital and savings, and the circumstances of you (and your partner, if you have one). To qualify for IBJSA, not only must you work for fewer than 16 hours per week but, if you have a partner, they should also work for fewer than 24 hours per week.[2] So, you may be able to get IBJSA if you are on a low income. Depending on your circumstances, you may qualify for IBJSA either from the start of your claim or later in your claim. See page 60, for more information about IBJSA.

Weeks 1 to 2 of your Jobseeker's Allowance claim – new jobseeker interview

Within about two weeks of contacting Jobcentre Plus to start your claim, you will have your first face-to-face interview with a personal adviser. If you need money quickly, you should ask for an interview sooner than this. This is called a 'new jobseeker interview'. The adviser will:

- outline some of the rules for JSA
- discuss the kinds of work you are looking for
- give you information about jobs, training and other opportunities
- draw up a Jobseeker's Agreement with you, and
- give you a log where you will write down the jobsearch steps you take each week.

The adviser should also talk to you about the extra help you can get to overcome job-hunting difficulties. Support will depend on your circumstances and where you live, but could include:[3]

- specialist help for things such as drawing up a CV, preparing for interviews, and building your confidence and work skills
- help to look for work, if you haven't experienced jobsearch for some time
- help to look for professional or executive jobs, if this is relevant to you
- help with basic skills such as reading, maths or English language
- opportunity for skills development, linked to local job vacancies
- help with one-off expenses so that you can get back to work quickly, such as the cost of buying formal clothes for an interview, or the cost of basic tools you need to take up a job
- help to cover travel costs to job interviews outside your local area through the Travel to Interview scheme.

Try to bring relevant evidence and information to your interview (for example, letters about your last employment ending, your P45, and proof of income and savings if you are making a claim for IBJSA). You will be told what documentation you need to bring. Do not delay your interview if you do not have all of the information at hand, because you can send it later.

Jobcentre Plus can arrange for you to have an interpreter at the interview, if you need one.[4]

Jobseeker's Agreement

Your Jobseeker's Agreement will set out your availability for work and the ways in which you will search for a job. It will usually include:

- the hours you are available for employment
- where you are available to work
- any restrictions on your availability
- a description of the type of employment you are seeking
- the action you will take to seek employment
- the action you will take to improve your prospects of finding employment
- the start and finish dates of any permitted period (see page 50), and
- a statement of rights.

If you are not happy with something in the Jobseeker's Agreement, try to discuss it (or take time to seek independent advice) before you sign the Agreement. It can be harder to re-negotiate your Agreement after you have signed it, though you can ask to make changes at any stage after signing.[5] You can always explain why you feel that any restrictions you want to place on your Agreement are reasonable.

Weeks 2 to 13 of your Jobseeker's Allowance claim

Every week, you need to take action to find work, and you must be able to give information about your jobsearch to Jobcentre Plus. You may record evidence that you have been actively seeking work by using the jobsearch log you received during your first interview with Jobcentre Plus. To get your JSA payments, you will have to sign on at the Jobcentre at least once per fortnight, where you will talk to a member of staff about what you have been doing to find work and show them your jobsearch log. Jobcentre Plus staff might also talk to you about the changes you need to make to improve your chances of finding a job, and any extra help you think you need. You will not be paid travel expenses to sign on. In between your fortnightly visits to the Jobcentre, you will be expected to search for jobs on your own, taking more than two jobsearch actions per week.

You may sign on by post if you:

- live more than an hour's travel time (door to door) from the nearest Jobcentre

- have to walk more than three miles to the Jobcentre
- would be absent from home for more than four hours, or
- have a physical or mental disability that restricts your mobility.[6]

If you don't sign on at the right time or day, your JSA claim will stop.[7] However, if you show, within five working days, that you had 'good cause' for signing on late, your claim can continue.[8] It is best to sign on at the right time and day to avoid problems.

Back to Work session

At some time during the first three months of your JSA claim, often around Week 6, you might be asked to attend a 'Back to Work' session. Usually, this is a group session with other jobseekers, which is supposed to help you look over the steps you've taken to find work and get advice on ways to improve your chances of finding work.[9]

As part of the session, you may draw up a Jobsearch Action Plan.

Week 13 of your Jobseeker's Allowance claim – review meeting[10]

Once you have been claiming JSA for about 13 weeks, Jobcentre Plus will ask you to attend a review meeting with a personal adviser. This meeting is in addition to your regular jobsearch reviews. The main point of the meeting is to make sure that you are taking steps to find work, and that Jobcentre Plus is giving you all the help you need. Jobcentre Plus will tell you where and when your interview will take place, and you should contact them straight away if you cannot attend. If you don't attend the interview, and you don't contact Jobcentre Plus to tell them, then your benefit may be reduced or even stopped. After the meeting, you may have to attend more regular jobsearch reviews, usually every week for six weeks. During your interview, you will set up a date for these future meetings.

At the review meeting, the personal adviser should:

- review your Jobseeker's Agreement
- make suggestions for updating your CV

- discuss what you have been doing to look for work
- talk to you about applying for the widest possible range of jobs
- help you find and apply for job vacancies
- find out any barriers that may be stopping you from getting a job, such as health problems, debt or childcare
- give advice on training and ways to improve your skills, and
- do a 'better off in work' calculation based on your circumstances and tell you about the benefits you may be able to claim when you start working.

If you attended a Back to Work session and drew up a Jobsearch Action Plan in the first three months of your JSA claim, your personal adviser will review your plan with you during your 13-week review.

Weeks 14 to 20 of your Jobseeker's Allowance claim – directed jobsearch

After your 13-week review, your regular jobsearch reviews will become more frequent for a time: you will have to sign on and attend jobsearch reviews once a week for six weeks. You must continue to make sure that you are available for work and actively seeking it during this six-week period, carrying out any steps agreed at your 13-week review.

If you incur any costs (such as travel expenses) when attending your weekly jobsearch reviews, you will be reimbursed. You may not be offered these, so do ask if they are not offered. Your costs will only be covered for the weeks you would not normally have attended Jobcentre Plus. Since you would normally attend the Jobcentre once per fortnight to sign on, during your weekly review period you will get help with expenses for every additional week you attend Jobcentre Plus – that is, for the weeks in between your usual attendance pattern.[11] If you are away from home during your directed jobsearch period, you will have to attend Jobcentre Plus once per week after you return, until you have made up a full six-week period of weekly reviews.[12]

Weeks 21 to 26 of your Jobseeker's Allowance claim

During Weeks 21 to 26 of your JSA claim, you will continue to sign on fortnightly at Jobcentre Plus and take at least two actions to find work each week.

Week 26 of your Jobseeker's Allowance claim – Restart Interview[13]

When you have been claiming JSA for about six months, you will have a formal review with your personal adviser, called a 'Restart Interview'. This meeting will be in addition to the regular jobsearch reviews you attend every fortnight. The main point of the meeting is to make sure that you are taking the agreed steps to find work, and that Jobcentre Plus is giving you all the help you need. Jobcentre Plus will tell you where and when your interview will take place, and you should contact them straight away if you cannot attend. If you don't attend the interview and you don't contact Jobcentre Plus to tell them, or if you don't have 'good cause', then your benefit may be sanctioned. During your interview, you will set up a date for future meetings which will take place every week for the next six weeks, in addition to your regular jobsearch reviews.

Your personal adviser will help you draw up and follow a personal action plan. You may need several meetings with your adviser to draw up the plan, which aims to provide you with the best chance of finding work. During your Restart Interview, and at following meetings, your personal adviser should:

- review your Jobseeker's Agreement with you to make sure it's still useful
- talk about how you can improve your chances of getting a job, by looking at the full range of jobs you are able to do
- talk about the jobsearch support you may need, such as help with writing job applications and your CV
- discuss the option of doing a skills assessment
- try to find and solve any barriers to work, such as health problems, debt or childcare

- give you access to specialist help, if you need it, for things such as building your confidence, handling debt, and communicating your skills to employers
- help you find and apply for job vacancies, and
- do a 'better off in work' calculation based on your circumstances, which tells you about the benefits you may claim when you start working (however, there are concerns about the quality of these and you should obtain independent advice).

Your adviser will also discuss the help you can get in your particular area or circumstances. This could include:

- help setting up your own business, or becoming self-employed
- skills training that is available in your area
- help finding volunteer work, so you can keep your skills up-to-date and get experience that will improve your chances of getting a job, or
- access to subsidised jobs, where your employer receives £1,000 as a recruitment subsidy, along with up to £1,500 to pay for your training.[14]

At your 26-week review, you should receive an employment subsidy voucher, which you can use to market yourself to employers to encourage them to offer you work.[15] Any wage restrictions will end at this point so that jobs at the National Minimum Wage form part of the Jobseeker's Agreement.

Weeks 27 to 52 of your Jobseeker's Allowance claim[16]

After your Restart Interview, you will have extra follow-up meetings with your personal adviser. You will usually meet your adviser every week for six weeks (from approximately Week 27 of your claim to Week 32, though the weekly review period could occur later),[17] in addition to attending your regular fortnightly jobsearch reviews at Jobcentre Plus. During these extra meetings, your adviser should help you to draw up and carry out a personal action plan, as described in the previous section.

Once your weekly review period is over, you will meet with your personal adviser regularly. You will search for jobs with your adviser at these meetings, and by yourself in between meetings. You will continue to attend fortnightly jobsearch reviews. You will be expected to take more than two jobsearch actions per week.

During Weeks 27 to 52 of your claim, you will also be required to take part in up to three activities designed to improve your employability (the number will depend on how difficult or challenging the activities are). These will be agreed and detailed in your action plan, and you will only have to do one activity at a time.[18] Your adviser is responsible for deciding which activities you should do, but your activities could include:

- basic skills assessment
- occupational skills assessment
- completing modules at a programme centre
- researching a new place or work area to identify job opportunities
- enquiring about training opportunities
- doing a short period of work experience or volunteer work, and
- seeking advice about debt, housing or health issues, if these are a barrier to employment.[19]

If you fail to participate, or if you can't give proof that you have participated (such as a letter from your training provider or confirmation of enrolment), you could face a benefit sanction.[20] You will also have access to Skills Health Checks during this time (see page 146), and your adviser may direct you to undergo a check.[21]

If you stop claiming JSA during Weeks 27 to 52, and then return later to re-claim the benefit, you will usually start again from the first stage of the customer journey. However, if you return within 28 days of leaving, you will keep your entitlement to the recruitment subsidy, volunteer work, work focused training and self-employment credit.[22] If you leave JSA during this time to start full-time training supported by allowance payments, and you return to JSA immediately after finishing your training, you will also keep your entitlement to the recruitment subsidy, volunteer work, work focused training and self-employment credit. [23]

Months 6 to 24 of your Jobseeker's Allowance claim – employment programmes

Once you have been claiming JSA for a certain amount of time, you will be required to take part in one of the compulsory employment programmes:

- Flexible New Deal (after 12 months of claiming)
- Young Person's Guarantee (at around 10 months of claiming)
- Future Jobs Fund employment (6 to 12 months of claiming)
- New Deal for Young People (after 6 months of claiming)
- New Deal for 25 Plus (after 18 months of claiming), or
- Employment Zones (after 18 months of claiming).

Before your adviser refers you to a programme, you will have to attend a review at Jobcentre Plus.[24] If you have been claiming JSA for 12 months, but have to wait until 18 months into your claim to start an employment programme, then you will retain access to the recruitment subsidy, volunteer work, work focused training and self-employment credit discussed earlier, until you start your programme.[25]

The programme you take part in depends on where you live. Jobcentre Plus is replacing New Deal for Young People (NDYP), New Deal 25 Plus (ND25+) and Employment Zones (EZs) with Flexible New Deal (FND) in phases. So, if you live in a Phase 1 area, and you had done six months of Supported Jobsearch by October 2009, you will be required to take part in FND. Until October 2010, NDYP, ND25+ and EZs will run in Phase 2 areas. If you live in a Phase 2 area, FND will be introduced from October 2010 for those who have done six months of Supported Jobsearch. See page 78 for a list of Phase 1 and Phase 2 areas.

Flexible New Deal

While you are taking part in FND, you will continue to get JSA and you will have to sign on at the Jobcentre once every fortnight. However, the programme is run by an independent provider (a private, public or voluntary organisation), and the provider will take the place of your Jobcentre Plus personal adviser in giving you jobsearch support.

At a minimum, FND will require fortnightly contact with your programme provider, an in-depth assessment of your needs, drawing up a personal action plan, and a compulsory period of full-time work experience or work in the community. See page 77, for more information on the FND programme.

Young Person's Guarantee

If you are aged 18 to 24, you are promised an offer of a job, work focused training, or other meaningful activity through the Young Person's Guarantee, at around the 10-month stage of your JSA claim. Participation in the work or training you are offered is compulsory, if you want to continue to receive JSA. The Guarantee is being rolled out nationally from early 2010, but parts of it will have started in some areas from as early as October 2009. Effectively, this means that you will be required to undertake some activity for your benefits.

Future Jobs Fund

As from October 2009,[26] as part of the Young Person's Guarantee, if you are aged 18 to 24, and have been claiming JSA for between 10 and 12 months,[27] you will be eligible for a six-month paid job supported by the Future Jobs Fund. The job will usually take 25 hours per week or more. It is up to your Jobcentre Plus personal adviser to decide whether or not you can apply for a job supported by the Fund.[28]

If your JSA claim has been fast-tracked because you were not in education, training or employment prior to making your claim, you may be able to apply for a job through the Future Jobs Fund after you have been claiming JSA for six months, rather than 12 months.[29] You may also be able to get work through the Future Jobs Fund if you are aged over 24, have found it particularly difficult to get a job, and live in an 'unemployment hotspot'.[30]

New Deal for Young People

If you are aged 18 to 25, and FND is not yet running in your area, you will take part in NDYP. The first part of the NDYP programme is called the Gateway, and it lasts for up to four months. During your time on the Gateway, you will continue to get JSA, provided you sign on at the Jobcentre each fortnight and meet the rules about taking steps to find work. While you are on the Gateway, you will attend weekly interviews with Jobcentre Plus (or your programme provider), draw up an action plan and address your barriers to work.

If you have not found work after four weeks of being on the Gateway, you will do a two-week Gateway to Work Course. If you have not found work after taking part in NDYP for four months, you will work with your programme provider to get a suitable place on one of the following options:

- full-time education or training option
- employment option
- voluntary sector option
- environmental task force option.

If you do not have a job by the time you complete your option, you will have a Follow-through period in which Jobcentre Plus gives you intensive help to find work. For more information on the NDYP programme, see page 85.

New Deal 25 Plus

If you are aged over 25 and FND is not yet running in your area, you will take part in ND25+. The first part of the ND25+ programme is called the Gateway, and it lasts for up to four months. During your time on the Gateway, you will continue to get JSA, provided you sign on at the Jobcentre each fortnight and meet the rules about taking steps to find work. While you are on the Gateway, you will draw up an action plan with Jobcentre Plus, and address your barriers to work.

If you have not found work after being on the Gateway for four months, you will enter the Intense Activity Period, which lasts for up to 13 weeks (or 26 weeks for people who need extra help). During the Intense Activity Period, you will do 30 hours of activity spread over five days each week. You will get a New Deal Allowance instead of JSA.

If you have not found a job by the time you finish the Intense Activity Period, you will go on to a Follow-through period, in which Jobcentre Plus will give you intensive jobsearch support. The Follow-through period can last for between six and 13 weeks, depending on the amount of support you need. If you have not found a job by the end of the Follow-through period, you will have to re-claim JSA. For more information on ND25+, see page 95.

Employment Zones

There are four EZs across the country, in areas that have a high rate of long-term unemployment. See page 109, to find out if you live in an EZ area.

The EZ programme is made up of three stages. The first two stages are compulsory, and the third stage is voluntary. Stage 1 lasts for up to 28 days.[31] Your EZ provider will appoint you a personal adviser, who will help you to decide on the kind of work you are looking for and understand what may be stopping you from getting that work. You will draw up an individually tailored Action Plan with your adviser. Stage 2 can last for up to 26 weeks. During Stage 2, your EZ contractor will help you to carry out the activities in your Action Plan. After Stage 2, if you have not got a job you can choose to have follow-on support for a maximum of 22 weeks. Stage 3 begins once you have started work, and lasts for 13 weeks. During Stage 3, your EZ provider will give you in-work support to help you keep your job.

While you are taking part in the EZ programme, you are guaranteed an income that is equal to your total weekly benefit claims for as long as you stay unemployed. If you have not found a job by the end of Stage 2, you will return to Jobcentre Plus to claim a benefit. If you did not find a job after spending 26 weeks actively searching during Stage 2 of the programme, you will have to re-join EZ once you have been re-claiming JSA for 13 weeks. See page 103, for more information on EZ.

Eligibility rules for Jobseeker's Allowance

Are you the right age?

In order to claim JSA, you must be aged between 18 and the pensionable age. Once you reach pensionable age, you should claim retirement pension (between ages 60 and 65, you can either claim JSA or Pension Credit).

Those aged 16 and 17

Those aged 16 and 17 usually can't claim JSA because they are unlikely to satisfy the NI contribution requirements for CJSA, and there are special rules for people under 18 who claim IBJSA. More information can be found in the Centre for Economic and Social Inclusion's Young Person's Handbook. However, it is still possible for many aged 16 or 17 to make successful claims.

Are you capable of work?

To be entitled to JSA you will have to show that you are capable of work. If you are not capable of work, you may be eligible for an incapacity-related benefit such as Employment and Support Allowance. If you have been judged as capable of work under the Work Capability Assessment for Employment and Support Allowance, then Jobcentre Plus will automatically decide that you are capable of work, without exceptions.[32] If you wish to appeal against being found fit to work, you can continue to be paid ESA at the basic rate (which is the same as JSA).

Are you available for work?[33]

In general, you will be considered available for work if you can show that you are willing and able immediately to accept all offers of employment brought to your notice. You will not be expected to look for or accept work as a self-employed person.

Being available does not only mean that you are willing to work, it also means you are able to work a certain number of days or hours each week. You must be able to work for 40 hours per week to be deemed 'available', although this rule is not set in stone. Your JSA can be suspended immediately, if a personal adviser believes that you have failed to show that you are available for work.

Note: If you are still on a New Deal programme, you still have to satisfy conditions about being available for work.

The 40-hour rule

Generally, to be considered available for employment, you must be willing and able to take up work of at least 40 hours per week. At your first interview with a personal adviser, you will agree the number of hours you are available to work in your Jobseeker's Agreement, before you are entitled to receive JSA. You will need to tell the adviser:

- the days of the week you are available to work, and
- your earliest start time and latest finishing time each day, and
- the maximum number of hours you can work each day and, in total, during the week.[34]

This is called your pattern of availability.

If you would like to work for at least 40 hours per week, but you are offered work of fewer hours, you will be expected to accept it. However, you can refuse any job that offers fewer than 24 hours of work per week. Similarly, if you have been allowed to restrict your availability to fewer than 24 hours per week, you will be able to refuse jobs that offer fewer than 16 hours of work per week.

Monitoring your availability

Doubts about your availability to work can arise at any time (including from the way that you answer questions at your first interview). When you answer questions, you must make sure that you meet the availability conditions set out in your Jobseeker's Agreement. This form is the main way of monitoring your availability. During your claim, your availability for work will be checked whenever you sign on and attend your fortnightly jobsearch review. A more intensive check of your availability is carried out at advisory interviews.

If at any point Jobcentre Plus staff think that you need more help with finding work, or if they think that you may be working while claiming and not declaring all of your earnings, you may have to attend extra compulsory interviews. You may be asked to attend extra interviews because a member of staff is not satisfied with your progress, or because you have been 'caseloaded', which means that you get extra attention from Jobcentre Plus for a period of time, to help you into work as quickly as possible.

If your benefit is suspended, it is important to keep on showing that you are available for and are actively seeking work, and that you are attending the Jobcentre Plus office every fortnight to sign on. Also, you should press for a decision to be made quickly about your entitlement. If your benefit is reinstated later on, arrears will be paid only for the days on which you met these conditions. You should also obtain independent advice to challenge any suspension – you have a right to appeal a decision you think may be wrong.

Restricted availability[35]

You are allowed to be available for fewer than 40 hours per week, if you have:

- caring responsibilities (including for your children, if you are a lone parent)
- a disability or health problem, or
- been laid off or are on short-term work.

You will have to show that you are continuing to meet these conditions each time you sign on at the Jobcentre. You also have to show that you have a reasonable prospect of obtaining work.

You can place additional restrictions on your availability, if you:

- are within your permitted period (see to page 50), or
- can show that you have reasonable prospects of securing employment, or
- have a sincerely held religious belief or conscientious objection.

The opportunity to place additional restrictions on your jobsearch after your permitted period is fairly limited for most people. You will be able to place restrictions on the nature, rate of pay or location only if you can show that you have reasonable prospects of securing employment despite your restrictions.

People with children

If you are responsible for a child, and your caring responsibilities mean that it is unreasonable for you to start work in less than one week or attend a job interview with fewer than 48 hours' notice, you can restrict your availability to say that you can start work with 28 days' notice and attend a job interview with seven days' notice.[36]

You have to be available for jobs that your caring responsibilities allow. If your caring responsibilities are such that it is unreasonable for you to make childcare arrangements during holidays, breaks, or other times when your child is not at school, then you will still count as being available for work, so that you can meet the benefit criteria and get your payments. Even though you will be treated as available for work, you will not actually have to find work that your caring responsibilities do not permit. This gives you a lot of flexibility to adjust your work availability according to family and personal circumstances.[37]

You can also place reasonable limits on the number of hours you are willing to work if you are subject to, or have agreed to, a legally prescribed 'Parenting Contract'.[38]

Some special groups[39]

Certain categories of JSA customers are excused from the requirement that they should be immediately available to take up employment:

- If you have caring responsibilities – defined as caring for someone over 65, or someone who has mental or physical difficulties – you can give one week's notice before taking up a job and you should be available to attend a job interview within 48 hours.

- If you have a part-time job while claiming JSA, you are not required to be immediately available for a full-time job, provided that you are willing to start a job with 24 hours' notice (or up to one week, if you have to give your employer statutory notice). Once you have started a job, it is possible also to continue with your part-time job provided it fits into the pattern of work you agreed with Jobcentre Plus.

- If you do voluntary work, you are permitted to give one week's notice before starting a job, but you must be available for an interview within 48 hours.
- If you are providing a service (including jury service, being a witness in court proceedings, serving as a justice of the peace or as a member of a tribunal, or serving a community service order) you may be excused from the requirement to start a job immediately.

People with caring responsibilities

Under the JSA regulations, if you have certain caring responsibilities you are allowed to be available for work (or to refuse vacancies of) fewer than 40 hours a week – though you must be available to work for as many hours as your caring responsibilities allow, as long as this totals at least 16 hours per week.

Jobcentre Plus will not accept that someone has caring responsibilities if they are caring for a friend or a neighbour. Caring responsibilities mean caring for a close relative or those within the same household. However, if you are caring for someone else and they get Disability Living Allowance, you may be able to get Carer's Allowance (see page 203) instead of JSA. With the additional carer's premium paid with Income Support (IS), this may mean a higher income than JSA. Seek advice about changing to IS.

You should consider your options carefully if you have caring responsibilities. People looking after a disabled person who receive Carer's Allowance, or lone parents with children aged under 10, may be entitled to claim IS instead of JSA (see page 268).

Volunteers

Unemployed people are allowed to do voluntary work. You may even be encouraged to participate in voluntary activities. Voluntary work is work for an organisation whose activities are not-for-profit, and where no payment is received by you except for reasonable expenses, or work for anyone except a member of your family where no payment is received.

CONCESSIONS FOR VOLUNTEERS

The government recognises the importance of voluntary work, so there are a number of concessions for volunteers.

Volunteers can give 48 hours' notice before starting a job, or attending a job interview or jobsearch interview. However, you could be contacted at any time by Jobcentre Plus staff. Providers of voluntary work can help you to meet this condition by making sure that you are contactable whenever you are volunteering.

Voluntary work is also taken into account when deciding whether you meet the criteria of actively seeking work. For example, voluntary work may help you develop skills or bring you into contact with people who are able to offer you a job.

People with disabilities and health problems

If you have a disability or health problem, you 'May restrict [your] availability in any way providing the restrictions are reasonable in the light of [your] physical or mental condition'.[40]

You do not have to show that you have reasonable prospects of obtaining employment with the restriction, so this means you can restrict the hours you are available to work each week. There is no minimum number of hours per week for which people with disabilities and health problems must be available.

You may also place any other restrictions on the nature, rate of pay, location or other terms and conditions of employment.

While staff can ask for medical evidence to check the validity of your physical or mental condition, they must first check other sources to see if they can gain the necessary information.

Religious beliefs or conscientious objections

You can place restrictions on the type of work (but not the number of hours) for which you are available on the grounds that you have a sincerely held religious belief or a sincerely held conscientious objection.[41] However, you must show that you 'have reasonable prospects of employment notwithstanding these restrictions and meet all the other standard availability rules'.

Common restrictions include:

- not working on a Sunday on religious grounds (or on another day, if this is appropriate to your religion)
- refusing to work in certain jobs (for example, working in an abattoir or doing work that involves the supply and handling of alcohol or weapons).

Laid-off and short-time workers

If you have your hours of work reduced by your employer (known as 'short-time work'), or you are temporarily laid off because adverse industrial economic conditions have affected your employer, you are entitled to claim JSA for up to 13 weeks without needing to be available for alternative full-time work, provided you are willing and able immediately to take up your previous employment.[42] To count as being laid off or on short time, you must still have an employment contract with your employer, but you must have a temporary gap in your work for that employer or a temporary reduction in your hours that the employer will increase at a later date.

If you are doing occasional casual work (work that does not require you to give an employer notice) the usual rules will apply after 13 weeks.

Remember that any pay you get from short-time or casual work could affect your right to JSA, especially if it's the means-tested version, as well as other benefits.

Short periods of sickness when claiming JSA[43]

You are able to receive JSA for up to two weeks during short periods of illness. You will have to fill out a form declaring that you are unfit for work.

In each 12-month period, you are entitled to receive JSA while ill for two fortnight-long occasions (based on the date of your first claim). Once you have been unemployed for more than a year, you again become eligible to receive JSA during two periods of sickness in the following 12 months. If you are sick for more than two weeks, you will need to make a claim for Employment and Support Allowance.

Deaths, funerals, domestic emergencies, and holidays

If you are unavailable for work because of an emergency, Jobcentre Plus will continue to pay JSA for up to one week. You can only make yourself unavailable based on an emergency for a maximum of four times in any 12-month period.

For a two-week period each year, you can take a holiday in the UK during which you will be counted as meeting the available for work rule. However, Jobcentre Plus must be able to contact you while you are away from home. In addition, you must be willing to return home immediately to take up a job opportunity.

Are you actively seeking work?[44]

You have to take steps each week to find employment. Your Jobseeker's Agreement will set out what you have agreed to do to seek work actively each week.

An oral or written application for employment is counted as a single step to seek work. You can apply to:

- people who have advertised job vacancies
- people who appear to be in a position to offer employment
- employment agencies and employment businesses, and
- employers.

Other single steps include:

- registering with an employment agency or employment business
- looking for advertised job vacancies (on paper or on the Internet)
- appointing a third party to help you look for work
- seeking specialist advice to improve your prospects of finding work (such as advice from a disability employment adviser)
- drawing up a CV
- drawing up a list of employers to contact about the possibility of a job, and/or
- doing research on employers.

The above lists are not exhaustive.

How many steps do you have to take to seek work actively?

You should take more than two steps each week, unless one or two steps are all that it is reasonable for you to take. (For example, one or two steps might be reasonable if you are homeless and are spending most of your time looking for somewhere to live.)

It does not matter whether you take steps to seek work every day of the week, or concentrate your jobsearch into a few days (or even one day), so long as you take those steps that are reasonable to satisfy the benefit rule. Jobcentre Plus will take your circumstances into account to decide whether you are actively seeking work.

Your Jobseeker's Agreement may specify in greater detail what you will do. The two steps are the legal minimum below which you will be regarded as ineligible for JSA as not actively seeking work.

The following things will be considered:[45]

- your skills, qualifications and abilities
- your physical or mental condition
- the length of time since you were last in employment
- your work experience
- the steps you have taken in previous weeks

- the availability and location of vacancies
- whether you are treated as available for employment
- whether you are on, or applying to, an EU-funded course, and
- whether you have no living accommodation.

Jobcentre Plus will also take into account any time during which you were:

- carrying out lifeboat or part-time fire-fighting duties
- engaged in duties for the benefit of others in an emergency
- attending an Outward Bound course
- doing a course of training in the use of guide dogs (if you are blind)
- doing a course of training in the use of special aids to improve your job prospects (if you have a disability)
- engaged in duties with the Territorial Army
- participating as a part-time student in an employment-related course
- participating for fewer than three days in an employment or training programme for which a training allowance is not payable, or
- doing voluntary work.

People who are highly skilled or qualified may be allowed to restrict their jobsearch (for instance, because they are within their 'permitted period'), and they will have greater flexibility in how they look for work (including registering with specialist employment agencies). Those who are looking for semi-skilled or unskilled work have less flexibility about how they look for work.

How to show you are actively seeking work

At your first interview, you will receive a jobsearch activity log. You should complete the log and show it at your fortnightly review. Evidence of jobsearch can include proof of applications for work, copies of job advertisements for which you have requested more details, lists of employers, and copies of application letters or application forms. Jobseeking activities could include drawing up a CV, seeking a reference, and finding information about potential employers or occupations.

Permitted period[46]

When you become unemployed and start claiming JSA, you may have a short period during which you are allowed to restrict your jobsearch to your usual occupation and your usual level of pay. This is officially called your 'permitted period'. Your permitted period lasts for a minimum of one week, but no longer than 13 weeks from the start of your claim. During the permitted period, you can also refuse any job offer that is not in your usual occupation or at your usual rate of pay. Once the permitted period ends (or from the beginning of your claim, if you are not granted a permitted period), you must widen the range of jobs you will consider taking and that you can reasonably be expected to do.

The adviser's decision on whether you are allowed a permitted period will be based on the answers you give on the Helping You Back to Work Form (ES2) and the JSA Claim Form (JSA1). The duration of your permitted period will be set out in the Jobseeker's Agreement that is completed by you and an adviser at your interview.

Usual occupation in the permitted period

You will not be given any permitted period if you do not have a usual occupation – such as if you are a school leaver, have never worked before or your former occupation has died out or been replaced. If you have suffered injury or disablement that makes you incapable of resuming your former occupation, you will also be ineligible for a permitted period.

However, if you have temporarily left your occupation (for example, on health grounds or because of a temporary industrial economic recession) it remains your usual occupation.

If you have received training for an occupation but have not been employed in it, you do not qualify for a permitted period. However, if you have undertaken vocational training for at least two months, you are allowed four weeks from the end of the training during which you can restrict your jobsearch.

You are allowed to restrict your jobsearch to self-employment during your permitted period, so long as you are still prepared to take a job as an employee. To qualify for restricting your jobsearch to self-employed work, you must have been self-employed at some stage during the last 12 months.

Accustomed rate of pay in the permitted period

When you are within your permitted period, you can restrict your jobsearch to the rate of pay you are accustomed to receiving (that is, the rate of pay in your usual occupation).[47]

Length of permitted period[48]

The length of your permitted period depends on several factors, including:

- your usual occupation and any relevant skills or qualifications
- the length of any relevant training you have done
- the length of time that you have been employed
- the length of time since you were last employed, and
- the availability and location of employment.

You should be told at your first interview that, if you are still unemployed at the end of the permitted period, you will have an advisory interview at which your Jobseeker's Agreement will be revised to broaden your jobsearch.

Restrictions after the permitted period

You can keep restrictions on your jobsearch (including your level of pay) after the permitted period, if you have shown there are still reasonable prospects of securing employment. However, you can only do this for a maximum of six months from the beginning of your claim, or if it is reasonable in the light of your physical or mental condition.

The reasonable prospects of employment criteria can also be used to restrict your availability for work. The DWP's benefit Decision Makers are told that any assessment of this should take into account:

- your skills, qualifications and experience
- the type and number of vacancies within daily travelling distance
- the length of time you have been unemployed
- any job applications you have made and their outcome, and
- whether you are willing to move home to take up a job.[49]

The restrictions you place on your availability affect the jobseeking steps that you are expected to undertake (as detailed in your Jobseeker's Agreement).

See page 43, for rules affecting people with children.

Actively seeking work and travelling time

For the first 13 weeks of a JSA claim, you do not have to be available for work that involves travelling more than one hour in each direction. After 13 weeks of claiming, you will be expected to take jobs that involve up to one and a half hours' travel each way, and you will also have to sign on at the Jobcentre once a week for the next six weeks.

You will receive help with fares and overnight costs to attend job interviews, if you qualify for the Travel to Interview Scheme (see page 256).

Actively seeking work and special needs

Jobcentre Plus staff are told to be aware of the particular jobsearch difficulties faced by some customers. These difficulties include health problems or disabilities, problems with reading and writing, or speaking English as a second language. It is likely that Jobcentre Plus will soon be conducting 'skills audits' to identify literacy and numeracy problems, and will make it part of the Jobseeker's Agreement that someone gets help with those skills. There are also proposals that people who misuse drugs will have to disclose this to Jobcentre Plus and seek treatment as a condition of getting JSA.

Actively seeking work and homelessness

If you are homeless, Jobcentre Plus staff must consider the following factors when deciding what is reasonable for your jobsearch:

- difficulties in contacting employers and employment agencies
- the need to spend time during the week looking for accommodation, and
- the fact that you may have less time for active jobsearch and therefore less need to fulfil steps.[50]

Deliberately avoiding employment

A jobseeking step will not count as actively seeking work, if there is evidence that you deliberately lowered your chances of gaining employment. Examples of deliberately lowering your chance include:

- violent or abusive behaviour towards the employer during a job interview
- an inadequate written application for a job
- drawing up an inadequate CV, or
- failing to use appropriate behaviour or appearance at a job interview.

You can appeal if your benefit is refused on these grounds because you might think that your CV, application form, appearance or behaviour weren't at fault.

Suspensions

If an adviser believes that you have been deliberately avoiding employment, they can suspend your benefit immediately. You can argue good cause for your behaviour or appearance only if the Decision Maker accepts that the circumstances were beyond your control. Your argument may be accepted if you have a history of mental illness. It may also be accepted, if you can show that inappropriate behaviour on your part was beyond your control because of an alcohol or drug-related condition. However, you will have to prove that you have a known problem.

Are you resident in the UK?

Generally, you must be present in the UK to be eligible for JSA. You may be able to claim CJSA while in the EU, if:

- you have been claiming CJSA and signing on as available for work for at least four weeks before you go abroad, and
- you are going abroad to look for work, and
- you register within seven days as unemployed with the employment service of the other country.

Note: that you should get advice from your local Jobcentre Plus office before going abroad.

You may also keep your JSA, if you go abroad:

- for a job interview
- for up to eight weeks to take a child or young person for whom you receive benefits or tax credits for medical treatment, and
- for NHS treatment.

You must inform Jobcentre Plus, if you think any of these might apply to you.[51]

People from abroad

If you are from abroad, but you have worked in the UK and paid NI contributions, then you can claim CJSA like anyone else. To qualify for CJSA in the UK, you may also use NI contributions paid in another EU country, or contributions paid in a country that has a Reciprocal Agreement with the UK and that covers JSA. You may also combine contributions paid in your country with any paid in the UK to qualify for CJSA. If you are from an EU country, you may want to claim an unemployment benefit from your home country and have it paid via the Jobcentre Plus office.

To qualify for IBJSA you need to have a right to reside in the UK (for example, because you have worked in the UK) and to be habitually resident.

Education

Full-time education

You will not be able to claim JSA, if you are in full-time education, unless you are in one of the following situations:

- If your partner is also a full-time student, you can claim during the long summer vacation, providing you or your partner is responsible for a child or young person.[52]

- If you are taking a full-time employment-related course for no longer than two weeks, you can claim JSA providing you agreed your course attendance with Jobcentre Plus before the course started. You will be treated as available for employment and actively seeking employment in any week where you participate in a course for three days or more. You can only take one course in any 12-month period.[53]

- If you are following an Open University course and there is a residential element, you can claim JSA.[54]

- If you are a full-time student and you have 'abandoned' your course, or been 'dismissed' from it,[55] or if you stopped studying with the agreement of the college or university because of illness or caring responsibilities, and you are waiting to resume the course after your illness or caring responsibilities have ended, you can claim JSA.[56]

Part-time education

You are allowed to do part-time education or training while looking for work. Certain people doing flexible courses can take advantage of a concession called Regulation 11.[57] This rule relaxes some of the requirements and makes it easier for some part-time students or trainees to keep their benefit. If you study part-time, you still have to be actively seeking work and available to start work immediately.

Part-time study is not considered an active step towards finding a job. In addition to attending your course, you are expected to carry out a list of active steps each week to find work. In addition, you must be:

- willing and able immediately to take time off the course to attend an interview

- able to be contacted promptly so that notification to attend an interview will reach you in time, and
- willing and able immediately to rearrange the hours of your course to fit in with employment.

You will normally have to agree a work pattern of 40 hours per week. The pattern of availability you agree with the Jobcentre Plus adviser will depend on the type of work you are looking for. For example, if you are allowed to restrict yourself to shop work, your adviser may insist that your pattern of availability includes Saturdays. It is important that your part-time study fits with your pattern of availability.

If you are already claiming JSA, it is your responsibility to inform your local Jobcentre Plus if you have enrolled or intend to enrol on a course. When you first sign on for JSA, you are asked this question in the Helping You Back to Work form. You may also be asked about part-time study when your jobsearch activities are reviewed at interviews.

When you tell the Jobcentre Plus adviser that you are taking or intend to take a course, you will be given a questionnaire to complete. This form assesses whether you can follow your part-time course and continue to receive benefit. The form asks three test questions:

1 Are you a part-time student?

2 Are you still available for and actively seeking employment?

3 Are you available for and actively seeking employment, when matters relating to the course are taken into account? This relates to how much importance you have attached to doing the course instead of taking any job that is offered to you. For example, if you are doing a two-year course in catering because you say it's your life's ambition to be a chef, would you take a job in a burger restaurant and give the course up after you've been on it a year?

Are you a part-time student?

If you are judged to be a full-time student, you will not be entitled to JSA. The definition of a full-time student changes depending on where you attend the course, the level of the course and who funds it. Some young people under the age of 21 who are in full-time, non-advanced education may be able to receive IS instead of JSA – for example, if they have to live away from their parents and are estranged, if they are a lone parent, or if they have a disability. If you are not sure how your course is funded, you should ask the welfare officer where you attend your course. Most courses are funded or part-funded by the Learning and Skills Council in England until August 2010 (or by Local Authorities, the Skills Funding Agency and Young People's Learning Agency from August 2010). In Wales, similar rules apply to Welsh Assembly government funded courses. Learning and Skills Council rules are that full-time study involves more than 16 guided learning hours per week. Your learning agreement shows your number of weekly guided learning hours, the name of the college/course provider, your personal details and the signature of a representative of the college/course provider. Jobcentre Plus staff will accept a copy of the learning agreement from you. Time spent on unpaid work experience that is part of your course does not normally count as guided learning hours. For higher education courses, the rule is that there is no hourly definition of full-time. (An approximate guide is 21 hours per week.)

Are you available for and actively seeking employment?

Regulation 11 makes the availability requirements easier to meet. If you satisfy Regulation 11, you will not have to move on to the third test. You qualify for Regulation 11, if you are a part-time student, you are willing and able to re-arrange the hours of your course to take up employment, you can take up employment immediately, and for a period of three months immediately before the course you were receiving JSA (or IS or support group ESA/Incapacity Benefit (IB) because you were incapable of work). For example, if you can rearrange the hours of your course by doing evening classes or open learning in order to fit around a job, then you are likely to qualify under Regulation 11.

Are you available for and actively seeking employment, once your course design is taken into account?

If you do not qualify under Regulation 11, then Jobcentre Plus will apply the third and stricter test to your claim. Under this third test, Jobcentre Plus staff will ask questions about your course and take your answers into account when deciding whether you are available for work. You therefore need to think very carefully about the answers you give. You might be doing a part-time course in order to improve your employment prospects in a year or two's time. That's very good, but Jobcentre Plus might think that you are therefore not willing to give up the course and get a job right now. Remember, it's JSA that you are claiming, so you have to make it clear that the course is less important to you than getting a job is.

Types of JSA

Contribution-Based Jobseeker's Allowance

You must meet two NI contribution conditions to qualify for CJSA:

1 You must have paid Class 1 contributions for one of the last two complete tax years before the start of the benefit year in which your JSA claim began. Your earnings for that tax year must have reached a total of at least 25 times the Lower Earnings Limit during that tax year; and

2 You must have paid Class 1 contributions and/or been credited with Class 1 contributions for both of the previous two tax years before the start of the benefit year in which your JSA claim began. Your earnings and/or credits must total at least 50 times the Lower Earnings Limit during each tax year.

The jargon explained

The Lower Earnings Limit is the level of weekly earnings on which you begin to pay National I contributions as an employee. It changes every year. For 2009–10 the Lower Earnings Limit is £95 per week. If you earn between £95 and £110 per week, you will not pay NI contributions but you will be treated as having paid them (which means you may still claim benefit based on NI contributions).

Class 1 contributions are paid by employees. Self-employed people, who pay Class 2 and Class 4 contributions, cannot qualify for CJSA (though they may still qualify for CJSA based on Class 1 contributions they paid when they were an employee in previous years).

When you are signed on as unemployed, each week you are automatically credited as having made a Class 1 contribution on earnings equivalent to the Lower Earnings Limit in that year. So, if you have accumulated enough contribution credits, you can meet the second contribution condition even if you were not earning (or only earning for part of the tax year).

The benefit year is based on the calendar year but starts on the first Sunday in January and ends on the Saturday immediately before the first Sunday in January in the following calendar year.

The tax year starts on 6 April and runs through to 5 April of the following year.

Duration of Contribution-Based Jobseeker's Allowance

CJSA lasts for a maximum of 28 weeks. If you are unemployed for longer than this, you will continue to receive benefit only if you qualify for IBJSA.

Breaks in claim

If you are claiming CJSA and you sign off for fewer than 12 weeks, the JSA linking rule states that you have not broken your claim. Your entitlement will resume on the same basis from where you left off. For example, if you have been paid eight weeks of JSA, then you work for three weeks and afterwards claim CJSA again, you will have another 20 weeks CJSA.

If you are claiming CJSA and you break your claim for more than 12 weeks, you are then treated as a fresh claimant and have to re-qualify.

Part, or in some cases all, of your six-month entitlement to CJSA can be used up if you are not getting the benefit because of a sanction. In principle, this means that you can lose all of your entitlement to CJSA if you are sanctioned at the beginning of a claim (for leaving a job voluntarily or because of misconduct) and a Decision Maker imposes the maximum six-month sanction.

You also count as receiving CJSA if you meet the benefit conditions but are not paid the contribution because of the income you are getting from an occupational or personal pension. Your CJSA is cut pound for pound for any weekly pension above £50 per week.

Re-qualifying for Contribution-Based Jobseeker's Allowance

To re-qualify for a new period of entitlement to CJSA:

- your last claim for CJSA must have ended more than 12 weeks ago
- the NI contribution test must be applied to at least one new tax year that was not used in your most recent claim for CJSA, and
- you must meet all of the NI contribution conditions – again, using the new tax year(s).

Because a new tax year must be used for your contribution test to re-qualify for CJSA, this means that you are not able to make a new claim in the same benefit year. So, in some cases it may be worth delaying your re-application for CJSA if you know that you will re-qualify soon by claiming in a new benefit year.

Income-Based Jobseeker's Allowance

IBJSA is means-tested and you can claim for your partner and children. You receive IBJSA regardless of previous NI contributions. It is possible to register as unemployed, sign on regularly and look for work without receiving JSA, and you might want to do this so that your NI record is credited. However, most people claim one type of JSA.

Rules for Income-Based Jobseeker's Allowance

IBJSA is a means-tested benefit, so your capital and your partner's circumstances are taken into account. If you or your family has capital above £16,000, you will not qualify for IBJSA.

How is Income-Based Jobseeker's Allowance calculated?

The means test for IBJSA is identical to the test for IS (see pages 271–273). Also, see the benefit rates table (page 344) for more information.

THE MEANS TEST

According to the rules of the means test, you will not qualify for any IBJSA in any week where:

- your partner works for 24 hours or more
- the total capital (for example, savings and lump sum redundancy payments) held by you and/or your partner exceeds £16,000, or
- your income and/or your partner's income is more than the amount the DWP says you need to live on (the 'applicable amount').

Weekly income from other sources as well as part-time work is taken into account for IBJSA. Once your weekly income has been calculated, your IBJSA will be cut by the amount of net earnings minus an 'earnings disregard' of between £5 and £20 (depending on your circumstances) plus half of any pension payments you are making.

If you or your partner has capital above £16,000, you will not qualify for any IBJSA. If you or your partner has capital between £6,000 and £16,000, then £1 is deducted from your IBJSA for every £250 of capital above the £6,000-mark. For example, capital of £7,500 would lead to a weekly cut of £6 in your IBJSA.

Even if you only receive a small amount of IBJSA, you are automatically eligible for:

- free prescriptions
- free school meals and possibly other local education benefits, such as school uniforms
- free dental care
- free sight tests and glasses
- Healthy Start vouchers for milk and healthy food, and tokens for vitamins if you have children under school age, or if you are an expectant or nursing mother
- refunds of fares for hospital visits
- Social Fund grants and loans, and
- maximum Housing and Council Tax Benefit, or possibly help with your mortgage (after a waiting period).

National Insurance credits

When you are out of work and not paying NI contributions, gaps appear in your NI record. These can affect your future entitlement to benefits or pension. In many circumstances, you are automatically given credits to cover periods when you are not working –for example, if you have been a student or cared for children or someone with severe disabilities.

You also receive these credits automatically when you are unemployed and signed on for JSA. However, if your entitlement to JSA is completely disallowed because of any income, earnings, or savings, you are no longer entitled to your contribution credits unless you continue to sign on for them. This may affect you if you do not qualify for any JSA because you fail to qualify for IBJSA under the means test and you are not receiving CJSA. In these circumstances, you are normally advised to continue signing on even though you are not entitled to any money, in order to be awarded weekly NI contribution credits.

You may not be directly encouraged by Jobcentre Plus staff to sign on for your credits. However, it is your right to do so and it can be important for your future entitlement to contributory benefits (especially Retirement Pension).

Joint claims for Jobseeker's Allowance

If you are a member of a couple that lives together (including a same-sex partners who live together as a couple), you have no children, and you and your partner were born after 28 October 1947, you will have to claim IBJSA jointly and both of you will have to meet the conditions of entitlement.[58] (Note: The joint claim rules only apply to IBJSA, not CJSA). If one of you fails to meet the conditions for entitlement, then there are special rules for reducing benefit and paying it to the customer who does meet them. If one of you is sanctioned (see pages 67–77), your IBJSA will be reduced by half.

If you are a joint claim couple, and one of you fits into a certain category, then that person will not have to meet the labour market rules for JSA. The most common categories are:[59]

- working 16–24 hours per week
- some carers
- aged 60 or older
- incapable of work because of illness or disability
- mentally or physically disabled, with earnings or hours of work 75 per cent or less than the earnings or hours of work for people who don't have a disability
- registered blind
- incapable of work because of pregnancy.

Three common problems with Jobseeker's Allowance claims

1 Payments at the end of a job;

2 Trade disputes;

3 Income Tax.

1 If you receive holiday pay or pay in lieu of notice or wages, you will be treated as if you are still in work and not entitled to JSA (though you may still qualify for National Insurance Credits). However, do not delay making a claim, because you can claim JSA up to three months in advance, so there is less delay in receiving payments when you qualify. By making a claim, you may also receive National Insurance Credits during your pay in lieu period. Redundancy pay, to which you have a contractual right, can also affect your JSA, but other redundancy payments will normally be treated as capital.[60] Seek advice if you are unsure. The precise wording of documents you receive from your employer on the ending of your job can affect a Jobcentre Plus Decision Maker's view. Seek advice from your trade union or your employer to minimise problems.

2 If you are on strike, or have a direct interest in a trade dispute at your place of work on any day, you are not entitled to claim JSA for the week that includes that day. You become entitled to JSA during the dispute, if you get another bona fide job and then lose that second job. Your dependants may also have entitlements. You should get advice from your trade union.

3 You may be entitled to a refund of some or all of the Income Tax you have paid after the end of the tax year in which you claimed JSA, or if you return to work within the same tax year in which you claimed JSA. Jobcentre Plus should issue you with form P45U, which you should give to your new employer or send to the Tax Office after the end of the tax year.

Leaving a job

Leaving a job voluntarily

You will lose your JSA for between one and 26 weeks if a Decision Maker decides that you have voluntarily left your job without just cause.[61] The length of the sanction will depend on how 'reasonable' it was for you to leave your job. If you left because you were being bullied, abused or harassed, for example, you should have no sanction (as that is usually good cause, especially if you tried to find other work or to solve the problem before leaving). But if it's not clear how severe the mistreatment was, the sanction could be anything from one to 26 weeks. The sanction does not apply if you have left self-employment.

Voluntary departure or dismissed for misconduct?

You should immediately sign on for JSA even if you think you will face problems, because you may win on appeal and you may also qualify for IBJSA on hardship grounds and/or other benefits – for example, Housing Benefit.

The voluntary unemployment sanction applies to jobs within the last six months. A number of factors are taken into account when working out the length of a sanction, and there may also be an overlap of sanctions.

Just causes for leaving a job voluntarily

You must show 'just cause' for leaving a job voluntarily to avoid a benefit sanction (though the DWP must prove you left voluntarily).

Normally, you must show that you went through the processes and procedures in place to try to correct your work situation before deciding to leave your job:

- You can have just cause to leave, if your employer tries to change the terms and conditions of your employment to make them less favourable than before without your agreement. In this case, your employer may also have ended the employment by breaking your contract of employment.

- You can show just cause for leaving a job, if you had a genuine and substantial grievance about the employment and had tried, in a proper and reasonable way, to get it settled. For example, you may have been asked to do work that was not covered by your contract of employment.

- You will have just cause for leaving, if your employer ordered you to do something that conflicted with your sincerely held religious or conscientious principles.

- Personal and domestic circumstances can be just cause to leave a job, provided they are pressing. For example, you may have just cause for leaving if you had to look after your child.

- You can show just cause, if you give up work for health reasons. You could give up work because the job is either beyond your physical or mental capacity, or harmful to your health. Medical evidence is preferred but not required.

- Moving home beyond the daily travelling distance of your job may give you just cause for leaving.

- Leaving work for another job could be just cause, if you had a firm offer of another job that started immediately but it fell through unexpectedly or did not last long. Again, there are several limitations that need to be considered.

- Giving up a new line of work because you are unsuited to it will be just cause for leaving, particularly if you leave during the early weeks of the job, because it prevents an employer from having an unsuitable employee.

- Taking voluntary redundancy when your employer has a need for redundancies should not be viewed as leaving voluntarily.

Employment lost through misconduct

There is no definition of misconduct, but some examples include wilful disobedience of instructions, failure to observe rules and regulations, refusal to perform particular work, negligence, carelessness or inefficient work, offensive behaviour, dishonesty, unauthorised absence or bad time-keeping, disqualification from driving (if employed in a driving capacity) and the conviction of a criminal offence inside or outside of work.

If you have been dismissed without a warning for being a 'slow worker', or if you have been dismissed in unfair circumstances, you may be able to argue against having a sanction imposed, because you did not lose your job through 'misconduct'.

The procedure for deciding whether you left your job with just cause

Jobcentre Plus will send an ES85 form to your employer. Your employer does not have to complete this but, if they do, it will give their view about why you left your job, which might be different to yours.

You are allowed to comment on your employer's allegations by writing a response on the ES86LV form, and it is important that you do give comments. This form must be returned to the Jobcentre Plus office within seven days of the date of issue, if your comments are to be taken into account by the benefits Decision Maker.

The above process can be bypassed, if Jobcentre Plus issues you directly with an ES84 form, which also requests details of how you left your last job. If you are taking action against your employer for discrimination or unfair dismissal, you should seek legal advice before replying to enquiries from Jobcentre Plus. If the reasons for dismissal that your employer gives to Jobcentre Plus are different to the reasons your employer gave to you, this may be significant for your unfair dismissal claim. A JSA sanction does not depend on an Employment Tribunal's hearing/decision of an unfair dismissal or discrimination case.

Once all the evidence is submitted, Jobcentre Plus will send you a Notification of Adjudication Submission letter (ES48S). If you are going to be sanctioned, this letter should contain a copy of the JSA9 leaflet that explains how to apply for hardship payments. If you receive one of these letters, you should immediately tell Jobcentre Plus that you want to apply for a hardship payment, and you should also appeal against both the sanction and the length of the sanction. (It is possible to have the length of the sanction reduced or to have the whole sanction removed.) These appeals have a high success rate, especially if you are represented.

Employment on Trial

Employment on Trial is a concessionary period during which you can leave a job voluntarily but you will not be disqualified for JSA under the voluntary unemployment sanction.[62]

To qualify for Employment on Trial, you must have been unemployed for at least 13 weeks before you started the job, you must leave the job from the beginning of the fifth week onwards but no later than the end of the 12th week, and you must have been working for 16 hours per week or more.[63] Vocational training for which you are referred by Jobcentre Plus also counts toward the qualifying period of 13 weeks.

Suspension of Jobseeker's Allowance, and other sanctions

If an adviser feels that you are not actively seeking or being available for work, they are instructed to suspend your benefit immediately[64] and to give you a Notification of an Entitlement Doubt letter. This letter says for how long your JSA will be suspended (one week minimum) and whether you can apply for hardship payments of IBJSA.

You will only get money from the beginning of your suspension period (or from the beginning of your claim), if you qualify for hardship payments as someone from a vulnerable group, or if Jobcentre Plus accepts that you were available for and/or actively seeking work.

If you are not classified as being in a vulnerable group, you can apply for hardship payments of IBJSA only after your JSA has been suspended for two weeks. In some cases, this means that you cannot apply for hardship payments during the whole period of suspension (that is, if you lose JSA for only one or two weeks).

Whatever the circumstances, if you are not receiving any money, you should immediately ask to apply for an IBJSA hardship payment. If you are told that you can't because your claim has been terminated, you should then ask to make a new claim for JSA.

If your JSA is suspended for not actively seeking work, it is normally only suspended for one or two weeks. Jobcentre Plus staff should explain that your jobsearch activity will be reviewed when you next attend the Jobcentre Plus office, so it is in your interests to show that you meet the actively seeking work/availability condition.

It is very important to appeal against any sanctions or benefit suspensions. If you can find someone to represent you at the appeal hearing, you have a good chance of success.

Refusing employment

You can be disqualified from JSA for up to six months (and for a minimum of one week) if Jobcentre Plus can show that, without good cause, you have refused or failed to apply for a job vacancy that Jobcentre Plus has informed you about. You can also be sanctioned if you are offered the job but refuse to take it without good cause.

You cannot be sanctioned if you refuse to take a job lasting fewer than 24 hours per week (or a job of fewer than 16 hours per week, if you have restricted your availability for work to fewer than 24 hours per week in your Jobseeker's Agreement).

The definition of 'refusing employment'

For the purposes of imposing a benefit sanction, 'refusing employment' means more than simply refusing or failing to apply for or to accept a job notified to you by Jobcentre Plus. It includes behaving in such a way that you lose the chance of employment. This includes:

- not turning up or arriving late at an interview
- going to the wrong place through your own negligence
- imposing unreasonable conditions on acceptance of a job offer
- behaving or appearing at the interview in such a way that the employer decides not to offer you the job

- refusing to give references
- delaying acceptance of the job until it has been taken by someone else, and
- accepting a job but then failing to start on the agreed day.

Moreover, Jobcentre Plus staff now have power under the Jobseeker's Direction to instruct you to improve your employability by taking steps to make yourself more acceptable to employers. In law, a Direction must be reasonable, taking account of your needs and the circumstances of the local labour market, and must also be in writing.

Notification of vacancies

To be sanctioned for refusing to apply for or accept a vacancy (including temporary work), the vacancy must be notified to you personally by a Jobcentre Plus member of staff. You must be given enough information so you can apply for the vacancy or to decide whether to apply for it.[65]

If you are offered vacancies by employment agencies or external providers (for example, programme centres or Connexions/careers services), these vacancies are not classed as being notified to you by Jobcentre Plus. However, if Jobcentre Plus staff become aware that you have been offered a vacancy by an external agency, they are within their rights to offer it to you again. This changes it to a vacancy that has been officially notified to you by Jobcentre Plus. The same applies for other types of vacancies, such as jobs from a newspaper.

Reading a job advertisement on the self-service boards in a Jobcentre Plus office does not count as notification of a vacancy. Vacancies need to be discussed with you personally by Jobcentre Plus staff.

FND providers may count as Jobcentre Plus staff for this purpose.

Types of vacancies

You cannot be sanctioned for refusing employment that is vacant because of a trade dispute.

You cannot be disqualified under the refusal of employment rule for refusing or failing to follow up self-employed jobs. However, if you are restricting your jobsearch to self-employment during your permitted period, neglecting to follow up these types of vacancies may call into question whether you are available for and actively seeking work.

Refusing a reasonable opportunity of work

The sanction for refusing employment can also be imposed for neglecting to avail yourself without 'good cause' of a reasonable opportunity of employment in your previous employment.[66]

'Neglect to avail yourself' of employment means that you have refused to take advantage of a reasonable opportunity of work that has arisen with a previous employer.

When deciding whether you had good cause to refuse employment or neglect to avail yourself of an opportunity of work, some important issues are:[67]

- the job offer was fewer than 24 hours per week, or 16 hours per week for some customers (jobs with 24 hours of work in one week and less work in other weeks are considered to be less than 24-hour-per-week jobs).
- you recently did training for a particular kind of employment for a period of not less than two months (you can refuse work for up to four weeks from the day your training ends).
- the vacancy did not fit within the restrictions on your availability for work (set out in your Jobseeker's Agreement).
- the vacancy did not fit within the restrictions you placed on the type of employment and level of pay during your permitted period.
- the vacancy would have caused you health problems or excessive physical or mental stress (the best evidence of this would come from your doctor or an allied professional).
- you have a sincerely held religious or conscientious objection to the job (you must give evidence that it genuinely conflicts with your principles and that your objection was sincere).
- you have caring responsibilities that would have made the job unreasonable (inconvenience is not enough for good cause).

Examples of unreasonable conditions include working at night, having a very early start or finish, and overnight stays away from home. You also have good cause for refusing work if the job would have conflicted with your restrictions on availability, or with the 48-hours' notice you are allowed to have before taking up employment.

- the travelling time was excessive (for example, over one and half hours, once you have been claiming JSA for 13 weeks).

- the work-based expenses would have used up an unreasonably high proportion of the wages of the job.

This is not an exhaustive list.

Rate of pay, on its own, is not a good cause for refusing work but it must, of course, be in line with the National Minimum Wage legislation. Examples of times when financial grounds do not give you good cause to refuse work include particularly high financial commitments, and the fact that you or a member of your household would lose the right to other benefits and concessions that are available to unemployed people. However, there are times when financial grounds do give you good cause for refusing work. This occurs when you are within your permitted period, when you are allowed to restrict your rate of pay for the first six months, when you are allowed to restrict your level of pay on health grounds, when a job pays on a commission-only basis, and when work-based expenses would be unreasonably high.

Any matter you put forward as good cause for refusing work must be considered. This includes having a real chance of another job that will start in the near future, that is likely to last as long as the current job offer, and that will be lost if you accept the current job offer.

Jobseeker's Direction

The Jobseeker's Direction is power that lets Jobcentre Plus staff instruct you, under threat of a sanction, to take steps aimed at improving your chances of finding employment.[68] The Direction given to you by Jobcentre Plus staff must be reasonable for your circumstances.

The instructions must be given in writing in order to qualify as a Direction.

If you refuse or fail to comply with a Direction that is reasonable and you cannot show good cause, your JSA personal allowance is cut for two weeks. This is the same sanction that is imposed if you do not attend a compulsory programme (see page 67).

Though the law does not list them, Jobseeker's Directions fall into one of the following four categories:

1 Your jobsearch activities;

2 Referral to Jobcentre Plus programmes;

3 Referral to other employment and training programmes;

4 Your behaviour and appearance – it may be possible to challenge this using Human Rights law.

1 You can be directed to do jobsearch activities such as applying for a specific vacancy (typically part-time), applying for advertised vacancies not notified to Jobcentre Plus, sending your CV to a particular employer, and making speculative approaches to employers in a particular trade;

2 A Jobseeker's Direction can be used to refer you to employment and training programmes that you may not wish to attend and that, under normal circumstances, are not compulsory;

3 A Jobseeker's Direction can refer you to other employment. If you are instructed to apply for a job of fewer than 24 hours per week you must apply, otherwise you can be sanctioned for a two- or four-week period for not following a Jobseeker's Direction. However, once you have applied, you cannot be sanctioned for refusing to take a job of fewer than 24 hours per week. So you should follow the Jobseeker Direction, but you can refuse the job offer;

4 For directions involving behaviour and appearance, you have between two and four weeks to comply. You will only be sanctioned if you ignore the advice from Jobcentre Plus staff. No personal directions that are discriminatory because of gender, sexuality, religion, disability, race or nationality can be given. Also, no directions that would be at odds with

conscientious belief can be given. An example of a direction involving appearance would be if you have a nose ring and the adviser knows that a certain employer will not tolerate nose rings, and so tells you either to remove the nose ring or to change your job goals.

How and when can a Jobseeker's Direction be issued?

Jobcentre Plus advisers can give a Jobseeker's Direction at any stage of your JSA claim. However, they should not issue a Direction:

- when referring the problem to a Decision Maker is more appropriate, or
- as a means of filling programmes, or
- when it is unlawfully discriminatory, or
- when it at odds with a sincerely held conscientious belief.

Good cause for not carrying out a Direction

A benefit sanction can only be imposed on you for refusing or failing to carry out a Direction if:

- the Direction was given in writing to you by a Jobcentre Plus adviser, and
- the Direction was reasonable taking your circumstances into account, and
- you were not referred to a job that was vacant because a trade dispute had stopped work, and
- you do not have good cause for refusal or failure.

All the guidance on good cause for refusing employment applies to Jobseeker's Directions with one exception: you do not have good cause for refusing or failing to carry out a Direction because the employment is fewer than 24 hours (or fewer than 16 hours in certain circumstances (see page 70) per week.

Certain restrictions on the kind of employment you are available for (for example, if you are within a permitted period) may also give you good cause for refusing or failing to carry out Directions.

You can refuse to follow a training-related Direction, if:

- you have finished another training course fewer than four weeks ago, and
- your training course lasted for at least two months, and
- the Direction is intended to find you a different type of employment than your previous training.

Good cause justifications

You will have good cause for refusing to comply with a Direction for the following reasons:

- health reasons
- conflict with a sincerely held religious belief, or a conscientious objection
- conflict with caring responsibilities
- unreasonably high expenses in carrying out the Jobseeker's Direction.

When deciding whether you had good cause to refuse to follow a Direction, the following things will be considered:

- any availability restrictions imposed by you that have been accepted by Jobcentre Plus
- any medical conditions or personal circumstances that have been accepted by Jobcentre Plus, or
- any religious or conscientious belief, such as:
    - religious objections to handling alcohol or certain foodstuffs
    - religious objections to working on a certain day
    - objections to working with materials that may be used for the destruction of life, or
    - religious objections to working with the opposite sex.

Compulsory programmes

If you receive a Jobseeker's Direction that refers you to a compulsory programme or to a voluntary scheme and you fail to attend, your JSA can be cut for two or four weeks. Your benefit is automatically cut for four weeks if you have already had a sanction in the last 12 months. Otherwise, it is cut for two weeks. Your benefit cannot be cut until a Decision Maker has examined all the evidence and written to ask you for your version of events and your comments on any evidence that is being used against you. It is important that you comment on any evidence.

What happens if you change your mind?

If at first you refused or failed to take a place on a compulsory programme, and then later changed your mind and took the place before the provider had filled it and before the course had started, you can be exempted from a benefit sanction or have the decision revised in your favour.

Good cause for not attending a compulsory programme[69]

You have good cause for not attending a compulsory programme, if you:

- have a physical or mental health problem that means that you cannot attend because your attendance would either risk the health of others on the scheme or risk your own health and safety
- have a sincerely held religious or conscientious objection
- have to travel more than an hour each way to attend the programme, or have to travel a long distance from home to attend, or travel makes it very difficult for you to attend
- have caring responsibilities and no close relative who can take over your duties
- are attending court for jury service or appearing as a witness
- are attending the funeral of a close relative or close friend, or dealing with an emergency.

Losing a place on a compulsory programme because of misconduct

The rules about misconduct and loss of employment (laid out on page 64) are also used to decide whether or not your benefit will be stopped when you lose your place on a compulsory programme because of alleged misconduct.

The procedure

The penalty process for refusing employment, neglecting to avail yourself of an employment opportunity, refusing a Jobseeker's Direction or failing to attend a compulsory programme is as follows:

- If Jobcentre Plus staff propose a benefit sanction they are legally obliged to give you a chance to comment on the circumstances on an official form. This form is sent to the Decision Maker and must be used in deciding if you had good cause for your actions. If you show you had a good cause, your benefit should not be sanctioned. It is very important to get independent advice and to fill out and return this form.

- If your benefit is sanctioned, the evidence you provide on the form may reduce the length of the sanction. The form gives you the chance to give your reasons and show good cause, but you have to complete it and return it to the Jobcentre Plus Office within seven days of the issue date (not the date you received it). It is important for you to give your views.

- You should continue to sign on. Your JSA will only be cut if the Decision Maker decides against you and is obliged to inform you by sending you a notice. You should also apply for a hardship payment.

- You may also want to request a revision of the decision, or appeal against the decision. Many appeals are successful, especially if you attend the appeal or have someone to help you make your case. You may appeal against the length of a sanction as well as the sanction itself.

Ways to deal with sanctions

- Always seek independent advice and appeal against a sanction – most appeals succeed.

- Continue to sign on as unemployed.

- Reply quickly to enquiries from Jobcentre Plus. If necessary, seek independent advice before replying.

- Do not delay making a claim, if you think you may be sanctioned.

- If you have been sanctioned, and you have a partner, and you are also not a Joint Claim Couple (see page 62), you can avoid loss of income if your partner makes a claim for JSA instead of you (so long as they are eligible for JSA).

- Do you qualify for another benefit instead of JSA? Sanctions only apply to JSA and you will not be sanctioned, for example, if you qualify for IS rather than IBJSA.

Compulsory programmes to help you into work

Flexible New Deal

What is Flexible New Deal?

Flexible New Deal (FND) is a compulsory programme for all those who are unemployed and eligible to receive JSA. The programme replaces:

- ND25+
- NDYP
- EZ, and
- New Deal for 50 Plus (ND50+).

FND will be introduced in phases, so programme availability will depend on where you live. If you live in a Phase 1 area, and you have done six months of Supported Jobsearch, you will have moved on to FND. Those who live in a Phase 1 area and were taking part in any of the programmes listed above before October 2009 will have also moved on to FND. If you live in a Phase 2 area, FND will be introduced from October 2010 for those who have done six months of Supported Jobsearch, and for those who are taking part in any of the programmes listed above at the time. This means that the above programmes will run in Phase 2 areas up until October 2010.

Phases 1 and 2

FND is being introduced into Jobcentre Plus districts in two phases, as follows:[70]

Phase 1

- Ayrshire, Dumfries, Galloway and Inverclyde
- Birmingham and Solihull
- Black Country
- Cambridgeshire and Suffolk
- Central London
- Coventry and Warwickshire
- Derbyshire
- Devon and Cornwall
- Edinburgh, Lothian and Borders
- Greater Manchester Central
- Greater Manchester East and West
- Kent
- Lambeth, Southwark and Wandsworth
- Lanarkshire and East Dunbarton
- Leicestershire and Northamptonshire
- Lincolnshire and Rutland
- Norfolk
- North and East Yorkshire and Humber
- North and mid-Wales
- Nottinghamshire
- South East Wales
- South Wales Valleys

Phase 2

- Bedfordshire and Hertfordshire
- Berkshire, Buckinghamshire and Oxfordshire
- Cheshire, Halton and Warrington
- City and East London
- Cumbria and Lancashire
- Dorset and Somerset

- Essex
- Forth Valley, Fife and Tayside
- Glasgow
- Gloucestershire, Wiltshire and Swindon
- Hampshire and Isle of White
- Highland, Islands, Clyde Coast and Grampian
- Merseyside
- North and North East London
- Northumbria
- South London
- South Tyne and Wear Valley
- West London
- West of England
- West Yorkshire

Who is required to join Flexible New Deal?

If you remain unemployed and on JSA for 12 months, you will then be required to join FND.[71]

Programme Elements[72]

Technically, the FND programme has four stages, with the first three stages related to claiming JSA with Jobcentre Plus. The fourth stage, which is often the only stage actually called 'Flexible New Deal', is an employment programme delivered by private or third-sector providers.[73]

Improved jobseeking with Jobcentre Plus

Stage 1 (months 1–3): Self-managed Jobsearch

Stage 1 FND includes an initial interview, fortnightly jobsearch reviews and help from an adviser, similar to the current JSA process.

At the beginning of your claim for JSA, you will have a New Jobseeker's Interview with a personal adviser, in which you will draw up a Jobseeker's Agreement and identify your main needs. The adviser will also explain that you must attend a Back to Work Session six to nine weeks after making your JSA claim, or you will face a one-week sanction.

If there is a large gap in your skills, you will be referred to a Skills Health Check at this stage. You may be fast-tracked immediately to Stage 3 if you need a lot of help with getting into work – for example, if you are aged 18, and not in employment, education or training.

As with the current JSA regime, at Stage 1 you will be given access to job vacancies and have a review every fortnight with an adviser. You must attend the mandatory group Back to Work Sessions at Week 6 to go through how to look for work and what you need to do to look for work, in order to encourage effective job hunting.

Stage 2 (months 3–6): Directed Jobsearch

If you are still claiming JSA after three months, you will move on to the Directed Jobsearch stage, in which you will expand your jobsearch and have more intensive reviews.

Similar to the current process for JSA, if you reach this stage, you will have a formal review of your Jobseeker's Agreement. You will be expected to expand your jobsearch based on travel to work distances, wage and working hours, rather than simply based on your preferred employment. You will be submitted to suitable vacancies.

After this review of your Jobseeker's Agreement, you will have six-weekly jobsearch reviews. As from October 2009, if you need extra help during Stage 2, advisers will identify this and you will have two targeted interviews during this stage.

Stage 3 (months 6–12): Supported Jobsearch

If you are still claiming JSA after six months, or if you have been fast-tracked because of particular disadvantage in the job market, you will enter the Supported Jobsearch stage, which builds on current New Deal Gateways.

Six months into your JSA claim, you will have a formal review with a personal adviser, and they will help you to draw up a back-to-work action plan that includes a range of activities aimed at improving your chances of getting a job. Jobcentre Plus will work with local partnerships to make sure that there is a range of employability training options to choose from, and you will be required to complete between one and three of these activities. You will not have a choice in this matter, because the increase in support means an increase in your responsibility, and you will be sanctioned if you do not co-operate.

Your formal review will be followed by six-monthly interviews with a personal adviser. In the first of these interviews, the adviser will assess you, conduct an in-depth skills screening, and help you draw up a revised Jobseeker's Agreement.

Jobseeking support outside Jobcentre Plus

Stage 4 (months 12–24): Flexible New Deal[74]

If you are still unemployed and claiming JSA after the Supported Jobsearch stage, you will be referred to the FND programme, which is delivered by public, private, and third-sector providers. This stage will be flexible and tailored to your personal employment and skills needs. During FND, you will remain on JSA and will still be required to sign on at the Jobcentre every fortnight. Jobcentre Plus will continue to monitor your journey into work for as long as you are claiming JSA.

You will receive a lot of personalised support on FND, but in return for increased help, you will be expected to take increased responsibility for making the most of this support. If you do not live up to your responsibilities, you risk losing your benefit. The minimum level of support you can get on FND includes:

- fortnightly contact with your FND provider
- an in-depth assessment of your needs
- drawing up of a challenging personal action plan
- a compulsory period of full-time work experience or work in the community, if you cannot find work early in Stage 4. This will help to refresh your skills and remind you of work patterns.[75]

Work for your benefit pilot[76]

For those who are have not found work after claiming JSA for two years, the government will pilot a 'work for your benefit' programme in some Jobcentre Plus districts from October 2010 to October 2012. In Greater Manchester, Norfolk, Cambridgeshire and Suffolk, those who have gone through FND, remain unemployed, and do not return to the Supported Jobsearch stage will be required to participate in either:

- a full-time work for your benefit programme, involving full-time work experience for up to six months, or
- an alternative programme delivered by Jobcentre Plus, involving increased support and interaction.

The aim of the work for your benefit programme is to help people who have been out of work for a long time to learn skills or refresh their existing skills, and to get into the routine of working. If you are unemployed after FND because of a gap in your skills, the work for your benefits programme could help you.

You will continue to receive JSA while you are taking part in the programme. If you refuse to participate, you could face benefit sanctions.

Young Person's Guarantee

If you are aged 18 to 24, through the Young Person's Guarantee you are promised an offer of a job, work focused training, or other meaningful activity before you reach the 10-month stage of your JSA claim.

The Guarantee is being rolled out nationally from early 2010, but parts of it will have started in some areas from as early as October 2009 (for example, the Future Jobs Fund will have started in some places in October 2009 – see page 84 for further details).

The Guarantee will provide you with one of the following four options:

- support to take an existing job in a key employment sector with funding for sector-specific training, recruitment subsidies and training on the job

- a work focused training place, lasting up to six months, which should lead to a job after the training has finished
- a place on the Community Task Force – this is unpaid work experience focused on improving your employability through jobs that benefit local communities (you will continue to receive JSA in this period)
- a new job supported by the Future Jobs Fund (see page 84).

To decide which of these options to take part in, you will have a discussion with your Jobcentre Plus adviser as you approach the 12-month stage of your JSA claim. Participation in one of the options is compulsory, if you want to continue to get JSA after 12 months.[77]

If you are aged over 24 and are finding it particularly difficult to get a job, then some parts of the Guarantee, including access to the Future Jobs Fund, could be made available to you at the discretion of your Jobcentre Plus personal advisor.

Community Task Force

Where a subsidised job or training is unavailable or unsuitable, and you have been claiming JSA for 10 months, you may be required to take part in the Community Task Force option as part of the Young Person's Guarantee. This is a work experience placement designed to increase your employability and benefit the wider community. The placement is offered alongside training and will last for up to six months.[78] You will receive a Training Allowance worth the same amount as your benefit, plus a top-up of £15.38.[79]

The Community Task Force option will be voluntary from January 2010, and mandatory from spring 2010.[80] It is possible that you could be fast-tracked to the Community Task Force part of the Young Person's Guarantee. This decision is made by your personal adviser, if they feel it would benefit you to be fast-tracked.[81]

The work experience you gain while taking part in the Community Task Force should show that you can carry out tasks similar to those in a normal working environment. The tasks should give you work-related skills and increase your chances of finding paid employment. [82]

If you do not find work at the end of the placement, you will go back to claiming JSA, returning to the point at which you left the claims process.[83] If you choose to end your work experience through the Community Task Force and stop claiming JSA, but you then return to re-claim JSA within 28 days of leaving, the usual linking rules will apply, and you will return to the stage of the process you were at when you left the benefit. If the break is longer than 28 days, you will return to the start of the process.[84]

While taking part in the Community Task Force option, you are still subject to sanctions as you would be if you were on New Deal (see page 67).[85]

Future Jobs Fund

As from October 2009,[86] if you are aged 18 to 24 and have been claiming JSA for between 10 and 12 months,[87] you will be eligible for a six-month paid job supported by the Future Jobs Fund. The job should be for 25 hours per week or more, and you will be paid at least the National Minimum Wage.[88] [89]

If your JSA claim is fast-tracked because you were not in education, training or employment prior to making your claim, you may be able to apply for a job through the Future Jobs Fund after claiming JSA for six months, rather than 12 months.[90] You may also be able to get work through the Future Jobs Fund if you are aged over 24, have found it particularly difficult to get a job, and live in an 'unemployment hotspot'.[91]

Jobs supported by the Future Jobs Fund are not limited to people claiming JSA, but can be available to those on Income Support (IS), Incapacity Benefit (IB), or Employment and Support Allowance (ESA) as well. However, you will have to claim one of these benefits for 12 months before you become eligible to access the Fund.[92] It is up to your Jobcentre Plus personal adviser to decide whether or not you can apply for a job supported by the Future Jobs Fund.[93]

Jobs are designed to improve the local community. You will be referred to potential jobs following discussions with your personal adviser, who will decide the jobs for which you are likely to be eligible.[94] The type of work on offer could include sports coaching, crime prevention, social care, hospitality, tourism, working with children, and jobs that improve the environment.[95]

Once you have started your job, you should receive extra help from your employer to get any training and support you need in the workplace, and you may also be eligible for Train to Gain funding to help pay for training. In addition, you should get help with finding employment once your job is over.[96]

Future Jobs Fund jobs could also potentially form the first six months of an apprenticeship. As with other jobs through the Fund, if you're doing a job as part of your apprenticeship, you should be working for at least 25 hours per week and you should receive at least the minimum wage. Apprenticeships will normally continue beyond six months and are subject to different rules.

Future Jobs Fund employers should offer an exit interview to assess your experience of the job, and provide you with a reference that details your performance, attendance record and any skills that you have developed while in work. [97]

If you think that you may need some training before starting a Future Jobs Fund job, then you should discuss this with your personal adviser at Jobcentre Plus, since they can authorise up to eight weeks of full-time training for people on JSA in these circumstances.[98]

You may not be on FND (or any New Deal options) at the same time that you are doing a job through the Future Jobs Fund.[99]

New Deal for Young People

NDYP was replaced by the FND programme in Phase 1 districts as from October 2009, and will be replaced in Phase 2 districts from October 2010. So, until October 2010, NDYP will still be running in Phase 2 districts.

What is New Deal for Young People?

The primary aim of NDYP[100] is to move you into sustainable work. It provides a wide variety of support, including training, advice, jobsearch support and work experience.

NDYP consists of three stages:

- Gateway
- Four NDYP options
- Follow-through.

Who is eligible for New Deal for Young People?

If you are aged 18 to 25, and have been claiming JSA for six months, you must take part in NDYP.[101]

Early entry

In some circumstances, you are allowed early entry to NDYP. Usually, personal advisers use their discretion to decide whether it would be best for you to enter the programme early,[102] but you may be eligible if you fall into one of the special groups listed below. Some people in the special groups may be able to access other help through Progress2Work or Progress2Work-Link-up (see page 224).

Special groups:

- refugees
- ex-offenders
- homeless people (including rough sleepers)
- people affected by drug addiction (including alcoholism)
- people who have been in residential care
- ex-regular members of the armed forces
- benefit recipients with language, literacy or numeracy problems
- lone parents, people with disabilities and carers on JSA (instead of other benefits).

Gateway

The Gateway period is the first stage of NDYP. It can last up to four months and may put you into contact with a number of organisations. During this time, you will remain on JSA and be subject to the normal JSA rules about taking steps to look for work and being available to start work. The Gateway prepares you for work by addressing any barriers to work, and by helping you to find work. In each Jobcentre Plus district, the Gateway focuses on meeting the needs of the local labour market, along with meeting your needs.[103]

Your Jobseeker's Agreement will be reviewed and the steps you should take included in it may be changed.

Gateway content

The activity you do during the Gateway will depend on your particular needs. Certain activities from the following list are available to everyone, while other activities are only available to those with particular needs.

The Gateway can include:

- jobsearch advice and help
- individual careers guidance (an hour-long interview with a qualified adviser, to discuss your options for learning and work)
- help with working towards Level 1 Basic Skills qualifications (if your Basic Skills are between Entry Level 3 and Level 1)
- help with pre-ESOL and ESOL courses
- skills training in communication, IT, problem solving and teamwork
- help to build your confidence and motivation for work
- specialist help to improve your chance of getting a job (especially if you have a problem relating to crime, homelessness, drug and alcohol misuse or debt)
- special help if you have a disability, are part of an ethnic minority, or come from a rural area
- advice about your training needs, including guidance on further and higher education, and open and distance learning, and
- employment and training for up to two weeks.[104]

Your Jobseeker's Agreement will be reviewed and the steps you should take included in it may be changed.

Initial interview

The Gateway starts with an initial interview with a Jobcentre Plus personal adviser. The interview will:

- tell you about New Deal, how it operates locally and the involvement of partner organisations
- begin the process of drawing up an action plan that will record any action you intend to undertake and that you do undertake to move closer to work
- screen for basic skills needs
- where appropriate, refer you to partner organisations that deliver relevant activity.

Further interviews

Following the initial interview, you will attend interviews with your adviser on at least a weekly basis.[105] These interviews will last around 30 minutes. If you have significant barriers to employment because of health or disability, you should be referred to the Disability Employment Adviser, who will take on the role of a personal adviser.

Gateway courses

If you have not found work after four weeks on the Gateway, you must attend a Gateway to Work course. The course is aimed to help you to improve:

- your communication skills
- how you present yourself
- your punctuality, time-keeping and time-management
- your team-working and problem-solving skills
- your ability to search for jobs
- your CV, and
- your performance in interviews.

The course is mandatory, and if you do not go, your benefits may be affected. If no course is running, then you must attend the next available one. The courses last two weeks, and you are required to attend for a minimum of 30 hours each week.[106]

End of the Gateway

At the end of the Gateway period, if you have not found work, your adviser will work with you to find a suitable placement on one of four options. You will also be referred to a provider for mentoring, although you can opt out of this.[107]

Flexible options

Once you enter the flexible options period, you will be able to choose between four different options. Your adviser will help you decide which is most appropriate for you. As well as doing your chosen option for 30 hours each week, you will spend the equivalent of one day per week on jobsearch.

When taking part in any of the options, your provider should fill in an action plan review record and give you a copy to keep. This keeps a record of any changes to the action plan and any progress you have made, ensuring that you are keeping in line with your goals.[108]

At the end of Week 10 of your chosen option, you will need to go to your local Jobcentre Plus to discuss your progress with your personal adviser. You will talk about whether you have achieved the aims of your action plan, and assess how ready you are to go into employment. Your adviser will decide whether you stay on your option for longer than 13 weeks and, if so, for how long.[109]

1. Full-time education or training

The full-time education or training option is designed to help you reach Level 2 or equivalent, or offer support if you have basic skills needs. If you do not have a relevant Level 2 qualification, or equivalent, the option will help you to get employability and occupational skills for work.

There are two types of programme:

- a short, job focused course that lasts two, four, six or eight weeks, with a certificate awarded on completion, and

- a course of between 13 and 52 weeks, with an education and training provider, which leads to a Level 2 Scottish or National Vocational Qualification, involving work experience.

Work placement

It is important that any education or training you receive provides links to a work environment, because the NDYP aims to increase your employability and help you to get a job. Therefore, you must complete a work placement with an employer during the full-time education or training option. The length and timing of your work placement depends on local needs and circumstances.[110]

2. Employment option

The employment option offers a job with an employer, who is paid a subsidy to employ you.

You can participate in the employment option at any time during NDYP, including during the Gateway and Follow-through, and even after a spending the full amount of time on the other options.[111] The aim of the employment option is to help improve your chances of finding permanent employment by offering a period of work with training to an approved level. The length of the employment option is up to 26 weeks.

Employers will be expected to pay you the going rate for the job. They will be offered a subsidy towards the cost of employing you. If they take you on full-time (30 hours or more per week), they will receive up to £60 per week, and if they take you on part-time (between 24 and 29 hours per week), they will receive up to £40 per week. They may also receive up to £750 towards the cost of vocational training.

The employer will sign an agreement stating that they will:

- keep you on as long as you show the aptitude and commitment needed
- provide or arrange training as appropriate
- monitor and record your progress, and identify areas of action – in the same way that they would for any other employee, to help them settle in and make progress.[112]

It is important for your personal adviser to monitor your progress in the employment option. Your hours of work must be specified on your Learning Development Plan and may be monitored by Jobcentre Plus.[113]

You can also choose a Self-Employment Option, which prepares you to set up and run a successful business, and equips you with the skills to help you into work with another employer, if appropriate. It involves a one-day awareness and information session, one-to-one counselling and a short part-time course that includes developing a business plan.[114] These parts of the Self-Employment Option are also available during the Gateway and Follow-through. The Self-Employment Option can also include test-trading for up to 26 weeks and some training.

3. Voluntary Sector Option

The Voluntary Sector Option (VSO) involves a work placement or employment in the voluntary sector to benefit your local community. It will also include support and education or training at an approved level. This option lasts for a minimum of 13 weeks but, in special circumstances, your personal adviser can extend it by between one and 13 weeks.[115]

4. Environment Task Force Option

The Environment Task Force Option (ETFO) involves a work placement or employment designed to improve the environment. It includes support and education or training towards an approved level. As with the VSO, this option lasts for a minimum of 13 weeks, and can be extended by between one and 13 weeks.[116]

Finance and your choice of options

If you are on:

- the employment option, you will be paid a wage by your employer and you will be eligible for tax credits and other in-work benefits (see page 248), but you will not be eligible for passported benefits, such as free prescriptions or free dental care;

- the self-employment option, you will receive a training allowance from Jobcentre Plus, which includes a top-up payment of £400 paid to you in instalments. You may start trading whilst on this scheme;[117]
- the full-time education and training option, you will receive a training allowance equivalent to your JSA plus £15.38 per week, and your travel expenses will be paid;
- the work experience placement, you will receive a training allowance, which includes a top-up payment of £400 paid to you in instalments. (This may be referred to as ETF or VSO. Monetary values and conditions are the same.)[118]

Support while on a New Deal Option

While you are on a NDYP Option, you will still have access to your personal adviser, and you should contact them if you have any problems. The adviser is supposed to keep in touch with you and monitor your progress throughout your option. You are not required to attend weekly or fortnightly meetings.

The referral process

If you find it difficult to choose an option, you can do a taster that gives you the opportunity to try out one of the options for a short time. You can stay on JSA while doing a taster.[119]

Once you have agreed to start an option, you will have a pre-entry interview with your personal adviser, who will formally refer you for an interview with the provider of the option you have chosen. You will be asked to agree a personal development plan that will form part of your New Deal Action Plan.

Although you have a choice about which option you join, once your decision is made participation on the option is mandatory. If you repeatedly fail to start, you may be sanctioned.

Transferring between Options

If you do not get on well with your chosen option, you may be able to move onto a different option.[120] You should speak to your personal adviser, and they can agree to a transfer between providers and options. If you simply leave your option and try to claim JSA at a Jobcentre Plus office, you will face possible sanctions for leaving your option.

There used to be a time limit that stopped participants moving between options. This has been removed. You should be fully involved in the discussions with your personal adviser when agreeing which New Deal option best suits your needs. However, if at any time you feel you are attending the wrong option, then you should notify your personal adviser, who will arrange a transfer to a more suitable option for the rest of time that is left.

If you transfer to a different programme or provider within the same option, you can only have a total of:

- 26 weeks on the employment option (including the Self-Employment route)
- 13 weeks on the VSO or ETF option (with extensions allowed in special circumstances), and
- 52 weeks on the full-time education or training option.[121]

Follow-through

If you have completed your option and have not found a job, you will have to re-claim JSA. At this point, you will be referred back to your personal adviser, who will start a Follow-through period.

You will receive intensive help to find jobs, as well as advice and guidance to identify further action to improve your chances of finding work. You will receive similar assistance as you were offered in the Gateway period, including:

- jobsearch advice and help
- individual careers guidance
- help with basic skills
- key training in communication skills, problem solving, working with others and basic IT skills
- help with attitude, motivation and confidence

- specialist assistance to deal with problems such as homelessness and drug abuse
- assessment of training needs, including advice and guidance about further and higher education and distance learning
- employment and training for up to two weeks.

The Follow-through period can last for up to 16 and 26 weeks,[122] during which time you will have interviews with your adviser. There is no set frequency for these meetings, and your adviser will agree a course of action that best suits you.

Sanctions

Leaving the programme

If you are seriously considering giving up your option placement, you should discuss this with your personal adviser, who may be able to resolve the issues causing problems with your option, or refer you to a different placement.

If you fail to complete an option, and you return to the Jobcentre to reclaim JSA within 13 weeks of your leaving date, your adviser will decide whether to:

- submit you to unsubsidised jobs
- re-refer you back to the same option
- refer you to a different option, or
- move you straight into Follow-through.[123]

You may leave NDYP if you are eligible to receive another benefit (such as IS or ESA). Similarly, you can leave NDYP if you join a full-time education course or take up a job.

NDYP is only available to JSA claimants, and if you cease to claim for any reason other than starting an option or getting a job, then you automatically leave NDYP.

You can be sanctioned for repeatedly failing to start an option, for leaving an option without agreeing this with your personal adviser, or for being dismissed due to misconduct or leaving voluntarily without just cause.[124] Jobcentre Plus is the only organisation that can sanction you.

A sanction could involve taking away two weeks' worth of benefit, unless you have already been sanctioned in the last 12 months whilst on NDYP. If so, this amount could increase to four weeks. It can go up to 26 weeks, if you have been previously sanctioned two or more times for an offence whilst on NDYP.[125] Seek independent advice and appeal, if you are sanctioned.

If you still require assistance to find employment, a further range of help is available through more intensive employment and training measures.

New Deal for 25 Plus

New Deal for 25 Plus (ND25+) was replaced by the FND programme in Phase 1 districts from October 2009, and will be replaced in Phase 2 districts from October 2010. So, until October 2010, ND25+ will still be running in Phase 2 districts.

What is New Deal for 25 Plus?

ND25+[126] aims to help unemployed adults into lasting work. The programme offers a wide range of personalised support, including training, advice, guidance and work experience.

ND25+ has three stages:

1 Gateway;

2 Intensive Activity Period;

3 Follow-through.

Who is eligible for New Deal for 25 Plus?

Compulsory participation

You must join ND25+, if you:[127]

- are aged 25 or over but under State Pension age, and
- have been claiming JSA for 18 of the past 21 months (even if you

have just been receiving National Insurance Credits), and

- do not live in an EZ area or have not been directed to join an EZ programme (to find out if you live in an EZ area see page 109).[128]

Both members of a Joint Claim couple must join ND25+ if their claim is eligible.

If you are a Joint Claim couple, Jobcentre Plus will keep the following things in mind when deciding whether you should join ND25+:

- the date when your Joint Claim started
- the date when you claimed extra JSA for your partner, or your partner claimed extra JSA for you
- whether you have children who are no longer in full-time education, or children who are over 18 years old.

Voluntary participation and early entry

In some cases, you may be granted early entry to ND25+. Personal advisers use their discretion to decide whether you can enter early,[129] but you may be eligible if you fall into one of the groups below:[130]

- ex-offenders
- refugees
- homeless people (including rough sleepers)
- people affected by drug addiction (including alcoholism)
- people who have been in residential care
- ex-regular members of armed forces
- benefit claimants with language, literacy or numeracy problems
- lone parents, people with disabilities and carers on JSA (instead of other benefits).

Programme elements

The Gateway

The Gateway is the first stage of ND25+ and it lasts for up to four months. It aims to help you find work or prepare you for work by giving you skills and training. You will have a Basic Skills screening during the Gateway, and you might also have to do an in-depth assessment. Once you have done the Basic Skills screening, you will immediately have access to support and help for your Basic Skills needs.

The Gateway will vary according to individual needs. So, some people will attend a series of one-off interviews as part of the Gateway, while other people will attend training and other activities for several days.[131]

While you are on the Gateway, you will still get JSA and you will have to meet the JSA rules about taking steps to look for work and being available to start work.

Your personal adviser and his or her managers will check your progress at the end of the first and third months of the Gateway. They will agree on suitable help that should be given to you.[132]

Gateway content

The things you do during the Gateway will depend on your needs. You may get:[133]

- jobsearch advice and help
- individual careers guidance (an hour-long interview with a qualified adviser, to discuss your options for learning and work)
- help with working towards Level 1 Basic Skills qualifications (if your Basic Skills are between Entry Level 3 and Level 1)
- help with pre-ESOL and ESOL courses
- skills training in communication, IT, problem solving and teamwork
- help to build your confidence and motivation for work
- specialist help to improve your chances of getting a job (especially if you have a problem relating to criminality, homelessness, drug and alcohol misuse or debt)
- special help if you have a disability, are part of an ethnic minority, or come from a rural area
- advice about your training needs, including guidance on further and higher education, and open and distance learning
- employment and training for up to two weeks.

At your first interview, you will begin to draw up a New Deal Action Plan, which will record any action you plan to undertake and do undertake to become more work-ready.

Intensive Activity Period

If you have not found work by the end of the Gateway, you will move into the Intensive Activity Period (IAP). The IAP aims to increase your employability by:

- addressing 'deep-seated' barriers to work
- giving you experience in the world of work, and
- getting you to do full-time hours of activity, to encourage you to move into work.

If you are aged 25 to 59, you must participate in the IAP.[134] If you do not take part in the IAP, you could lose your benefit.

If you are aged over 60, but you are still below pension age, you will have to participate in the Gateway, but entry to the IAP will be voluntary.

Length and requirements of IAP

For most people, the IAP lasts for 13 weeks but, for those who need extra help, the IAP can last for up to 26 weeks. (In some cases, the IAP can even last for up to 12 months.)[135] After about 11 weeks, there will be a review to finalise the length of your IAP.

In almost all cases, you will have to do at least 30 hours of IAP activities spread over five days each week.[136] If you have a health condition, a disability or caring responsibilities, and your Jobseeker's Agreement sets out your restrictions, you will be able to discuss reducing your IAP hours with your personal adviser.[137] If you are working or studying part-time, you will still have to take part in 30 hours of IAP activity per week. Your adviser will help you to arrange your study or work around IAP activities, and, in certain cases, they may be able to reduce your IAP activity time to 20 hours per week. The study that you are doing must be helping you towards getting a job.[138]

During the IAP, you will get a New Deal Allowance instead of JSA. The amount of allowance is equal to the amount of JSA you have been getting. You will also get a top-up (currently £15.38), unless you are on some kind of paid training or work placement.

IAP content

During your IAP, you will receive at least one of the following things:

- help with basic skills problems
- work placements with employers (see also page 100) (the employer must give a reference for you)[139]
- work experience placements
- training linked strongly to the labour market
- help with motivation, soft skills and jobsearch skills
- any other support that will help you to get past barriers to work
- help with becoming self-employed.

Subsidised employment

You can take up subsidised employment after the fourth week of the Gateway, during the IAP, or during Follow-through. You should expect your subsidised employment either to be permanent or to last for at least 26 weeks. ND25+ is different from NDYP because, under ND25+, employers do not make a formal commitment to give you training, and they do not get extra money towards your training. However, employers should still give you the same training that they give any of their other employees.

If you take up subsidised employment, you will be paid a wage (employers should pay you the going rate for the job). Your employer will also be given a subsidy towards the cost of employing you, so long as your job is still available to you once the subsidy ends. If your job is full-time (30 hours or more per week), your employer can get £75 per week for 26 weeks. If your job is part-time (16 to 29 hours per week), your employer can get £50 per week for 26 weeks.[140]

The employer where you complete your work experience or placement must complete a reference for you as part of your IAP. It can be included in, or additional to, your Record of Achievement and Capabilities. It should be completed at the end of your placement by the employer and will provide potential employers with first-hand evidence of your skills and abilities.

A positive Employer Reference is something that you will work towards throughout your time on work experience or placement. Your personal adviser should work closely with you to ensure you are doing enough tasks to get a substantial reference. The Employer Reference must be personalised, of high quality and include some or all of the following:

- the skills you have demonstrated
- significant achievements while working with the employer
- your personal qualities
- your reliability, timekeeping, communication skills and other performance issues
- any other attributes the employer feels you have demonstrated.

IAP Training

During the IAP, training may be available to you.

Work experience during the IAP

Work experience aims to help you find paid work, and where this is not possible, to improve your readiness for work.

Work experience placements give you the chance to:

- build on or renew your soft skills and abilities
- update your CV
- get a recent work reference, and
- search for jobs (which may include attending Jobcentre interviews).

Work-related experience takes place in a work environment with a Jobcentre Plus provider, but it offers more support and supervision than you might usually get at work. After your work experience placement, you may have a work placement with an employer. This work placement could either make up part of your overall period of work experience, or it could be separate to your work experience. You may also be able to gain experience by volunteering.

Education and Training Opportunities

Once you have done the Basic Skills screening, Basic Skills assessment and further training, you may be able to take up Education and Training Opportunities (ETO) if you still face barriers to work.

If you are ready for work but you need some help with Basic Skills, you can do an ETO course for eight or 10 weeks to bring your Basic Skills up to speed. If you need help with more than just Basic Skills, your ETO course can be longer, covering work and skills training in addition to Basic Skills. Your ETO can last for up to 12 months and can help you to get qualifications up to NVQ/SVQ Level 3 or equivalent. In special cases, you may be able to get higher qualifications through ETO.[141]

You will have to spend 30 hours per week on your ETO course, spread out from Monday to Friday. Most (or all) of your time should be used to study towards your qualification but, in some cases, your time can include getting help with IT skills, counselling for personal problems, financial advice, and so on. Sometimes, work experience and work placements can also count towards your 30 hours.[142]

Self-Employment Provision

Self-Employment Provision (SEP) gets you ready to set up and run your own business. It can also help you to get skills that you can use to find work with another employer later on. SEP offers:[143]

- good-quality, ongoing advice and support
- the chance to do test-trading for up to 26 weeks, while still getting an allowance or Working Tax Credit
- the chance to experience the realities and responsibilities of being self-employed, and
- training to help you get through the test-trading period, if you need it.

SEP is made up of the following three stages:[144]

1 one-to-one assessment to make sure that you understand what self-employment means in reality, and to make sure that you have a business idea and the ability to see it through;

2 one-to-one counselling and training to help you draw up a business plan. You will receive this support for one day each week, for a maximum of eight weeks;

3 a period of test-trading that lasts for up to 26 weeks.

You can do the first and second stages during the Gateway, and the third stage during your IAP. You can also do the first and second stages during your Follow-through, but you can't do the third stage at this time.

Unlike NDYP, you do not have to do training as part of the ND25+ SEP. It is open to you if you need some specific help in order to make it through your test-trading, but your training does not necessarily have to be towards an approved qualification.

Follow-through support

If you reach the end of ND25+ and you have not found employment, you will move into the Follow-through part of ND25+ and go back to getting JSA. Follow-through aims to help you move into work as quickly as possible by making the most of the extra support you received during the Gateway and IAP. Follow-through usually lasts for six weeks but, if you need extra help, it may last for 13 weeks.[145]

The support you get during Follow-through will be tailored to your needs. It can include jobsearch help, guidance, training and specialist support. If your Follow-through is extended to 13 weeks because you still face barriers to work, you will be able to access the things offered during IAP as well as what is usually offered during Follow-through.[146]

Leaving the programme and sanctions

If you haven't found work by the time you finish ND25+, you will have to re-claim JSA.

If you leave ND25+ before you have finished the programme, and without getting approval from your personal adviser, your benefit may be sanctioned. If you fail to attend any part of the ND25+ programme, or if you turn up late to activities or behave with misconduct, your benefit may be sanctioned. If you try to re-claim JSA within 13 weeks of leaving ND25+ early, you will have to re-enter ND25+. Your personal adviser will decide which part of ND25+ you should return to (either the Gateway, IAP or Follow-through).[147]

Employment Zones

Employment Zones (EZs) were replaced by the Flexible New Deal programme in Phase 1 districts as from April 2009, and will be replaced in Phase 2 districts from April 2010. So, until April 2010, EZs will still be running in Phase 2 districts (Glasgow, Liverpool and Sefton, Tower Hamlets and Newham, and Brent and Haringey).

What are Employment Zones?

EZs aim to help people who have been out of work for a long time to find and stay in work. There are four EZs across the country, in areas that have a high rate of long-term unemployment. If you take part in the EZ programme, you are guaranteed an income that is equal to your total weekly benefit claim/s for as long as you stay unemployed.

Each EZ is run differently, but they all follow the same broad guidelines. EZs combine funding for training with Jobcentre Plus support and benefit amounts, so that you can have more flexibility and more say in choices that affect you.

The government runs EZs through contractors. There are two types of contract: single provider EZs (where one contractor provides the service for the whole zone), and multiple provider EZs (where more than one contactor provides service in the zone). If you live in an EZ where there is more than one contractor, you may be able to choose which service to use.

Who is eligible for Employment Zones?[148]

Jobcentre Plus is responsible for identifying, referring and re-referring eligible jobseekers to the EZ programme. If you are found to be ineligible after starting EZ, you should be given the chance to continue. If you choose not to continue, you will be issued an end date notification (Form EZ9) by your provider and return either to full JSA or to your existing benefit.

Compulsory participation

If you are aged 25 to 60, you must take part in EZ if:

- you live in an EZ area, and
- you have been claiming JSA for 18 of the last 21 months.

You may apply to join EZ earlier, if your circumstances make it particularly difficult for you to find work.

If you are aged 18 to 24, you must take part in EZ if:

- you live in an EZ area, and
- you have taken part in NDYP in the past.

If you have taken part in E Z in the last 12 months, but you did not finish the programme, then you must return to the programme.

If you have been referred to another programme and are waiting to start, you won't be referred to EZ. If you are awaiting a decision on a JSA eligibility question, you will not be referred to a provider.

Lone parents

If you are a lone parent, you can volunteer to take part in an EZ programme, if:

- you live in an EZ area, and
- you are unemployed, or working for fewer than 16 hours per week, and
- you are not claiming JSA.

In the multiple-provider EZs, you can choose which contractor to work with. If you choose to take part in EZ, you can no longer participate in New Deal for Lone Parents. You can decide to leave the programme at any time and your benefits will not be affected.

Warning: If you are a lone parent claiming JSA, and you meet the criteria for compulsory participation in EZ, then you must take part in the programme.

Lone parents living in London

In EZ strands in London (Tower Hamlets and Newham, and Brent and Haringey), EZ has replaced the New Deal for Lone Parents. The EZ programmes are run by multiple providers and you can choose which one you work with. When EZ is replaced by FND, Jobcentre Plus will have to provide New Deal for Lone Parents services in those areas.

People claiming Pension Credit

If you are claiming Pension Credit, you can volunteer to take part in an EZ programme so long as you are unemployed, or working for fewer than 16 hours per week.

In the multiple-provider EZs, you can choose which contractor to work with. You can choose to leave the programme at any time and your benefits will not be affected.

Early entry[149]

In some circumstances, you may be given early entry to EZ. Jobcentre Plus advisers will use their discretion to decide whether you can enter the programme early, but you may be eligible if you fall into one of the following groups:

- people with a physical or mental disability
- people who need help with reading, writing or numbers
- people whose first language is not English, Welsh or Gaelic
- lone parents who do not live with a partner and are responsible for at least one child living in their household
- people who have served in the regular armed forces

- people who were looked after as a child by a local authority
- people with a criminal record
- people with a drug problem
- people who have participated in Progress2Work
- people who have been told by the Home Office that they are officially a refugee
- people who have been given humanitarian or discretionary protection by an immigration office.

If you live in a multiple-provider EZ and you are granted early entry to the programme, you will not be able to choose which contractor you go to. The contractor will be randomly chosen for you. Once you start the programme, you must stay on the programme.

Referral to interview[150]

Once Jobcentre Plus has confirmed your eligibility, they will contact the contractor and send you a Referral to Interview letter. The contractor must make an appointment within two weeks of your being referred from Jobcentre Plus. Jobcentre Plus will forward a copy of this letter and an EZ1 form to your EZ provider.

Choosing an Employment Zones provider if you live in a multiple-provider zone[151]

If you live in an EZ area where there is more than one programme provider, you will have the chance to choose which provider to go with. Once you have chosen a provider, you must stay with that provider for the whole programme.

If you do not choose a provider, you will be randomly allocated to one of the providers in your zone.

Once you have been claiming JSA for 18 months (if you are aged 25 or over), or six months (if you are aged 18 to 24 and have taken part in NDYP in the past), then you will be given an information leaflet about the different EZ providers in your area. You will usually have up to four weeks to look into the options that are open to you, and you may have the chance to visit the providers before making your choice.

Jobcentre Plus advisers will help you to choose a provider where appropriate, but must remain neutral during the process.

Programme elements

The EZ programme is made up of three stages. The first two stages are compulsory, and the third stage is voluntary. Each EZ contractor designs their own programme, but must follow basic guidelines.

Stage 1

You will only do Stage 1 if you are a compulsory participant. Volunteers will not enter Stage 1.

Stage 1 lasts for up to 28 days.[152] Your EZ provider will appoint you a personal adviser. The adviser will help you to decide on the kind of work you are looking for and understand what may be stopping you from getting that work. You will draw up an individually tailored Action Plan with your adviser. An Action Plan is an agreed plan of activities that will help you move closer to work. When you have agreed on an Action Plan, your EZ provider will tell Jobcentre Plus, and you will move on to Stage 2.

During Stage 1, you will continue to sign on at the Jobcentre every fortnight and you will be paid JSA.[153]

Stage 2

Stage 2 can last for up to 26 weeks. During Stage 2, your EZ contractor will help you to carry out the activities in your Action Plan. You may get help with the cost of travel and clothes for interviews. You may also get help to move into training or self-employment. You will also carry out an intensive jobsearch.

During Stage 2, your provider will pay you an amount equal to your benefits, so you will no longer need to attend Jobcentre Plus.[154]

If you find a job before entering Stage 2, you will move straight from Stage 1 to Stage 3.[155]

Stage 3

Stage 3 begins once you have started work and lasts for 13 weeks. During Stage 3, your EZ provider will give you in-work support to help you keep you job.

Your provider will get a payment when you start work and another payment if you are still employed after 13 weeks. As a result, your provider has a strong motive to find you a job that lasts.

Follow-on

If you are a compulsory participant in EZ, and you have not found a job by the end of Stage 2, you will return to Jobcentre Plus office to claim a benefit. You can choose to continue on EZ, if you wish. If you did not find a job after spending 26 weeks actively searching during Stage 2 of the programme, you are will have to re-join EZ once you have been re-claiming JSA for 13 weeks.[156]

Benefits and entitlements

If you volunteer to take part in EZ, your benefits will not be affected. If you are a compulsory participant, you will continue to get your benefits from Jobcentre Plus during Stage 1 and, during Stage 2, your contractor will pay you an amount that is equal to your benefit payments.

Leaving early

If you leave EZ during Stage 1 and you sign on at the Jobcentre within 13 weeks of leaving, you will be referred back to EZ straight away. If you leave during Stage 1 and you don't sign on at the Jobcentre within 13 weeks of leaving, you must re-qualify for EZ.

If you leave EZ during Stage 2 or Stage 3, and your time on the programme combined with your time in employment is fewer than 22 weeks, Jobcentre Plus will immediately refer you back to EZ. If you leave EZ during Stage 2 or Stage 3, and your time on the programme combined with your time in employment is more than 22 weeks, you must re-qualify for EZ.

If you enter Stage 3, but you lose your job before you have been employed for 13 weeks, you will return to the stage that you were at immediately before starting work. You will stay at that stage until you reach the maximum number of weeks allowed for that stage.[157]

Sanctions

If you are a compulsory participant, and you fail to do what is expected while you are on the EZ programme, your benefits may be affected. Reasons for benefit sanctions include:

- failing to turn up to appointments
- failing to follow your Action Plan
- being dismissed from an employment programme, and
- leaving the EZ programme early.

If you have already been sanctioned and referred to EZ by mistake, you will not be able to take part until your sanction ends, when you will be referred back to EZ at the point you left.

Employment Zones[158]

The current EZs are:

- Glasgow
- Liverpool and Sefton
- Tower Hamlets and Newham
- Brent and Haringey.

Other programmes to help you into work

New Deal for 50 Plus

What is New Deal for 50 Plus?

New Deal for 50 Plus (ND50+)[159] offers a route for older workers back into paid employment from being out of work. ND50+ differs from New

Deals for other groups in its recognition of the difficulties that older people have in re-entering the labour market after becoming workless.

Note: The programme is entirely voluntary, which means that you will not lose any benefits if you decide not to take part.[160] You can take a job (including becoming self-employed) if you want to, regardless of whether or not you will be better or worse off.

Who is eligible for New Deal for 50 Plus?

You are eligible[161] for ND50+, if you are aged 50 or over and have received one of the following benefits for at least 26 weeks:

- Income Support
- Jobseeker's Allowance
- Incapacity Benefit or Employment and Support Allowance
- Severe Disablement Allowance

JSA claimants aged 50 and over are also eligible for ND25+ (see page 95) or EZ (see page 103), which include mandatory elements.

You may be eligible, if you have been receiving National Insurance Credits, Carer's Allowance or Bereavement Allowance.

Programme elements

There are three elements to ND50+:

1 Help to find paid employment through a New Deal personal adviser or to move into self-employment;

2 Help in claiming the 50+ return to work element of the Working Tax Credit once you have secured paid employment;

3 Access to a training grant, once you have secured paid employment.

You do not have to take part in all three elements of the programme. So, for example, you can find work or become self-employed without using the services of the Jobcentre or the help of a personal adviser, and still claim your Training Grant.

Finding paid employment (caseloading)

Caseloading is a series of about six 30-minute interviews with your personal adviser over a period of between three and six months. The amount of time you spend with the adviser will depend on your needs. If you are disabled, you may have interviews with a Disability Employment Adviser instead.

During this caseloading period, your benefits will not be affected.

If you want to find paid employment, your personal adviser will help you by offering advice and assistance with writing CVs, writing application letters, and preparing for interviews, and by providing you with information about programmes and services that could help you. You will also receive money to cover the costs of travelling to interviews, including overnight stays.

Moving into self-employment

You could use ND50+ to start your own business and become self-employed.

You can participate in basic awareness and information sessions, one-to-one counselling and a short part-time course that will include the development of a business plan. You may also have the opportunity to do test-trading for up to 26 weeks, but this is not available to those claiming Incapacity Benefit or Employment and Support Allowance.[162]

Additional elements

While on ND50+, you may also have access to:

- Work Trials (see page 158)
- Travel to Interview scheme (see page 256)
- Programme Centres.

Your New Deal personal adviser may also discuss with you the benefits of doing voluntary work, which you could do to develop and maintain new and existing skills, provide an up to date reference, open up job opportunities, or provide you with a talking point at interviews.

The end of caseloading

Caseloading will end when:

- you move into a job or enter a training programme
- you no longer wish to participate (because the programme is voluntary)
- your personal adviser thinks this element is no longer appropriate
- you move into another New Deal or EZ.

Training Grant

Once you have taken up work with the help of ND50+ and have successfully claimed the 50+ element of Working Tax Credit, you can make a claim for a Training Grant up to the value of £1,500, where:

- £1,200 can be awarded at any time during the two-year eligibility period for training that is relevant to your current job
- £300 can be awarded at any time during the two-year eligibility period for lifelong learning.

The grant will be paid on production of a detailed receipt or invoice. It cannot be used to pay:

- for equipment (except workbooks or open learning)
- for job induction programmes
- for foreign language training, unless this is a requirement of the job.

If you are self-employed, you could use the Training Grant to go on general courses such as business administration or marketing, which you would use to run and develop your business.

To start the process of claiming the Training Grant, you must complete an Individual Learning Plan, which you can get from the Jobcentre. Once the Individual Training Plan has been approved, your personal adviser will help you complete the Training Grant Application Form.

It is up to you to take advantage of the Training Grant. You have two years in which to claim it.

Leaving the programme

The programme is voluntary, so you can leave at any time without your benefits being affected.

Rapid Response Service

What is the Rapid Response Service?

The Rapid Response Service (RRS) gives advice, information and help to people who lose their job because of large-scale redundancies. The RRS aims to help you move into a new job, training or further education as quickly as possible.[163]

Coverage

Currently, the RRS runs in Great Britain (England, Wales and Scotland) only.

Who is eligible to use the Rapid Response Service?

The RRS helps workers who are affected by a 'significant' redundancy. A 'significant' redundancy is a large-scale redundancy that has a substantial impact on the local area or labour market.[164]

Once the redundancy has been deemed significant, the RRS will help workers who are:[165]

- under threat of redundancy, or
- under notice of redundancy.

Who decides if a redundancy is significant?

Jobcentre Plus District Managers decide whether a redundancy is large-scale. They can declare the redundancy 'significant', if they think that giving workers early access to standard Jobcentre Plus services will not be enough to help the workers into new jobs.[166] RRS has been expanded in the recession.

How many workers make a redundancy significant?

Usually, to get help from the RRS, the redundancy has to affect 20 or more workers.[167] However, there are exceptions:

- If the redundancy affects fewer than 20 workers, but takes place in a small community where there aren't many other employment opportunities, the redundancy can count as significant.[168]
- If the redundancy affects more than 20 workers, but there are sufficient employment opportunities in the local area, the redundancy may not count as significant. However, the redundancy can still be deemed large-scale, and workers can get early access to standard Jobcentre Plus services.[169]

What does the Rapid Response Service offer?

The RRS brings together Jobcentre Plus, its local partners, and the company making the redundancies to respond to the situation. The help you get from the RRS will depend on your individual needs, your employer, and your local economy and labour market. It could include:[170]

- information, advice and guidance on your jobsearch
- help with your CV
- Skills and Training Analysis, to assess your skills in the context of the local labour market and find out if you have transferable skills, or need more training
- access to job focused training
- advice on claiming benefits
- information about other support organisations
- access to job vacancies
- access to Action Funding, which helps to address individual barriers to re-employment (for example, travel to work expenses).[171]

How can you access the Rapid Response Service?

Employers must tell the Insolvency Service when they make 20 or more workers redundant. Jobcentre Plus will contact every employer who reports to the Insolvency Service, to offer them support through the RRS.

If Jobcentre Plus hears about redundancies through a different source, it will still try to get in touch with the employer. It is up to your employer to decide whether you will have access to the RRS.[172]

When can you access the Rapid Response Service?

If you are 'under threat' of redundancy, you can access the following help before you get your official Notice of Redundancy:[173]

- information, advice and guidance
- Skills and Training Analysis.

If you are 'under notice' of redundancy, and you are within 12 weeks of your end date, you can access the full range of help from RRS (listed on page 115).[174] In addition, you may also be able to take part in tailored programmes that will help you to move into a new job quickly.[175]

You can get help from the RRS for up to 12 weeks after you have been made redundant.[176]

Local Employment Partnerships (Great Britain)

What are Local Employment Partnerships?[177]

Local Employment Partnerships (LEPs) are a deal between the government and businesses to work together to meet training and employment needs. Through LEPs, employers work with the government to give employment and training opportunities to disadvantaged jobseekers. In return, employers get a hassle-free chance to hire people who are eager to work and have the right skills.

Coverage

Currently, LEPs run in Great Britain only (England, Wales and Scotland).

Who can take part in Local Employment Partnership training?[178]

At the moment, LEP training programmes are aimed at certain people. You could get skills and training through an LEP, if you:

- have been out of work for more than six months
- are a lone parent
- are disabled
- have been out of work because of a long-term illness
- are a care-leaver
- are a former offender, or
- have very low qualifications.

If you have been unemployed for only a short time, you may be able to get help through LEPs at some point in the future. The government plans to extend LEPs to help people who are short-term unemployed, as well as the people who fall into the groups listed.[179]

The referral process[180]

If you are eligible to take part in training through an LEP, your current programme provider will refer you to the training. You can be referred to LEP training from a number of sources, including:

- Jobcentre Plus
- your Pathways to Work provider
- your EZ provider
- your New Deal provider
- the European Social Fund
- City Strategy, and
- an Employability Skills programme (funded by the Learning and Skills Council).

Local Employment Partnership training for disabled people[181]

If you are on New Deal for Disabled People, you can be referred to LEP training. However, if you have a complex health condition or disability, Jobcentre Plus staff might think about referring you to more appropriate programmes. This could include Work Preparation, Work Step (or Work Choice from October 2010) and the Job Introduction Scheme (see page 220). In October 2010, these schemes will be replaced by a new programme called Work Choice, which aims to provide a tailored, coherent range of specialist employment services.

What can you get through Local Employment Partnerships?

If you are eligible to take part in an LEP programme, there are a range of skills and experiences you could gain. Businesses that sign up to LEPs agree to do a number of things to help you into work. You could be offered things such as:[182]

- Work Trials, which last for between two and four weeks
- a place for you to do your subsidised employment option, work experience or work placement (if you are on a New Deal programme)
- one-to-one mentoring with company employees, to help you get ready for work.

Travel and childcare costs[183]

All people who do training through an LEP will have access to help with their travel and childcare costs. Usually, the programme provider who referred you to the training will pay your travel and childcare costs.

Training Premium[184]

If you are on New Deal for Lone Parents or New Deal for Partners, you may be paid a Training Premium while you take part in an LEP training programme.

What kinds of companies sign up for Local Employment Partnerships?

At first, the LEP scheme focused on giving unemployed people training and experience through retail businesses. However, companies from other sectors have now joined the scheme. They include companies that work in food processing, manufacturing, health, care, hospitality, tourism, security and facilities management, as well as retail.[185]

16-hour rule for people claiming Jobseeker's Allowance[186]

There is no minimum or maximum length of time for LEP training programmes. However, if you are claiming JSA, you will have to follow the 16-hour rule if you want to get your benefit. This means that:

- you can do only two weeks of full-time training in a 52-week period, or
- if your training lasts for longer than two weeks, then two of those weeks should be full-time training, and the rest of your training should take up fewer than 16 hours per week.

You can do part-time training that lasts for 16 or fewer hours per week.

Skills for Life (England)

What is Skills for Life?[187]

Skills for Life (SfL) is a free programme that helps people to develop the skills they use in everyday life, such as reading, writing and maths. Through the SfL programme, you can get a qualification that will help you to build up your CV, or go on to more difficult study.

SfL qualifications can:

- improve your self-confidence
- prove that you have learnt certain things
- give you a nationally recognised qualification, and
- help you get onto other courses (for example, National Vocational Qualifications).

SfL qualifications are aimed at helping particular groups of people. You could benefit from an SfL qualification, if you are:[188]

- unemployed and on benefits
- a low-skilled adult in employment
- a prisoner, or supervised in the community
- a member of an ethnic minority, or
- living in a disadvantaged area.

Coverage

Currently, SfL runs in England only. Other options are available to meet these needs in Wales, Scotland and Northern Ireland.

Who can get a Skills for Life qualification?[189]

You can get a SfL qualification, if you:

- are aged 16 or over, and
- have left compulsory full-time education, and
- do not have an up-to-date English or maths qualification at Level 2 on the National Qualifications Framework (NQF).

If you are aged 14 to 16, you might be able to get an SfL qualification through school.

As from the 2009–10 academic year, the Learning and Skills Council have had a duty to make sure that adults who want to improve their literacy and numeracy at functional levels can do so. 'Functional levels' means Level 1 for literacy and Entry Level 3 for numeracy. The Council also has a duty to make sure that this training is free. English for speakers of other languages (ESOL) is not covered for free training.[190]

What is the National Qualifications Framework?

The NQF sorts qualifications into levels. This makes it easy to compare different qualifications and decide whether some are equal to others. The NQF starts at Entry Level and goes up to Level 8.

You can do an SfL course, if you do not have an up-to-date Level 2 qualification in English or maths. According to the NQF, a Level 2 qualification is a qualification that is equal to a GCSE at grades A* to C.

SfL qualifications are available at three different levels on the NQF: Entry Level, Level 1 and Level 2.

Subjects available through Skills for Life[191]

You can get an SfL Certificate in:

- adult literacy
- adult numeracy
- information and communications technology (ICT), and
- English for speakers of other languages (ESOL).

The certificate in ICT is available at Entry Level only.

At the moment, the Qualifications and Curriculum Authority is piloting new Functional Skills qualifications. There are plans to make Functional English, Mathematics, and ICT qualifications available across the nation in 2010.[192]

As from August 2009, there has been a new core curriculum for offender learning. It focuses on employment, getting ready for work, and vocational training.[193]

How are you tested?[194]

The kind of test or assessment you do will depend on the level of your qualification.

Entry Levels

There are three Entry Levels. To get an SfL qualification at any of the Entry Levels, you will do tasks that are assessed by your learning centre, college or school. Your tasks will be marked as either a pass or a fail.

Levels 1 and 2

To get an SfL qualification at either Level 1 or Level 2, you will do a National Basic Skills test. The test is made up of 40 multiple-choice questions, with a choice of four different answers for each question. You can do the test on paper, or you can do the test on a computer. If you are doing the literacy test, you will have one hour to finish the test. If you are doing the numeracy test, you will have one hour and 15 minutes. Your test will be marked as either a pass or a fail.

What happens if you don't pass the test?

If you don't pass the test, you can do it again, as many times as you like. Every time you take the test, you will get a different set of questions.

Where and when can you do a Skills for Life qualification?[195]

You can do an SfL qualification in your local learning centre, test centre, or (in some cases) at a driving test centre. To find your local learning and test centres, visit www.direct.gov.uk.

SfL qualifications are offered frequently, so you can do one whenever it suits you.

Better Skills for Life in the future

Because the SfL programme has been successful, the government plans to make it bigger in the future. SfL will focus more on making you work-ready, so that you have the skills and support to find work, stay in work, and make progress in your job. SfL will be improved in the following ways:[196]

- The government is trying to bring in new laws so that you have the right to ask your employer for time away from your core duties to do SfL training. If the laws are approved, they will come into force in 2010.[197]

- The Learning and Skills Council and Jobcentre Plus will combine employment and skills services, so that you can get the support you need.

- In the 2009–10 academic year, colleges and learning providers will be able to use their budget for qualifications at Level 2 and below with greater freedom, so that they can respond to the needs of local employers and learners.

- In 2009–10, there will be more support for learning providers, so that they can give you training at your place of work.

- In 2009–10, you will be able to get a SfL 'initial assessment' if you are doing training at Level 2 or below. An initial assessment will work out your current level of skills. If you are doing a literacy or an ESOL course, your numeracy skills will be assessed.

- In 2009, the government is running a pilot programme where learning providers get incentives if you find a job after your SfL qualification. This encourages learning providers to help you move into work.[198]
- In 2010–11, learning providers will get more funding so that they can help you to get work and make progress in your job.
- SfL qualifications will be included in other vocational programmes, such as National Vocational Qualifications (NVQs). So, if you're doing an NVQ, you could get SfL qualifications at the same time.[199]

Employability Skills Programme (England)

What is the Employability Skills Programme?

The Employability Skills Programme (ESP) is a course of learning that leads to basic skills qualifications and employability qualifications. ESPs can help you to:[200]

- improve your skills, to make you ready for work
- improve your literacy, language and numeracy skills
- find and stay in work, and
- continue to learn once you have started working.

Coverage

Currently, ESPs run in England only.

Who is eligible to take part in an Employability Skills Programme?[201]

You can take part in an ESP if you:

- are aged 18 or over, and
- have a literacy, language or numeracy need at Level 1 or below on the NQF (see page 120).

You will be able to take part in an ESP if you are getting benefit payments or credits, or a New Deal Training Allowance.

If you are part of a joint claim

If you are part of a joint claim for JSA, and you have to meet the JSA rules about availability for work, then you could be eligible to take part in an ESP.

If you are also eligible for a mandatory New Deal programme

If you are eligible for a mandatory New Deal programme (such as FND) at the same time you are eligible for an ESP, then you will have to do the New Deal programme, where appropriate.

If you are also eligible for Pathways to Work

If you are eligible for Pathways to Work at the same time you are eligible for an ESP, you will have to do Pathways to Work, where appropriate.

How do you get involved in an Employability Skills Programme?

A Jobcentre Plus adviser will decide if you are eligible to take part in an ESP. The adviser can make their decision by doing formal screening for basic skills needs, or through more informal methods. If they decide you are eligible, they will refer you to an initial assessment with an ESP provider. They will contact the provider to arrange an interview for you.[202]

If you hear about ESPs from a source other than Jobcentre Plus, you must still see an adviser at the Jobcentre to get a referral to an ESP.[203]

You will not be referred to a specific programme or skill level. It is up to the ESP provider to decide what is appropriate for you at the initial assessment.[204]

Jobseeker's Direction

Your adviser may give you a Jobseeker's Direction to attend the initial assessment with the ESP provider. They will do this whenever it is necessary to encourage attendance.[205] If you get a Direction, you must attend the ESP assessment, or you will risk losing your benefit.

Initial assessment

Deciding if you are suitable for an Employability Skills Programme[206]

At the initial assessment, the ESP provider will decide whether you are suitable for the ESP. They will follow some guidelines when making this decision. The provider cannot decide that you are unsuitable for the ESP based mainly on your level of need (for example, if your skills are at pre-entry level, the provider cannot use this as the main reason for deciding that you are not suited to the programme).

People with complex circumstances[207]

The Learning and Skills Council and Jobcentre Plus expect providers to work with people who have a number of issues and complex circumstances. This can include people who are facing homelessness or ongoing illness, or are taking part in a recovery programme.

If you are already taking part in another programme, such as a recovery programme, the ESP provider should try to fit your ESP around the other programme.

If you have a health issue, such as addiction, the ESP provider may refer you to a more appropriate programme or organisation to get help.

People with very poor English language skills[208]

If you have no English language skills, or very poor English language skills, your skills will have to be addressed before you can take part in an ESP. This is usually because:

- you may not be able to benefit from the employability aspects of the programme until you language needs are sorted out, or
- you may already have a high skill level, and you will not gain anything from an ESP once your language needs have been sorted out.

The ESP provider will refer you to a Skills for Life course in ESOL (English for speakers of other languages). See page 119 for information about Skills for Life.

Once you have finished your ESOL Skills for Life course, you should be given the chance to progress to an ESP, if this is appropriate for you. You should be referred back to Jobcentre Plus, so that an adviser can decide whether you are eligible to take part in an ESP.

Training needs assessment[209]

The ESP provider will do a training needs assessment as part of your initial assessment. The training needs assessment will work out:

- your past experience and achievements
- your current skills, and
- gaps in your knowledge, skills and experience that need to be addressed so that you can get your ESP qualification.

The provider must assess your numeracy needs along with your literacy or language needs.

Programme levels[210]

Once the ESP provider has worked out your current level of skills, they will be able to decide which programme level is best for you. Usually, you will do a programme that is one level above your current skills level. So, for example, if you have skills at Entry Level 3, you will do a Level 1 programme.

Programme elements

Basic skills and employability[211]

Usually, your ESP will include at least two basic skills learning aims at the appropriate level, ranging from Entry Level 1 to Level 2. Your two basic skills aims will be:

- literacy and numeracy, or
- ESOL and numeracy.

Basic skills will be taught in the context of employability. This means that you will learn basic skills through things like:

- jobsearch
- job interviews
- presentations
- time-management, and
- other skills, attitudes and behaviours that employers look for.

Work experience and work placements

You should experience a real workplace as part of your ESP. Your work experience or work placement can happen at any time during your ESP, and can be:[212]

- a regular activity for a few hours, one half-day or one whole day per week
- a 'taster' session, which lasts for a few hours and puts you in touch with a range of different employers, or
- a block placement of one or more weeks (this could also be a Work Trial).

This list is not exhaustive, and there may be other options.

If you are doing an ESP full-time, and you are getting a Training Allowance, you can take part in full-time work experience or placements for an unlimited number of weeks. Work experience or placements that last for more than 16 hours per week count as full-time.[213]

If you are doing an ESP part-time, you can do part-time work experience or work placements for an unlimited number of weeks. Work experience or placements that last for 16 or fewer hours per week count as part-time.[214]

If you are not able to achieve a full Employability Skills qualification

If the ESP provider decides that you are not capable of achieving a full Employability Skills qualification, you can still do specific units of learning.[215] You may also be able to do work experience or work placements.[216]

Programme length

The ESP provider will decide the length of your course by looking at:[217]

- how long it will take for you to achieve your learning aims
- the length of time you will be spending on work experience or work placements, and
- how many hours per week you can attend the course.

If you are doing the ESP full-time and you are getting a Training Allowance, your course can last for up to 15 weeks. Your course length can be extended in certain circumstances.

Definition of 'full-time' and 'part-time'

For the ESP, 'full-time' learning means learning of at least 20 hours per week. 'Part-time' learning means learning of 16 or fewer hours per week.[218]

The ESP provider will decide with you whether full-time or part-time learning best suits your needs and circumstances. Providers will usually assume that you can do the course full-time, unless you can show that your circumstances prevent this. You may be able to start doing the course part-time and then build up your hours until you attend full-time, or start the course full-time and then reduce your hours until you attend part-time.[219]

Training Allowance[220]

If you are claiming JSA and you are doing an ESP full-time, then you will be eligible to receive a Training Allowance. The Training Allowance is a weekly payment, and you can get the allowance for up to 15 weeks. You must attend a pre-entry interview at the Jobcentre before you start the ESP, so that Jobcentre Plus can arrange your Training Allowance.[221]

If you are doing an ESP part-time, you will not be able to get a Training Allowance. You will continue to get benefit payments instead.

If you are on New Deal for Lone Parents or New Deal for Partners, and you are doing an ESP for 16 or fewer hours per week, you can get a New Deal training premium. Jobcentre Plus will give you information about this. You must attend a pre-entry interview at the Jobcentre before you start the ESP, so that Jobcentre Plus can arrange your training premium.[222]

Unauthorised absences

If you are doing an ESP full-time, and you have unauthorised absences for more than 10 consecutive working days, your Training Allowance will be stopped. 'Unauthorised absence' is any time when you fail to attend the programme and your provider cannot authorise your reason for absence. Periods of sickness, and holidays abroad, count as unauthorised absences.[223]

If you are getting a Training Allowance and you are absent for 10 non-consecutive working days, the ESP provider can assume that you have left the course.[224]

Extending the Training Allowance

Your Training Allowance could be extended by up to five weeks, if you:[225]

- will be ready to do a national test or assessment for at least one of your learning aims within the next five weeks, and you are likely to achieve a pass, and/or
- you are applying for jobs and you will benefit from specific Employability Skill support.

Your ESP provider will contact Jobcentre Plus to ask for an extension of your Training Allowance. They should contact Jobcentre Plus no later than 12 weeks after you start your course.[226]

If your Training Allowance cannot be extended, and you are eligible for JSA, you can claim JSA and continue your course part-time (16 or fewer hours per week).[227]

Help with travel and childcare costs

If you are getting a Training Allowance and doing an ESP full-time, you can get help with travel and childcare costs. Jobcentre Plus will reimburse reasonable travel costs, excluding the first £4 per week. It will also reimburse reasonable childcare costs. Arrangements for payment will depend on your local ESP provider. Some providers will pay you directly but, in other cases, Jobcentre Plus will pay you.[228]

If you are not getting a Training Allowance and you are doing an ESP part-time, you can get help with travel costs only. Your ESP provider can reimburse you for your travel costs, and it will not affect your benefit.[229]

If you are on New Deal for Lone Parents or New Deal for Partners, you can get help with childcare or travel costs under the New Deal programme. Jobcentre Plus will give you more information about this.[230]

Taking part in the Employability Skills Programme more than once

Usually, if you haven't finished your ESP course after getting a Training Allowance for 15 weeks, you will continue the course part-time and get benefit payments instead. In exceptional circumstances, you may be given up to another 15 weeks to continue your course with a Training Allowance. This could happen, if:[231]

- you have not achieved a learning aim or found a job, and
- your provider can confirm that you are likely both to achieve your learning aims and to find a job after another 15 weeks of full-time learning.

However, if you have already started the ESP once, you can be referred for a second time in the following situations:[232]

- when you have had a short break for 28 or fewer calendar days, you can go back to your ESP for the remaining time of your Training Allowance period
- when you have had a break for more than 28 calendar days, a Jobcentre Plus adviser will use their discretion to decide whether you can go back to the course. The adviser may ask your ESP provider if you were making good progress before your break.

Training for Work (Scotland)

What is Training for Work?[233]

Training for Work (TfW) is a voluntary programme that gives training support to people who are unemployed and actively looking for work. Through the TfW programme, you can go on work placements and get access to formal training. In many cases, you will have a good chance of moving into a full-time job. TfW also helps people to start up their own businesses.

Who can take part in Training for Work?[234]

You can take part in TfW, if you:

- are aged 18 or over, and
- need training to help you get a job, and
- are not taking part in any other government-funded programmes, including:
    - a business start-up scheme
    - Positive Moves
    - Work Trials
    - Jobcentre Plus Rehabilitation Programme
    - Skillseekers
    - NDYP, and
    - ND25+.

How does the programme work?

If you join TfW, you will get help from a network of training providers. The programme covers a wide variety of skills and jobs, and local employers will give you on-the-job training as part of the programme. [235]

TfW offers two programmes to help people get ready for work:[236]

- occupational training – which is for specific jobs, and aims to improve and update your skills for re-entering employment, and
- customised training – which is flexible training for people who are capable of moving into work quickly (this training is often carried out in response to things such as large-scale redundancies).

Your TfW provider will assess your needs and draw up an Individual Training Plan. This plan sets out the kind of training you will do, activities to improve your 'core skills', and your employment goals.

You will do training at provider sites, at an employer's premises, or at a combination of these two places. You can do a mixture of skills training, work experience and test trading, depending on your needs. You may even work for an employer but continue to follow the steps set out in your Individual Training Plan.

How long is the programme?

There is no set length for a TfW programme. Your time on the programme will depend on your needs.[237]

How many hours per week does the programme take?

The amount of time you spend on the programme each week depends on whether you are doing TfW full-time or part-time. If you are taking part in the programme full-time, you will attend TfW for 30 hours per week, spread over five days. If you cannot do TfW full-time because of personal or domestic reasons, your TfW provider will decide if you can do the programme part-time instead. If you do TfW part-time, you will attend for 15 to 29 hours per week, spread over five to seven days.[238]

How do you join Training for Work?

Referral[239]

If you think you could be eligible to take part in TfW, contact your local Jobcentre Plus. They will do a 'Better off' calculation before referring you to TfW. The calculation tests your motivation, job readiness, and commitment to doing a training course.

If Jobcentre Plus decides that you are eligible for TfW, they will phone a TfW provider to arrange an appointment for you. They will give you written confirmation of the appointment and details of how to get to the TfW site.

A referral does not guarantee you a place on a TfW course. You may have to compete with other people for places on the course.

Interviews

At your appointment, the TfW provider will interview you. They will discuss the options that are open to you and assess whether you are eligible to join the programme. If you are eligible to join, and you decide to go ahead, you will have a Pre-entry Interview at your local Jobcentre Plus. You will be interviewed by a TfW officer.[240]

At the Pre-entry Interview, the TfW officer will make sure that:

- you are eligible for TfW
- you are fully aware of your responsibilities while taking part in TfW
- you have correct information about the benefits and/or allowances you will get while on TfW
- you have Form AT40, which you must use to tell Jobcentre Plus about any change in your circumstances.[241]

Re-joining Training for Work[242]

Once you have finished a TfW course, you will have to wait another 26 weeks to re-qualify for another TfW course.

If you stopped training because of sickness, maternity or Jury Service, you may be allowed to re-enter TfW. It is up to your TfW provider to decide whether you can re-enter the programme. If you were getting JSA after you stopped your training, this should not discount you from re-joining the programme. You will have to have another Pre-entry Interview at Jobcentre Plus before you can re-join TfW.

Training Allowance[243]

While you are taking part in TfW, you can get a training allowance that is equal to the amount of your benefits plus £10 per week, except in the following cases:

- if you are getting Incapacity Benefit, you will not be eligible for the extra £10 per week[244]
- if you are taking part in Discretionary Short Training, you cannot get the Training Allowance. You will continue to get your usual benefit.

Short training is for people aged over 25, and it lasts from two days to two weeks.[245]

- if you have 'employed status', you cannot get the Training Allowance because you already receive a wage from your employer.[246]

If you are taking part in self-employment training, the Training Allowance you receive during your test trading will be treated as part of your business profits. This means it is taxable income. Jobcentre Plus should tell you this at your Pre-entry Interview.[247]

If you get a job out of the TfW programme, you will be paid the usual rate for the job.

Help with costs[248]

You may be able to get some help with travel, meal and childcare costs. Skills Development Scotland and your TfW provider will decide the support you can get. You should be able to get advice from Jobcentre Plus.

Endnotes

1 Jobcentre Plus (2009) Find Your Way Back To Work.

2 Reg. 51 Jobseekers Allowance Regulations 1996 (JSA Regs).

3 Jobcentre Plus (2009) Find Your Way Back To Work: Day 1, p. 6.

4 Page 10 of leaflet published by DWP: 'Jobcentre Plus. Our Service Standards'.

5 S10 JS Act.

6 Regs 23 and 24 JSA Regs.

7 Regs 25 and 26 JSA Regs.

8 Reg. 27 JSA Regs.

9 Jobcentre Plus (2009) Find Your Way Back To Work: Day 1, p. 8.

10 Jobcentre Plus (2009) Find Your Way Back To Work: Your 13-Week Review Meeting.

11 Department for Work and Pensions (2009) House of Commons Deposited Paper DEP2009-2144, paras 39 and 41.

12 Department for Work and Pensions (2009) House of Commons Deposited Paper DEP2009-2144, para. 43.

13 Jobcentre Plus (2009) Find Your Way Back To Work: Your 26-Week Review Meeting.

14 www.jobcentreplus.gov.uk/JCP/Employers/AdvertiseaVacancy/recruitmentsubsidy/Dev_016226.xml.html Accessed on 12 November 2009.

15 Department for Work and Pensions (2009) House of Commons Deposited Paper DEP2009-2144, para. 18.

16 Jobcentre Plus (2009) Find Your Way Back To Work: Your 26-Week Review Meeting.

17 Department for Work and Pensions (2009) House of Commons Deposited Paper DEP2009-2144, para. 78.

18 Department for Work and Pensions (2009) House of Commons Deposited Paper DEP2009-2144, para. 120.

19 Department for Work and Pensions (2009) House of Commons Deposited Paper DEP2009-2144, para. 124.

20 Department for Work and Pensions (2009) House of Commons Deposited Paper DEP2009-2144, para. 126.

21 Department for Work and Pensions (2009) House of Commons Deposited Paper DEP2009-2144, para. 53.

22 Department for Work and Pensions (2009) House of Commons Deposited Paper DEP2009-2144, para. 181.

[23] Department for Work and Pensions (2009) House of Commons Deposited Paper DEP2009-2144, para. 183.

[24] Department for Work and Pensions (2009) House of Commons Deposited Paper DEP2009-2144, para. 54.

[25] Department for Work and Pensions (2009) House of Commons Deposited Paper DEP2009-2144, para. 186.

[26] http://research.dwp.gov.uk/campaigns/futurejobsfund/pdf/fjf-guide.pdf Accessed on 29 July 2009.

[27] http://research.dwp.gov.uk/campaigns/futurejobsfund/pdf/fjf-guide.pdf Accessed on 29 July 2009.

[28] http://research.dwp.gov.uk/campaigns/futurejobsfund/ Accessed on 29 July 2009.

[29] http://research.dwp.gov.uk/campaigns/futurejobsfund/ Accessed on 29 July 2009.

[30] http://research.dwp.gov.uk/campaigns/futurejobsfund/ Accessed on 29 July 2009.

[31] http://www.jobcentreplus.gov.uk/JCP/Customers/outofworkhelplookingforwork/Getting_job_ready/Programmes_to_get_you_ready/014878.xml.html Accessed on 5 March 2009.

[32] Reg. 10 Social Security and Child Support (Decisions and Appeals) Regulations 1999 and schedule 1 para. 2 JS Act.

[33] Regs 5–16 JSA Regs.

[34] Reg. 31 JSA Regs.

[35] Regs 7–10 JSA Regs.

[36] Regs 11(2) (b) and 5 (1A) and (1B) JSA Regs.

[37] Regs 72 and 73 JSA Regs.

[38] Reg. 13(3A) JSA Regs.

[39] Reg. 5 JSA Regs.

[40] Reg. 13(3) JSA Regs.

[41] Reg. 13(2) JSA Regs.

[42] Reg. 17 JSA Regs.

[43] Reg. 55 JSA Regs.

[44] Reg. 18 JSA Regs.

[45] Reg. 19(3) JSA Regs.

[46] Reg. 16 JSA Regs.

[47] Reg. 16(1) JSA Regs.

[48] Reg. 16(2) JSA Regs.

[49] Reg. 10(1) JSA Regs.

[50] Reg. 18(3) (j) JSA Regs.

[51] Reg. 14 JSA Regs.

[52] Reg. 15 JSA Regs.

[53] Reg. 14 JSA Regs.

[54] Reg. 14 JSA Regs.

[55] Reg. 1 (3A) (b) JSA Regs.

[56] Reg. 1(3D) JSA Regs.

[57] Reg. 11 JSA Regs.

[58] Reg. 3A JSA Regs.

[59] Schedule A1 JSA Regs.

[60] Reg. 52(3) JSA Regs.

[61] S19 (6) (a) and (b) JS Act.

[62] S20(3) JS Act.

[63] Reg. 74(4) JSA Regs.

[64] Reg. 16 (2) Social Security and Child Support (Decisions and Appeals) Regulations 1999.

[65] R(U) 32/52.

[66] S 19(6) (d) JS Act.

[67] Reg. 72 JSA Regs.

[68] S 19(5) (a) and (10) (b).

[69] Reg. 73(2) JSA Regs.

[70] http://www.dwp.gov.uk/supplyingdwp/what_we_buy/fnd_pqq.asp Accessed on 12 March 2009.

[71] http://www.workinglinks.co.uk/flexible_new_deal/about_flexible_new_deal.aspx Accessed on 26 January 2009.

[72] DWP (2008) No-One Written Off: Reforming Welfare to Reward Responsibility, DWP pp. 39–40.

[73] http://www.wlla.co.uk/media/file/Flexible%20New%20Deal-update.doc Accessed on 26 January 2009.

[74] DWP (2008) Raising Expectations And Increasing Support: Reforming Welfare for the Future, DWP p. 117.

75 http://www.docstoc.com/docs/2399216/Overview-of-flexible-New-Deal-(note-fND) and http://www.dwp.gov.uk/welfarereform/in-work-better-off/annex.pdf Accessed on 26 January 2009.

76 DWP (2008) Raising Expectations and Increasing Support: Reforming Welfare for the Future, DWP pp. 111–12.

77 www.dwp.gov.uk/docs/ctf-pqq-events-qa.pdf

78 www.dwp.gov.uk/supplying-dwp/what-we-buy/welfare-to-work-services/opportunities-to-tender/communitytaskforce.shtml Accessed on 29 July 2009.

79 www.dwp.gov.uk/docs/ctf-pqq-events-qa.pdf Accessed on 29 July 2009.

80 www.dwp.gov.uk/docs/ctf-pqq-events-qa.pdf Accessed on 29 July 2009.

81 www.dwp.gov.uk/docs/ctf-pqq-events-qa.pdf Accessed on 29 July 2009.

82 www.dwp.gov.uk/docs/ctf-pqq-events-qa.pdf Accessed on 29 July 2009.

83 www.dwp.gov.uk/supplying-dwp/what-we-buy/welfare-to-work-services/opportunities-to-tender/communitytaskforce.shtml Accessed on 29 July 2009.

84 www.dwp.gov.uk/docs/ctf-pqq-events-qa.pdf Accessed on 29 July 2009.

85 www.dwp.gov.uk/docs/ctf-pqq-events-qa.pdf Accessed on 29 July 2009.

86 http://research.dwp.gov.uk/campaigns/futurejobsfund/pdf/fjf-guide.pdf Accessed on 29 July 2009.

87 http://research.dwp.gov.uk/campaigns/futurejobsfund/pdf/fjf-guide.pdf Accessed on 29 July 2009.

88 http://research.dwp.gov.uk/campaigns/futurejobsfund/pdf/fjf-guide.pdf Accessed on 29 July 2009.

89 http://research.dwp.gov.uk/campaigns/futurejobsfund/ Accessed on 29 July 2009.

90 http://research.dwp.gov.uk/campaigns/futurejobsfund/ Accessed on 29 July 2009.

91 http://research.dwp.gov.uk/campaigns/futurejobsfund/ Accessed on 29 July 2009.

92 http://research.dwp.gov.uk/campaigns/futurejobsfund/ Accessed on 29 July 2009.

93 http://research.dwp.gov.uk/campaigns/futurejobsfund/ Accessed on 29 July 2009.

94 http://research.dwp.gov.uk/campaigns/futurejobsfund/pdf/fjf-guide.pdf Accessed on 29 July 2009.

95 http://research.dwp.gov.uk/campaigns/futurejobsfund/ Accessed on 29 July 2009.

96 http://research.dwp.gov.uk/campaigns/futurejobsfund/pdf/fjf-guide.pdf Accessed on 29 July 2009.

97 http://research.dwp.gov.uk/campaigns/futurejobsfund/pdf/fjf-guide.pdf Accessed on 29 July 2009.

98 http://research.dwp.gov.uk/campaigns/futurejobsfund/faq.asp Accessed on 29 July 2009.

[99] http://research.dwp.gov.uk/campaigns/futurejobsfund/faq.asp Accessed on 29 July 2009.

[100] DWP Provider Guidance ch. 11, and Jobcentre Plus Decision Makers' Guide, vol. 3, ch. 14.

[101] DWP Provider Guidance, ch. 11, para. 2

[102] http://www.direct.gov.uk/en/Employment/Jobseekers/ProgrammesandServices/ DG_173757 Accessed on 18 February 2009.

[103] http//:www.dwp.gov.uk/supplyingdwp/what_we_buy/pg_chapter_11.pdfaccessed on 18 February 2009.

[104] DWP Provider Guidance, ch. 6, sect. 5, para. 4.

[105] http://www.direct.gov.uk/en/Employment/Jobseekers/ProgrammesandServices/ DG_173757 Accessed on 20 February 2009.

[106] DWP Provider Guidance, ch. 6, sect. 6.

[107] DWP Provider Guidance, ch. 11, Introduction, para. 10.

[108] DWP Provider Guidance, ch. 11, para. 66 onwards.

[109] DWP Provider Guidance, ch. 11, para. 60

[110] DWP Provider Guidance, ch. 6, sect. 4, para. 6

[111] DWP Provider Guidance, ch. 11, para. 45

[112] Jobcentre Plus Decision Makers' Guide vol. 3, ch. 14, 14119. See also http:// www.smediversity.co.uk/GEC/dev_013527.pdf Accessed on 19 February 2009.

[113] DWP Provider Guidance, ch. 11, para. 19.

[114] Jobcentre Plus Decision Makers' Guide, vol. 3, ch. 14, 14113.

[115] DWP Provider Guidance, ch. 6, sect. 3, para. 5.

[116] DWP Provider Guidance, ch. 6, sect. 3, para. 5.

[117] Jobcentre Plus Decision Makers' Guide, vol. 3, ch. 14, 14133.

[118] Jobcentre Plus Decision Maker's Guide vol. 3, ch. 14, 14143.

[119] DWP Provider Guidance, ch. 11, para. 11–14.

[120] DWP 'New Deal streamlining changes' [June 2004] Touchbase 35, 20.

[121] DWP Provider Guidance, ch. 11, para. 35.

[122] http://www.direct.gov.uk/en/Employment/Jobseekers/ProgrammesandServices/ DG_173757 Accessed on 23 February 2009.

[123] DWP Provider Guidance, ch. 11, paras 38–40.

[124] DWP Provider Guidance, ch. 11, paras 73–5 and Jobcentre Plus Decision Makers' Guide, vol. 3, ch. 14, 14225.

[125] Jobcentre Plus Decision Makers' Guide vol. 3, ch.14, 14522.

[126] See DWP Provider Guidance, and Jobcentre Plus Decision Makers' Guide, for more information.

[127] Jobcentre Plus Decision Makers' Guide, vol. 3, ch. 14, 14335.

[128] Jobcentre Plus Decision Makers' Guide, vol. 3, ch. 14, 14626.

[129] DWP 'New Deal streamlining changes' [June 2004] Touchbase 35, 20.

[130] DWP. 'New Deal for Young People and Long-Term Unemployed People Aged 25+: Background Information'. In DWP Resource Centre. http://www.dwp.gov.uk/asd/ndyp.asp Accessed 28 February 2006.

[131] DWP Provider Guidance, ch. 9, paras 3-6.

[132] DWP Provider Guidance, ch. 9, para. 4.

[133] DWP Provider Guidance, ch. 6, sect. 5, para. 4.

[134] DWP Provider Guidance, ch. 9, para. 8.

[135] DWP Provider Guidance, ch. 9, para. 1.

[136] DWP Provider Guidance, ch. 9, para. 9.

[137] DWP Provider Guidance, ch. 9, para. 9.

[138] DWP Provider Guidance, ch. 9, para. 10.

[139] DWP Provider Guidance, ch. 9, para. 44.

[140] DWP Provider Guidance, ch. 9, para. 21.

[141] DWP Provider Guidance, ch. 6, sect. 2, paras 8-9 and 15.

[142] DWP Provider Guidance, ch. 6, sect. 2, para. 11.

[143] DWP Provider Guidance, ch. 6, sect. 10, para. 1.

[144] DWP Provider Guidance, ch. 6, sect. 10, paras 3-4.

[145] DWP Provider Guidance, ch. 9, paras 17-18.

[146] DWP Provider Guidance, ch. 9, para. 20.

[147] DWP Provider Guidance, ch. 9, paras 31 and 52.

[148] http://www.jobcentreplus.gov.uk/JCP/Customers/outofworkhelplookingforwork/Getting_job_ready/Programmes_to_get_you_ready/014878.xml.html Accessed on 5 March 2009.

[149] National Statistics, Employment Zones: Background Information, p. 3 http://www.dwp.gov.uk/asd/emp_zones/EZ_Background_Information.pdf Accessed on 6 March 2009.

[150] Employment Zone Guidance for Contractors, Chapter 1, para. 14. http://www.jobcentreplus.gov.uk/JCP/stellent/groups/jcp/documents/websitecontent/dev_014072.pdf Accessed 6 March 2009.

[151] Employment Zone Guidance for Contractors, Chapter 1, paras 15–19. http://www.jobcentreplus.gov.uk/JCP/stellent/groups/jcp/documents/websitecontent/dev_014072.pdf
Accessed 6 March 2009.

[152] http://www.jobcentreplus.gov.uk/JCP/Customers/outofworkhelplookingforwork/Getting_job_ready/Programmes_to_get_you_ready/014878.xml.html Accessed on 5 March 2009.

[153] National Statistics, Employment Zones: Background Information, p. 2. http://www.dwp.gov.uk/asd/emp_zones/EZ_Background_Information.pdf Accessed on 6 March 2009.

[154] Employment Zone Guidance for Contractors, ch. 3, para. 1. http://www.jobcentreplus.gov.uk/JCP/stellent/groups/jcp/documents/websitecontent/dev_014072.pdf
Accessed 6 March 2009.

[155] National Statistics, Employment Zones: Background Information, p. 2 http://www.dwp.gov.uk/asd/emp_zones/EZ_Background_Information.pdf Accessed on 6 March 2009.

[156] National Statistics, Employment Zones: Background Information, p. 2 http://www.dwp.gov.uk/asd/emp_zones/EZ_Background_Information.pdf Accessed on 6 March 2009.

[157] National Statistics, Employment Zones: Background Information, p. 2 http://www.dwp.gov.uk/asd/emp_zones/EZ_Background_Information.pdf Accessed on 6 March 2009.
158http://www.jobcentreplus.gov.uk/JCP/Customers/outofworkhelplookingforwork/Getting_job_ready/Programmes_to_get_you_ready/014878.xml.html Accessed on 5 March 2009.

[159] 'DWP. New Deal for 50 Plus' in Jobcentre Plus New Deals, http://www.jobcentreplus.gov.uk/JCP/Customers/outofworkhelplookingforwork/Getting_job_ready/Programmes_to_get_you_ready/New_Deal/New_Deal_50_plus/index.html and Jobcentre Plus Provider Guidance, ch. 1, para. 20 Accessed 16 February 2009.

[160] Jobcentre Plus Provider Guidance, ch. 1, para. 20.

[161] 'DWP. New Deal for 50 Plus'. In Jobcentre Plus New Deals, http://www.jobcentreplus.gov.uk/JCP/Customers/outofworkhelplookingforwork/Getting_job_ready/Programmes_to_get_you_ready/New_Deal/New_Deal_50_plus/index.html Accessed 18 February 2009.

[162] http://www.eurofound.europa.eu/areas/labourmarket/tackling/cases/uk007.htm Accessed on 18 February 2009.

[163] Morgan, B. (2008) Jobcentre Plus Rapid Response Service Standard Note SN/EP/4891.

[164] Morgan, B. (2008) Jobcentre Plus Rapid Response Service Standard Note SN/EP/4891.

[165] www.jobcentreplus.gov.uk/JCP/stellent/groups/jcp/documents/websitecontent/dev_010594.doc Accessed on 24 March 2009.

[166] Morgan, B. (2008) Jobcentre Plus Rapid Response Service Standard Note SN/EP/4891

[167] www.jobcentreplus.gov.uk Accessed on 24 March 2009.

[168] Morgan, B. (2008) Jobcentre Plus Rapid Response Service Standard Note SN/EP/4891.

[169] Morgan, B. (2008) Jobcentre Plus Rapid Response Service Standard Note SN/EP/4891.

[170] Morgan, B. (2008) Jobcentre Plus Rapid Response Service Standard Note SN/EP/4891.

[171] www.jobcentreplus.gov.uk Accessed on 24 March 2009.

[172] House of Commons (2009), Hansard Written Answers for 23 February 2009.

[173] Morgan, B. (2008) Jobcentre Plus Rapid Response Service Standard Note SN/EP/4891.

[174] www.jobcentreplus.gov.uk/JCP/stellent/groups/jcp/documents/websitecontent/dev_010594.doc Accessed on 24 March 2009.

[175] Morgan, B. (2008) Jobcentre Plus Rapid Response Service Standard Note SN/EP/4891.

[176] Morgan, B. (2008) Jobcentre Plus Rapid Response Service Standard Note SN/EP/4891.

[177] http://www.jobcentreplus.gov.uk/JCP/Employers/lep/ Accessed on 18 March 2009.

[178] DWP (2007) In Work, Better Off: Next Steps to Full Employment ch. 3, para. 8 and DWP (2008) Raising Expectations and Increasing Support: Reforming Welfare for the Future ch. 5 para. 72.

[179] Treasury (2008) Facing Global Challenges: Supporting People Through Difficult Times ch. 5, para. 33.

[180] DWP, Provider Led Pathways to Work Guidance, ch. 18, p. 6.

[181] DWP, Provider Led Pathways to Work Guidance, ch. 18, p. 8.

[182] DWP (2008) Raising Expectations and Increasing Support: Reforming Welfare for the Future ch. 6, para. 75.

[183] DWP, Provider Led Pathways to Work Guidance, ch. 18, p. 9.

[184] DWP, Provider Led Pathways to Work Guidance, ch. 18, p. 6.

[185] DWP (2007) In Work, Better Off: Next Steps to Full Employment ch. 3, para. 12.

[186] DWP, Provider Led Pathways to Work Guidance, ch. 18, p. 9.

[187] http://www.direct.gov.uk Accessed on 18 March 2009.

[188] DIUS (2009) Skills for Life: Changing Lives Executive Summary para. 6.

[189] http://www.direct.gov.uk Accessed on 18 March 2009.

[190] DIUS (2009) Skills for Life: Changing Lives p. 34.

[191] http://www.direct.gov.uk Accessed on 18 March 2009.

[192] DIUS (2009) Skills for Life: Changing Lives Executive Summary para. 11.

[193] DIUS (2009) Skills for Life: Changing Lives Executive Summary para. 11.

[194] http://www.direct.gov.uk Accessed on 18 March 2009.

[195] http://www.direct.gov.uk Accessed on 18 March 2009.

[196] DIUS (2009) Skills for Life: Changing lives Executive Summary para. 11.

[197] DIUS (2009) Skills for Life: Changing lives p. 34.

[198] DIUS (2009) Skills for Life: Changing lives p. 15.

[199] DIUS (2009) Skills for Life: Changing lives ch. 3, para. 3.

[200] LSC (2007) Employability Skills Programme for Jobcentre Plus Customers para. 2.1.

[201] LSC (2007) Employability Skills Programme for Jobcentre Plus Customers paras 3.1–3.4.

[202] LSC (2007) Employability Skills Programme for Jobcentre Plus Customers para. 4.1.

[203] LSC (2007) Employability Skills Programme for Jobcentre Plus Customers para. 4.4.

[204] LSC (2007) Employability Skills Programme for Jobcentre Plus Customers para. 4.2.

[205] LSC (2007) Employability Skills Programme for Jobcentre Plus Customers para. 4.2.

[206] LSC (2007) Employability Skills Programme for Jobcentre Plus Customers para. 5.1.

[207] LSC (2007) Employability Skills Programme for Jobcentre Plus Customers paras 5.1–5.2.

[208] LSC (2007) Employability Skills Programme for Jobcentre Plus Customers paras 5.3–5.4.

[209] LSC (2007) Employability Skills Programme for Jobcentre Plus Customers paras 6.1 and 6.3.

[210] LSC (2007) Employability Skills Programme for Jobcentre Plus Customers para. 6.2.

[211] LSC (2007) Employability Skills Programme for Jobcentre Plus Customers paras 7.1–7.2.

[212] LSC (2007) Employability Skills Programme for Jobcentre Plus Customers para. 7.8.

[213] LSC (2007) Employability Skills Programme for Jobcentre Plus Customers para. 7.7.

[214] LSC (2007) Employability Skills Programme for Jobcentre Plus Customers para. 7.7.

[215] LSC (2007) Employability Skills Programme for Jobcentre Plus Customers para. 7.5.

[216] LSC (2007) Employability Skills Programme for Jobcentre Plus Customers para. 7.7.

[217] LSC (2007) Employability Skills Programme for Jobcentre Plus Customers para. 7.14.

[218] LSC (2007) Employability Skills Programme for Jobcentre Plus Customers para. 7.11.

[219] LSC (2007) Employability Skills Programme for Jobcentre Plus Customers para. 7.13.

[220] LSC (2007) Employability Skills Programme for Jobcentre Plus Customers paras 7.11–7.12.

[221] LSC (2007) Employability Skills Programme for Jobcentre Plus Customers para. 8.1.

[222] LSC (2007) Employability Skills Programme for Jobcentre Plus Customers para. 8.1.

[223] LSC (2007) Employability Skills Programme for Jobcentre Plus Customers para. 8.3.

[234] LSC (2007) Employability Skills Programme for Jobcentre Plus Customers para. 8.4.

[225] LSC (2007) Employability Skills Programme for Jobcentre Plus Customers para. 8.8.

[226] LSC (2007) Employability Skills Programme for Jobcentre Plus Customers paras 8.7–8.9.

[227] LSC (2007) Employability Skills Programme for Jobcentre Plus Customers para. 8.11.

[228] LSC (2007) Employability Skills Programme for Jobcentre Plus Customers para. 10.1.

[229] LSC (2007) Employability Skills Programme for Jobcentre Plus Customers para. 10.2.

[230] LSC (2007) Employability Skills Programme for Jobcentre Plus Customers para. 7.12.

[231] LSC (2007) Employability Skills Programme for Jobcentre Plus Customers para. 9.2.

[232] LSC (2007) Employability Skills Programme for Jobcentre Plus Customers para. 9.1.

[233] http://www.hie.co.uk/trainingforwork.htm Accessed on 20 March 2009.

[234] DWP, Provider Led Pathways to Work Guidance, sect. 13, pt 2, para. 30.

[235] http://www.hie.co.uk/trainingforwork.htm Accessed on 20 March 2009.

[236] DWP, Provider Led Pathways to Work Guidance, sect. 13, pt 2, paras 6–8.

[237] DWP, Provider Led Pathways to Work Guidance, sect. 13, pt 2, para. 7.

[238] DWP, Provider Led Pathways to Work Guidance, sect. 13, pt 2, para. 15.

[239] DWP, Provider Led Pathways to Work Guidance, sect. 13, pt 2, paras 29 and 32–7.

[240] DWP, Provider Led Pathways to Work Guidance, sect. 13, pt 2, paras 49–50.

[241] DWP, Provider Led Pathways to Work Guidance, sect. 13, pt 2, para. 55.

[242] DWP, Provider Led Pathways to Work Guidance, sect. 13, pt 2, paras 61–4.

[243] http://www.hie.co.uk/trainingforwork.htm Accessed on 20 March 2009.

[244] DWP, Provider Led Pathways to Work Guidance, sect. 13, pt 2, para. 9.

[245] DWP, Provider Led Pathways to Work Guidance, sect. 13, pt 2, paras 20–1.

[246] DWP, Provider Led Pathways to Work Guidance, sect. 13, pt 2, para. 17.

[247] DWP, Provider Led Pathways to Work Guidance, sect. 13, pt 2, para. 19.

[248] DWP, Provider Led Pathways to Work Guidance, sect. 13, pt 2, para. 38.

2

3 Skills Health Check, Work Focused Interviews and Work Trials

Skills Health Checks, Work Focused Interviews and Work Trials are common to a number of different benefit claims, including Jobseeker's Allowance (JSA), Income Support (IS) and Employment and Support Allowance (ESA) claims. Rather than giving an in-depth explanation of checks, interviews and trials every time they arise in relation to a particular benefit throughout the handbook, detailed information is collated into one chapter, with cross-references where applicable in the benefit claim sections.

Skills Health Check

What is the Skills Health Check?

The Skills Health Check (SHC) will be introduced in autumn 2010. If you have a gap in your skills that could stop you from getting work, the SHC will work out your specific skills needs.[1]

Referrals to the SHC will be mandatory for those customers who have a basic skills need and have been claiming JSA for six months or more. Lone parents will be encouraged to attend a full SHC two years before they are due to lose eligibility for IS.[2]

Who is eligible for the Skills Health Check?

If you are claiming Jobseeker's Allowance

Jobcentre Plus will do a short skills screening for everyone who makes a new claim for JSA. If the screening shows that you're lacking certain skills, you will have to do a full SHC at the start of your claim, to work out your specific needs.[3]

If you don't do an SHC at the start of your JSA claim, you will have to do an SHC once you have been claiming the benefit for six months.

If you are claiming Employment and Support Allowance

The government is currently deciding if you will have to do an SHC when you start your claim.

If you are a lone parent on Income Support

It is not yet clear when you will have to do the SHC. The government has suggested that lone parents should do an SHC when their youngest child turns five years old.[4] However, you may have to do the check once your youngest child turns three years old. This is because the government is bringing in legislation that will allow your adviser to direct you to do an SHC once your child is three years old.[5]

If you are the partner of a benefit claimant

If you are:

- unemployed, and
- your partner is a lone parent claiming IS

you will have to do an SHC when your partner does their SHC.

How does the Skills Health Check work?[6]

Jobcentre Plus will refer you to the Adult Advancement and Careers Service (or a similar service in Scotland and Wales), which will start operating in autumn 2010. The Service will do the SHC.

Your personal adviser will discuss the results of the SHC with you. They will recommend that you do certain things (such as training) to address your skills needs. If you refuse to take action, your adviser can give you a Direction to do the things that they have set out.

Work Focused Interviews

What is a Work Focused Interview?

Work Focused Interviews (WFIs) aim to help unemployed people to overcome their barriers to work.[7] They:

- encourage you to see work as a realistic option, where appropriate
- help you build on your skills and potential
- help you tackle any obstacles to work
- give you ongoing support, and
- refer you to other opportunities (for example, New Deals).

If you don't attend an interview when required, your benefit may be affected.

If you attend an interview, you do not have to accept work.

Who is eligible for Work Focused Interviews?

People who are claiming JSA must attend a regular series of interviews and give proof that they are taking steps to find work.

People who are claiming certain benefits other than JSA must attend WFIs to talk about work options, where appropriate.

If your partner is claiming certain benefits, you may also have to attend a WFI.

If you are claiming benefits and you want to find out if you have to attend a WFI, answer these questions:[8]

Do you have to attend a Work Focused Interview?

	YES	NO
1 Age Are you of working age (aged from 16 to 59)?	YES	NO
2 Work Are you not employed, or working fewer than 16 hours a week on average?	YES	NO
3 Benefits Are you making a new or repeat claim for: • Employment and Support Allowance[9] • Income Support • Incapacity Benefit • Severe Disablement Allowance?	YES	NO

If you answered **YES** to every question, then you probably have to attend a WFI.
If you answered **NO** to any of the questions, then you do not have to attend a WFI.

If you have been claiming any of the benefits under Question 3 since before WFIs were made compulsory, and you answered 'yes' to the other questions, then you will have to attend trigger-point interviews (as discussed on page 153).

Work Focused Interviews for Partners

If your partner is claiming benefits and you want to find out if you have to attend a WFI, answer these questions:[10]

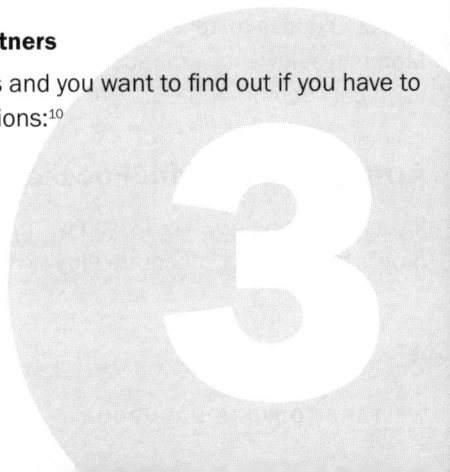

Do you have to attend a Work Focused Interview for Partners?

	YES	NO
1 Type of benefit Is your partner claiming one of the benefits below, plus extra for you: • Income-Related Employment and Support Allowance • Income Support • Income-Based JSA (excluding joint-claim JSA) • Incapacity Benefit • Severe Disablement Allowance • Carer's Allowance? (To find out if you are eligible for these benefits, see page 000)	YES	NO
2 Length of benefit claim Has your partner been claiming their benefit for at least 26 weeks?	YES	NO
3 Age Are you and your partner both aged under 60?	YES	NO
4 Work Are you working fewer than 24 hours per week?	YES	NO
If you answered **YES** to every question, then you probably have to attend a WFI. If you answered **NO** to any of the questions, then you do not have to go to a WFI unless your circumstances change.		

Who can volunteer to attend a Work Focused Interview?

You can choose to have a WFI if you are claiming Carer's Allowance, Maternity Allowance or Industrial Injury Disablement Benefit, or if you are aged between 60 and 65.

Arranging the Work Focused Interview

If you are claiming JSA or IS, you will have a WFI before your first claim is processed. Contact Jobcentre Plus to make a claim and arrange your WFI.

If you are claiming ESA or Incapacity Benefit (IB), you will have a WFI eight weeks after the start of your claim.[11] You must attend the interview, though it can be deferred or waived by Jobcentre Plus. If you fail to attend, your benefit may be affected.

If you have to attend a WFI because of the benefits your partner is claiming, Jobcentre Plus will contact you to arrange the interview when your partner has been making his or her claim for around 26 weeks. You must attend the interview. If you fail to attend, your partner's benefit may be affected.

Special cases

Location

In exceptional circumstances (for example, because of health problems or problems in arranging childcare), it may be possible to hold WFIs at home or away from the Jobcentre Plus office.

Translation

If you need someone to provide translation, Jobcentre Plus should arrange this for you. You can bring a friend or relative to your WFI, if you wish.

If you are deaf or have a hearing impairment, Jobcentre Plus should make arrangements to help you.

If you are aged 16 or 17

If you are aged 16 or 17 and making a benefit claim, you will have to attend a Learning Focused Interview (LFI). The LFI will be held at a Careers Service or at Connexions. The interview will cover education, training and future work options, but (unlike WFIs) you are not required to answer any particular questions. You may be entitled to help with travel costs. Your first claim will be processed after you have attended the interview.

You will have to attend follow-up LFIs, if you reach any of the trigger points listed above.

Assistance with costs

If you incur travel and/or childcare costs to attend your WFI, you may be eligible for help with these costs. You can get help if you:

- have a health condition or disability
- are a lone parent
- are a widow or widower, or
- are a carer.

Overview of a Work Focused Interview

When you attend your first WFI, you will meet with a financial assessor for about 20 minutes. The financial assessor will do an identity check and go over the details of your benefit claim. After this, the personal adviser will take over the meeting.

Your interview with the personal adviser will last about 40 minutes. You will not have to look for work in this interview, but the adviser will tell you about the help you can get from Jobcentre Plus. The adviser should take your individual situation into account when giving you advice.

Participating in the Work Focused Interview

To receive your benefit, you must participate in the WFI. This means that you must attend the WFI and answer questions about:[12]

- your educational qualifications
- your employment history
- work skills you have gained
- vocational training you have done
- whether you are currently doing any unpaid or paid work
- any medical conditions that could affect your work
- your caring or childcare responsibilities
- your aspirations for future employment, and
- any vocational training you wish to do.

These questions aim to find out basic information about you, so that the personal adviser can give you the right support. If you do not answer the interview questions, your benefit may be cut.

If you are a lone parent or you are claiming ESA or IB, you will have to complete an Action Plan with your adviser.

Trigger-point interviews

Trigger point interviews are basically follow-up interviews. They are similar to your first WFI, but you will not have to meet with a financial assessor.

Lone parents

If you have been claiming IS for 12 months or more, you will have to attend WFIs at least once every six months.[13] When you are in the last 12 months of your IS claim (based on the age of your child), you will have to attend quarterly WFIs.

Until recently, only lone parents with a youngest child aged [14] or over have been required to attend quarterly WFIs. However, from 25 October 2010, all lone parents with a youngest child aged six years or over will have to attend quarterly WFIs. These changes will be phased in over the next two years:

- From 24 November 2008, lone parents with a youngest child aged 9 to 11 years have been required to attend quarterly WFIs.
- From 26 October 2009, lone parents with a youngest child aged 8 to 10 years will have to attend quarterly WFIs.
- From October 2010, lone parents with a youngest child aged 6 to 8 years will have to attend quarterly WFIs.

From November 2011 onwards, lone parents will be required to attend quarterly WFIs from the time their youngest child is six years old.

Employment and Support Allowance claimants

People who make a claim for ESA will be divided into two groups: the work-related activity group, and the support group. If you are placed in the work-related activity group, you will need to attend regular WFIs. If you are placed in the support group, you will not have to attend WFIs unless you volunteer to do so.[14]

If you are in the work-related activity group, you will have to attend five more WFIs after your first WFI. The interviews will usually be held once a month. The interview schedule may differ according to where you live.[15]

Partners

Partners will only have to attend one WFI. There are no trigger-point interviews for partners.

Income Support, Incapacity Benefit and Severe Disablement Allowance claimants

Since December 2008, the rules for people claiming IS, IB or Severe Disablement Allowance (SDA) have been the same as the rules for those claiming ESA. If you are claiming IS, IB or SDA, and you are on the Pathways to Work scheme, then you will have to attend regular WFIs like those claiming ESA.[16]

Some people who have been claiming IB, IS or SDA continuously since before Pathways to Work began will have a different WFI schedule.[17]

If you are claiming IS only on the basis of being a lone parent, see the section on lone parents page 164.

If you do not fit into one of the claimant groups described above, but you are eligible for WFIs, you will be invited for further interviews at certain trigger points. You must attend these interviews.

Work Focused Interviews overview

Type of customer	2nd interview	3rd interview	4th interview	5th interview
Lone parent with youngest child aged 9 or over (until October 2009 – see 'Lone parents' section, page 164)	Three months after first interview	Three months later	Three months later	Three months later
Other lone parents on Income Support	Six months after first interview	Six months later	Six months later	Six months later
Other customer	Three years from date of last WFI or other face-to-face meeting with personal adviser	Three years later	Three years later	Three years later

Other trigger points

All people claiming benefits will have to attend a WFI at least once every three years.

You can arrange more interviews at any time by contacting your personal adviser.

However, there are other trigger points for attending a WFI, including:

- starting or ending part-time work
- staying on ESA, IB or IS after a Work Capability Assessment
- reaching the age of [18]
- finishing or reducing your caring responsibilities, and
- starting or ending a training course arranged by Jobcentre Plus.

Deferring Work Focused Interviews

Your WFI can be postponed, if it would not be helpful or appropriate for you to attend the interview at a given time. Your WFI may be deferred if you:

- are going through a time of major change (for example, you have recently given birth or become homeless)
- are emotionally distressed (because a close relative has died or a relationship has broken down)
- are too ill to attend a WFI (for example, you are recovering from surgery or a serious illness), or
- are likely to claim benefit only for a short time (for example, you are expecting to start full-time work soon).

Every situation will be considered on its own merits. If your WFI is deferred, you can still go ahead with your benefit claim and start getting benefits, as long as you agree to attend a WFI at a future time and actually do so.[18]

Waiving Work Focused Interviews

The WFI will be waived when:

it would not help you to attend an interview in the foreseeable future, or

- a WFI would not be appropriate in your circumstances.

This could be the case if, for example, you are very severely disabled.

If your interview is waived you can go ahead with your benefit claim straight away.[19]

What happens if you do not attend your Work Focused Interview?

If you fail to attend a WFI, your benefit (or your partner's benefit)[20] may be reduced.[21] You will have three chances to attend a WFI before your claim is affected.

If you are late for a WFI, or you make contact after the interview has passed, you may be treated as having failed to attend. It is important to contact an adviser as soon as you know that you are unable to attend.

In all cases, when your claim is terminated (or not processed) because Jobcentre Plus decides that you had no good reason for failing to attend an interview, you have a right to appeal[22] (see page 305, for details of the appeal procedure).

Showing 'good cause' for not attending a Work Focused Interview

If you show Jobcentre Plus within five working days that you had 'good cause' for not attending an interview, you will not be counted as having failed to attend. If you cannot show good cause for not attending your WFI, you may be counted as having dropped your claim for benefit, and you will have to make a new claim and attend an interview.[23]

If it is not possible to show good cause within five working days, you can try to convince Jobcentre Plus that you did have good cause for not attending, and that it was impossible for you to notify Jobcentre Plus within the time-frame. If you convince Jobcentre Plus of this, your benefit will not be affected. However, you must convince Jobcentre Plus within one month after the interview.

You have good cause for not attending an interview, if you can show that:[26]

- you did not understand that you had to attend an interview because of learning, language or literacy difficulties
- you did not understand that you had to attend an interview because your officer gave misleading information;
- you were attending a medical or dental appointment, or accompanying someone you have to care for to a medical or dental appointment, and it was not possible to rearrange the appointment
- you had transport problems and no reasonable alternative was available
- your religious practices stopped you from attending at the time or on the day of the interview

- you were attending an interview with a prospective employer
- you were actively following opportunities for work as a self-employed earner
- your dependant had an accident, a sudden illness or a relapse of a physical or mental health condition
- you were attending a funeral for a close relative or close friend on the day of the interview, or
- you suffer from a disability that made it impossible for you to attend.

Other factors may also be taken into account.

Work Trials

What is a Work Trial?[26]

Work Trials are short trial periods of working for an employer. Your Work Trial will usually be full time and will last no more than 30 working days. It will be a trial for a genuine job vacancy.

The main advantages to Work Trials are that:

- you can decide whether the job is suitable without losing your benefit (your benefit is not affected if you leave a Work Trial or decide you do not want the job)
- during a Work Trial, you will get help with meals (up to £3 per day) and travel expenses (up to £10 per day)[27]
- you have the chance to prove that you can do the job
- you can find out what problems you may have in a working environment and get support to overcome them.

Who is eligible for Work Trials?

Work Trials are widely available to those who claim benefits or take part in Welfare to Work programmes. You are normally eligible for a Work Trial if you:

- are aged 25 years or over, and
- have been out of work for more than 26 weeks, and
- you are claiming a qualifying benefit (such as JSA or IS).[28]

A Work Trial is voluntary and you can leave at any time.[29]

If you are claiming JSA, you should remember that refusing a job, whether you are offered a Work Trial or not, can result in benefit sanctions (see page 67).

Receiving benefits during your Work Trial

During your Work Trial, you will stay on your benefit. If you are already paid an allowance to do a Welfare to Work activity, you will stay on that allowance during your Work Trial. Jobcentre Plus staff will make arrangements so that your benefit does not stop.[30]

Your benefit will not be affected if you want to leave the Work Trial early, of if you turn down the job at the end of the trial.[31]

Arranging the Work Trial

Usually, your personal adviser will arrange your Work Trial for you. However, if you want to arrange your own Work Trial, you can do this by asking at your local Jobcentre Plus office. They will give you a copy of the letter 'Work Trials: Try it for yourself', which you can send to the employer with your application form, letter or CV. If the employer is interested, they will contact either you or Jobcentre Plus.[32]

Employer's contract

Before you start your Work Trial, your employer must sign a contract with Jobcentre Plus. The contract says that your employer will:

- give you the chance to do tasks that will provide suitable work experience
- interview you as a potential permanent employee for the vacancy (or for any other vacancy they think you may be suitable for)
- not fill the vacancy you are trying until you have finished your Work Trial and been interviewed, and
- have Health and Safety arrangements in place.

Absences during the Work Trial

If you do not attend the Work Trial for more than four days in a row, your employer and Jobcentre Plus will assume that you have withdrawn from the Work Trial. If you are sick and you are likely to be sick for more than a few days, your Work Trial may be stopped. Your employer can stop your Work Trial at any time because of changes in the needs of their organisation, or because of your behaviour or welfare.

The end of the Work Trial

If you are offered the job after the Work Trial and you accept it, then the Work Trial has been successful. If you do not get the job, your personal adviser will assess your performance during the Work Trial to find out why not.

Endnotes

[1] DWP (2008) Raising Expectations and Increasing Support: Reforming Welfare for the Future, DWP. para. 5.33.

[2] www.dwp.gov.uk/welfarereform/making-skills-work.pdf Accessed on 12 November 2009.

[3] DWP (2008) Raising Expectations and Increasing Support: Reforming Welfare for the Future, DWP. para. 5.33.

[4] DWP (2008) No-One Written Off: Reforming Welfare to Reward Responsibility, DWP. para. 2.69.

[5] DWP (2008) Raising Expectations and Increasing Support: Reforming Welfare for the Future, DWP. para. 6.68.

[6] DWP (2008) Raising Expectations and Increasing Support: Reforming Welfare for the Future, DWP. para. 5.33.

[7] Jobcentre Plus Decision Makers' Guide (DMG), vol. 1, ch. 5.

[8] Reg. 3, Social Security (Jobcentre Plus Interviews) Regulations 2002.

[9] Jobcentre Plus (2008) Notes sheet: Employment and Support Allowance ESA40 10/08 http://www.jobcentreplus.gov.uk/JCP/stellent/groups/jcp/documents/websitecontent/dev_015901.pdf Accessed on 4 February 2009.

[10] Reg. 2(1, 2), Social Security (Jobcentre Plus Interviews for Partners) Regulations 2003.

[11] Jobcentre Plus (2008) Notes sheet: Employment and Support Allowance ESA40 10/08 http://www.jobcentreplus.gov.uk/JCP/stellent/groups/jcp/documents/websitecontent/dev_015901.pdf Accessed on 4 February 2009.

[12] Reg. 11(2), Social Security (Jobcentre Plus Interviews) Regulations 2002.

[13] Newcastle City Council, Jobcentre Plus Work Focused Interviews http://www.newcastle.gov.uk/core.nsf/a/wr_jcpluswfi Accessed on 4 February 2009.

[14] Jobcentre Plus (2008) Notes sheet: Employment and Support Allowance ESA40 10/08 http://www.jobcentreplus.gov.uk/JCP/stellent/groups/jcp/documents/websitecontent/dev_015901.pdf Accessed on 4 February 2009.

[15] DWP (2008) Technical Factsheet T15: 'Work-Focused Interviews'. http://www.dwp.gov.uk/esa/pdfs/t15-esa-factsheet-work-focused-interviews.pdf p. 6. Accessed 4 February 2009.

[16] Newcastle City Council, Jobcentre Plus work focused interviews http://www.newcastle.gov.uk/core.nsf/a/wr_jcpluswfi Accessed on 4 February 2009.

[17] Newcastle City Council, Jobcentre Plus Work Focused Interviews. http://www.newcastle.gov.uk/core.nsf/a/wr_jcpluswfi Accessed on 4 February 2009.

[18] DMG, vol. 1, ch. 5, 05039.

[19] DMG, vol. 1, ch. 5, 05021.

[20] Reg. 3(1), Social Security (Jobcentre Plus Interviews for Partners) Regulations 2003.

[21] Reg. 4(2), Social Security (Jobcentre Plus Interviews) Regulations 2002.

[22] DMG, vol. 1, ch. 5, 05090.

[23] DMG, vol. 1, ch. 5, 05037, 05039.

[24] DMG, vol. 1, ch. 5, 05035.

[25] DWP Provider Guidance, Chapter 1, paras 14–15.

[26] http://www.jobcentreplus.gov.uk/JCP/Customers/Programmesandservices/Worktrial/index.html Accessed on 3 March 2009.

[27] http://www.jobcentreplus.gov.uk/JCP/Customers/Programmesandservices/Worktrial/index.html Accessed on 3 March 2009.

[28] http://www.jobcentreplus.gov.uk/JCP/stellent/groups/jcp/documents/websitecontent/dev_015630.pdf
Accessed on 3 March 2009.

[29] http://www.jobcentreplus.gov.uk/JCP/stellent/groups/jcp/documents/websitecontent/dev_015630.pdf Accessed on 3 March 2009.

[30] http://www.jobcentreplus.gov.uk/JCP/Customers/Programmesandservices/Worktrial/index.html Accessed on 3 March 2009.

[31] http://www.jobcentreplus.gov.uk/JCP/stellent/groups/jcp/documents/websitecontent/dev_015630.pdf
Accessed on 3 March 2009.

[32] http://www.jobcentreplus.gov.uk/JCP/stellent/groups/jcp/documents/websitecontent/dev_015630.pdf Accessed on 3 March 2009.

4 Out of work and a parent

Customer journey charts for lone parents

Over the next two years, the government is making big changes to the benefits system for lone parents. The following flow chart shows the journey that lone parents claiming Income Support (IS) can expect to take once all of the changes are in place in October 2010. The new system is being introduced in stages over the next 12 months or so. To find out how lone parents are affected during the interim stages, see page 168.

Lone parents claiming Income Support after October 2010

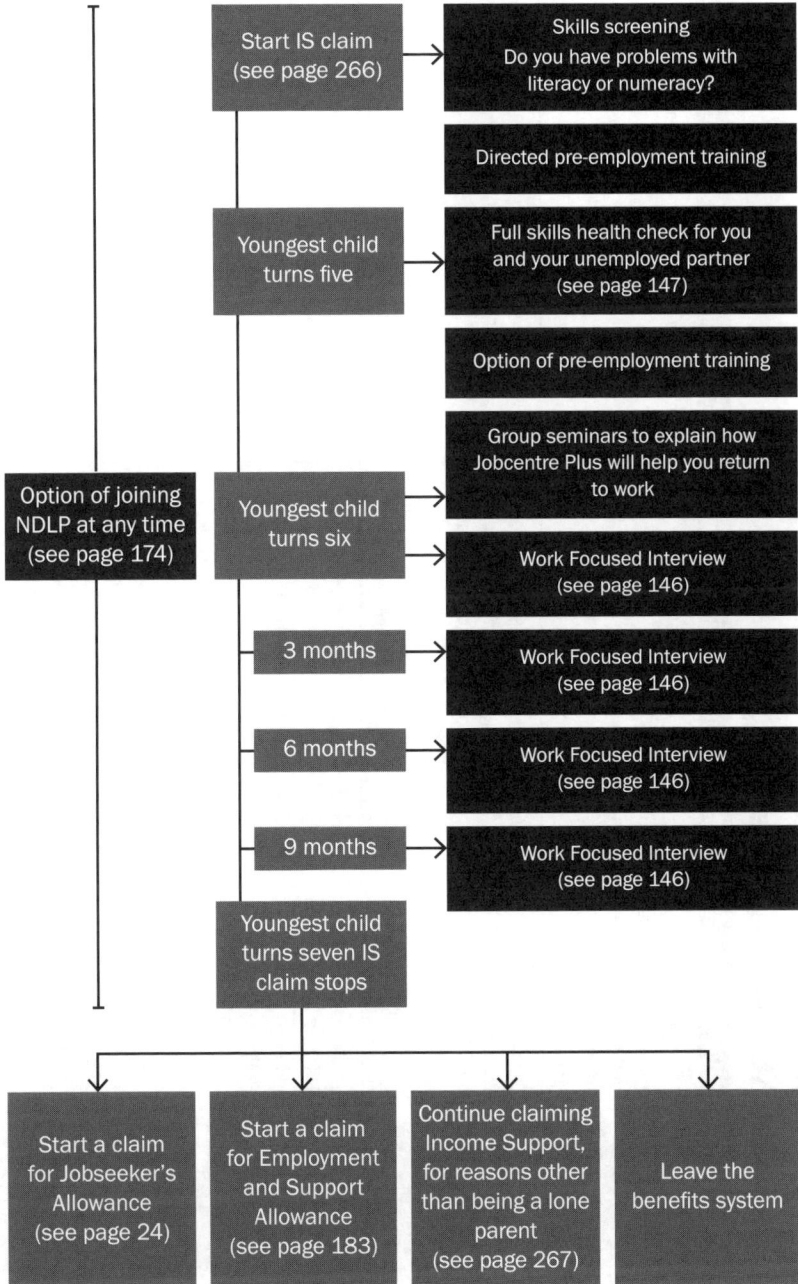

Start IS claim (see page 266) → **Skills screening** Do you have problems with literacy or numeracy?

Directed pre-employment training

Youngest child turns five → **Full skills health check for you and your unemployed partner** (see page 147)

Option of pre-employment training

Option of joining NDLP at any time (see page 174)

Youngest child turns six → **Group seminars to explain how Jobcentre Plus will help you return to work**

→ **Work Focused Interview** (see page 146)

3 months → **Work Focused Interview** (see page 146)

6 months → **Work Focused Interview** (see page 146)

9 months → **Work Focused Interview** (see page 146)

Youngest child turns seven IS claim stops

Start a claim for Jobseeker's Allowance (see page 24)

Start a claim for Employment and Support Allowance (see page 183)

Continue claiming Income Support, for reasons other than being a lone parent (see page 267)

Leave the benefits system

The following table sums up what lone parents can get during their (IS) claim, and what they will be expected to do once the new system is in place in October 2010, along with any possible future changes.

Lone parents and Income Support

	Start of Income Support claim	Youngest child turns five	Youngest child turns six	Three months later
What lone parents can get	Income Support 'Skills for work' premium, if you do training and education before your youngest child turns five (see page 171)	Income Support	Income Support	Income Support
What lone parents must do	Skills screening, to work out if you have problems with literacy or numeracy	Full Skills Health Check (unemployed partners must also have a full Skills Health Check) Appropriate training after your check (see page 147)	Work Focused Interview (see page 146)	Work Focused Interview (see page 146)
Optional extras	Training to address any lack of basic skills Can join New Deal for Lone Parents (see page 174)	Can join New Deal for Lone Parents (see page 174)	Can attend group seminars to find out how Jobcentre Plus will help you back to work Can join New Deal for Lone Parents (see page 174)	Can join New Deal for Lone Parents (see page 174)
Possible future changes	'Skills for work' premium is being tested in some areas, and may be either rolled out nationwide or discontinued (see page 171)	Full Skills Health Check may be moved to when your youngest child turns three, along with directed training (see page 147)	May have to attend Work Focused Interviews when your child is aged one or two (but will have no further jobsearch obligations) (see page 146)	

	Six months later	Nine months later	Youngest child turns seven	Switching to JSA
What lone parents can get	Income Support	Income Support	Income Support will stop	JCP will work with local authorities to make sure you get Housing Benefit and Child Benefit with no gap in payment (see page 169)
What lone parents must do	Work Focused Interview (see page 146)	Work Focused Interview (see page 146)	Switch to JSA, if you want to continue receiving benefits and are fit for work (see page 24) Switch to ESA, if you have a disability or health problem (see page 183) Continue on IS, if you can claim it for reasons other than being a lone parent (see page 267) Leave the benefits system	Meet all of the JSA benefit rules (see page 24)
Optional extras	Can join New Deal for Lone Parents (see page 174)	Can join New Deal for Lone Parents (see page 174)	Can join New Deal for Lone Parents (see page 174)	Can join New Deal for Lone Parents (see page 174)
Possible future changes				

Increased obligations for lone parents

Overview of the changes to lone parent benefits

Up until November 2008, lone parents could claim IS on the grounds of being a lone parent until their youngest child turned 16. Now, the government is reducing eligibility for IS, so that by 2010, only lone parents with a youngest child aged under seven will be able to claim IS on the grounds of being a lone parent (see page 267 for exceptions to this rule).

From October 2010, once their youngest child is seven years old, lone parents will no longer be able to claim IS and will have to claim a different benefit. If they are eligible, they can claim either Jobseeker's Allowance (JSA) or Employment Support Allowance (ESA), or they may leave the benefits system and/or enter work.

The government has announced that Jobcentre Plus advisers must take account of the wellbeing of the child and the availability of childcare when helping lone parents claiming benefits to look for work or start preparing for work in the future.

Timetable of changes

Changes to lone parent benefits will be phased in over two years, as follows:[1]

- From November 2008, lone parents with a youngest child aged 12 years or over could no longer claim IS on the grounds of being a lone parent. For those who are already claiming IS, this move away from the benefit is being phased in over the year. Those who are not currently getting IS cannot make a new claim or a repeat claim for IS once their child has turned 12 years old.

- From 26 October 2009, lone parents with a youngest child aged 10 years or over will no longer be able to claim IS on the grounds of being a lone parent. For those already getting IS, this move away from IS will be phased in over the year.

- From 25 October 2010, lone parents with a youngest child aged seven years or over will no longer be able to claim IS on the grounds of being a lone parent. For those already getting IS, this move away from IS will be phased in over the year.

Lone parents who have other grounds for claiming Income Support

If you are a lone parent, but you claim IS for reasons other than being a lone parent (for example, you get Carer's Allowance, you care for someone who gets the middle or highest rate of the care component of Disability Living Allowance, or you are fostering a child), then you can continue to claim IS once your youngest child passes the cut-off ages described above.[2]

If you are a lone parent with a disability or health problem, you may be able to transfer from IS to ESA, if you satisfy the conditions.[3]

How are Housing Benefit and Child Tax Credit affected when you move to Jobseeker's Allowance?

If you are claiming Housing Benefit and Child Tax Credit when you change from IS to JSA, Jobcentre Plus staff will work with local authorities and HMRC to make sure that you continue to get these benefits with no gap in payment.[4] To help you manage the change in payment schedule (IS is paid fortnightly, and JSA is paid weekly), you may be able to get a transition loan.

Extra obligations and support during your Income Support claim

If you are claiming IS on the grounds of being a lone parent, there are a number of new things you will have to do before your IS claim ends. Some of the obligations listed below are already in place, while others are still in the planning stage, and will be introduced later on.

Skills Health Check

The government is planning to introduce skills screening at the start of every new IS claim. Skills screening will work out whether you have any problems with basic literacy, numeracy and language skills, so that you can be referred to support and training to meet those needs.[5]

The government is setting out plans for all lone parents to do a full Skills Health Check (SHC) before their claim for IS ends.[6] The SHC will find any gaps in your skills that could stop you from getting work. After the SHC, you will be directed to appropriate training to get you ready for work.

It is not yet clear when you will have to do the SHC. The government has suggested that lone parents should do an SHC when their youngest child turns five.[7] However, you may have to do the check once your youngest child turns three. This is because the government is bringing in legislation that will allow your adviser to direct you to do an SHC once your child is three years old.[8] If your partner is unemployed, they will also have to do an SHC.

Work Focused Interviews

Currently, you have to attend a Work Focused Interview (WFI) once every three months in the year before your IS claim ends. While the changes to lone parent benefits are being put in place over the next few years, the following rules about WFIs will apply:

- From 24 November 2008, lone parents with a youngest child aged 9 to 11 years have been required to attend quarterly WFIs
- From 26 October 2009, lone parents with a youngest child aged 8 to 10 years will have to attend quarterly WFIs
- From October 2010, lone parents with a youngest child aged 6 to 8 years will have to attend quarterly WFIs
- From November 2011 onwards, lone parents will be required to attend quarterly WFIs from the time their youngest child is six years old.

These interviews will give you plenty of notice about the changes to your benefit entitlements. They will explain the differences between IS and JSA, and tell you about your new obligations under JSA.[9]

In the future, you may have to attend WFIs before your youngest child turns six years old. The government is thinking about bringing in changes so that lone parents with a youngest child aged one to two years old will have to attend WFIs. Lone parents with a child aged one to two years old will not have any other jobsearch obligations apart from attending WFIs, but they can volunteer for New Deal for Lone Parents (NDLP) if they want to.[10]

Pre-employment support and training

If you are a lone parent claiming IS, you will be able to take up all or some of the following before you lose your entitlement to IS:[11]

- group seminars, which explain how Jobcentre Plus and its partners will help you return to work, develop your skills and understand the labour market (for lone parents approaching their last 12 months of IS)
- guaranteed job interview with an employer
- pre-employment training (after you have done a skills screening or SHC)

The government is bringing in legislation that will allow your adviser to direct you to do work-related activity or training once your youngest child turns three years old.[12] If your partner is unemployed, they will also have to take part in these activities. However, the government announced in July 2009 that your obligation to prepare for work could be as minor as seeking advice on debt, if your youngest child is aged three to six years.

Skills for work premium

The government is thinking about piloting a 'skills for work' premium. This will pay extra money to lone parents who volunteer to do training and education before their youngest child is five years old.[13]

In-work support

In selected areas from 2010, the government will be running a new trial for lone parents who are claiming IS and working for fewer than 16 hours per week. If this describes you, the government will allow you to earn up to £50 per week before your benefit is affected. The trial was announced in July 2009 – previously, lone parents could only earn up to £20 per week before their IS benefit was affected.

Sanctions during your Income Support claim

If your child is younger than seven years old and you cannot meet your obligations under the IS rules because there is no appropriate or affordable childcare available to you, your benefit will not be sanctioned.

In addition, Jobcentre Plus advisers must consider the welfare of your children (no matter what age they are) before sanctioning your benefits for any reason.

Flexibilities for lone parents on Jobseeker's Allowance

If you move from IS to JSA, you will have to meet the JSA benefit rules. The government plans to support you by helping you to find appropriate and affordable childcare, flexible jobs, and training to meet your skills needs. You will not be forced to take a job that does not suit your individual circumstances. This means that you can look for part-time work, if that suits you and your family best. Jobcentre Plus advisers will have more discretion to weigh up your individual circumstances.[14]

Availability requirements

To get JSA, you will have to meet all of the JSA rules about being available for work (see pages 40-47). However, to make it easier for you to meet these rules, you may be able to reduce your availability for work and still get JSA in the following situations:[15]

- if you have more caring duties over school holidays
- if you are ill, or your child is ill
- if your child is disabled with special care needs
- if your usual childminder is ill
- if you have an unforeseen situation or personal crisis that has caused you to become a lone parent (such as domestic violence or a relationship breakdown)

You may be allowed to reduce your availability for work from 40 hours per week to as few as 16 hours per week, if your caring responsibilities do not allow you to work for more than 16 hours per week.[16]

Parents who have fallen victim to domestic violence will be exempt from looking for work for three months.

Childcare

Jobcentre Plus advisers will have extra discretion so that a lone parent who is claiming JSA will not face penalties for leaving a job, or failing to take a job, because appropriate, affordable childcare is genuinely unavailable.[17] However, under the Childcare Act (2008), local authorities have a duty to provide suitable and affordable childcare.

Sanctions

Since lone parents often need to be more flexible than other jobseekers, the government will try to give you some extra leeway with meeting JSA rules. So, if you have genuine reasons (or 'good cause') for not meeting JSA rules about looking for or accepting work, your JSA will not be sanctioned. Good cause for not looking for work or accepting a job can include the situations listed under the section 'Availability requirements' in this chapter. If you have transport problems, this may also count as good cause for not meeting the rules.[18]

If you cannot show good cause for not meeting the JSA rules, you will face sanctions and your benefit may be reduced. Jobcentre Plus will tell you about the sanction by either:

- making one attempt to phone you on the day from which your penalty will apply, or
- sending you a letter that tells you to contact Jobcentre Plus within five days.[19]

You can appeal to an Independent Tribunal against a sanction.

In-work support

To help you to stay in work, the government offers a range of support, including:[20]

- In Work Credit (IWC) (a payment of £40 per week, or £60 per week in London, see page 180)

- ongoing advice from your Jobcentre Plus adviser, who can help you to solve problems, and tell you and your employer about skills training opportunities

- eligibility to apply for payments from the In Work Emergency Discretion Fund, to help you get past unexpected financial barriers

- help with up-front childcare costs, such as registration fees, deposits and advance payments (this help will be piloted in London first), and

- a new credit payment expected to be rolled out nationally in 2009–10, which will guarantee that you're better off in work than on benefits by at least £25 per week (for lone parents who have been on benefits for at least 26 weeks).

New Deal for Lone Parents

What is New Deal for Lone Parents?

NDLP helps lone parents to improve their job readiness and increase their employment opportunities.

Who is eligible for New Deal for Lone Parents?

NDLP is a voluntary programme.[21] You do not have to be receiving any benefits to take part in the programme. If you are claiming Jobseeker's Allowance, you will be able to take part in NDLP until you are moved onto Flexible New Deal. You will usually be moved onto Flexible New Deal after 12 months, unless you are fast-tracked.[22]

You are eligible to participate in NDLP, if you:[23]

- are aged 16 or over, and

- have a dependent child under 16 years old, and

- are not working, or are working fewer than 16 hours per week, and

- are not an asylum seeker.[24]

If you are eligible but choose not to take part, your benefits or allowances will not be affected.

Programme elements

The programme is made up of a series of interviews between you and the New Deal personal adviser. The number and length of interviews will depend on you. Your adviser will give you help and advice about moving into work or training, as well as in-work support to smooth the move into work.

Role of the New Deal personal adviser

Your personal adviser will support you by:

- drawing up an Action Plan to monitor your progress
- giving advice about job vacancies, jobsearch, writing applications and CVs, and interview techniques
- arranging for you to attend job interviews or training to update your skills
- helping you to find good-quality registered childcare in your area, apply for child maintenance, or contact the Child Support Agency
- helping you with the cost of attending job interviews or training, including fares and registered childcare costs
- arranging payment of the Training Premium, if you are eligible
- helping you to contact employers
- helping to arrange a Work Trial, which could last for up to six weeks[25]
- calculating how much better off you could be in a job
- explaining the effect that starting work may have on your current benefits or tax credits
- explaining what benefits or tax credits you may be able to claim when you move into work, and helping you apply for them, and
- providing an in-work support service.

Help with costs

Interviews

When you attend an interview with a personal adviser or an employer, you can get help with some of the costs. These include travel and childcare costs. Remember to ask for this.

Childcare

You can get funding for childcare while you attend approved activities or interviews, so long as the childcare is either:

- provided by carers registered with Ofsted, or
- run on school premises or by the local authority.

You will not get funding for childcare provided by friends or family members, unless they are registered childminders.

You can get help with childcare costs until the first Tuesday in the September following your child's 15th birthday. The amount of help you get with childcare costs depends on the amount of time you spend doing approved activities or training, and on how many children you have. Childcare costs are paid directly to your childcare provider.

The government plans to pilot help for up-front childcare costs in London. This will include help with registration fees, deposits and advance payments.[26]

Training

You may get help with the fees and costs incurred by doing approved training courses.

If you are doing approved training for at least two hours per week, you could get the Training Premium. This is a sum of about £15, which is paid weekly in arrears. In most cases, if you are doing training, you will be expected to attend at least 16 hours of training per week. These hours can be split between training and jobsearch, according to your needs. If you get the Training Premium, it is your responsibility to tell the tax authorities (HMRC) that you are receiving NDLP funding and the Training Premium.

While on NDLP, you will have access to a range of training. This includes:[27]

- LSC, which you may have been referred to (in England) and Training for Work in Scotland (see page 130)
- Work Trials and work experience (as part of an approved training course) (see page 158)

- Jobcentre Plus training programmes (including other New Deal training programmes), and
- training programmes approved for one-off purchase.

Maintenance

From April 2010 it is planned that all child maintenance paid will be ignored when assessing benefits. For child maintenance, £20 a week is ignored when working out Income Support , income based Jobseeker's Allowance and income related ESA. It is all ignored for housing benefit and council tax benefit.

If you receive maintenance for yourself, £15 a week is ignored for housing benefit and council tax benefit if you have child or children and do not also receive other income-related benefits. For other means tested benefits, it counts in full as income.

In-work support

Childcare Subsidy

If you move into part-time work of up to 16 hours per week, you could get a Childcare Subsidy. This helps you with the cost of childcare while you are working. You are paid a maximum of £67.50 per week for one child and £100 per week for two or more children. You can get the Childcare Subsidy for a one-off period of 12 months from the time when you first start part-time work.

If you need help to cover the costs of childcare for the week immediately before you start work,[28] you can get help from the Childcare Assist scheme.

In Work Credit

If you have been claiming benefits for 12 months or more, and you go back to work for at least 16 hours per week, you could get In Work Credit (IWC). IWC is a tax-free payment of £40 per week to lone parents (£60 per week for parents living in London). IWC is paid for a period of 12 months from the time you start work.

The government has plans to pilot a new structure for paying IWC. After you have been receiving weekly payments of IWC for a certain period, you will receive your payments as a lump sum. The lump sum payment will depend on you attending a meeting with your personal adviser to discuss your progress in work and check whether you need any extra support.[29]

Additional courses

If you are a healthcare professional, you may be able to go on an NHS-funded return to practice course. These courses are aimed at encouraging former healthcare professionals to return to the NHS, and course availability varies according to your location, profession and how long you've been away from work. These courses are often funded by the NHS, depending on your local trust and their workforce needs.[30]

Leaving the programme

Since NDLP is voluntary, you can leave at any time without your benefits being affected.

New Deal Plus for Lone Parents

New Deal Plus for Lone Parents (NDLP+) adds an extra range of support to the regular NDLP programme. It will run as a pilot programme until March 2011 in selected Jobcentre Plus districts,[31] and is meant to help lone parents to stay in work. The range of extra support offered through NDLP+ includes pre- and post-employment support.

In addition to the things already offered by NDLP, NDLP+ offers:

- access to Discovery Events (three-day events where you can explore career paths and boost your self-confidence and motivation)
- more voluntary contact with your personal adviser
- help with up-front childcare costs (such as registration)
- more flexibility for advisers to buy training courses or other things to address your specific needs.[32]

The districts in which NDLP+ is available are:

- Leicestershire
- North and North East London
- South London
- Central London
- West London
- City and East London
- Lambeth, Southwark and Wandsworth
- Edinburgh and Lothian and Borders
- South West Wales (in Cardiff and Vale only)
- Black Country (in Dudley and Sandwell only)
- West Yorkshire (Bradford only).

Other programmes to help lone parents back into work

Along with NDLP, there are other programmes available to lone parents to help them back into work and training. If you are a lone parent, you could take part in:

- Local Employment Partnerships (see page 115)
- Skills for Life, provided you live in England, are aged 16 or over, and do not have an up-to-date English or maths qualification at Level 2 on the National Qualifications Framework (see page 119)
- the Employability Skills Programme, provided you live in England and are getting benefit payments, credits or a New Deal training allowance (see page 122)
- Training for Work, provided you live in Scotland, are aged 18 or over, and are not taking part in any other government-funded programmes (see page 130), and
- Working for Families, provided you live in Scotland are not on New Deal (see page 230).

Endnotes

[1] DWP (2007) Ready for Work: Full Employment in Our Generation, DWP. p. 37.

[2] DWP (2007) Ready for Work: Full Employment in Our Generation, DWP. p. 40.

[3] DWP (2007) Ready for Work: Full Employment in Our Generation, DWP. p. 40.

[4] DWP (2007) Ready for Work: Full Employment in Our Generation, DWP. p. 38.

[5] DWP (2007) Ready for Work: Full Employment in Our Generation, DWP. p. 47.

[6] DWP DWP (2008) Raising Expectations and Increasing Support: Reforming Welfare for the Future, DWP. para. 6.63.

[7] DWP (2008) No-One Written Off: Reforming Welfare to Reward Responsibility, DWP. para. 2.69.

[8] DWP (2008) Raising Expectations and Increasing Support: Reforming Welfare for the Future, DWP. para. 6.68.

[9] DWP (2007) Ready for Work: Full Employment in Our Generation, DWP. p. 38.

[10] DWP (2008) Raising Expectations and Increasing Support: Reforming Welfare for the Future, DWP. para. 6.64.

[11] DWP (2007) Ready for Work: Full Employment in Our Generation, DWP. pp. 44–5.

[12] DWP (2008) Raising Expectations and Increasing Support: Reforming Welfare for the Future, DWP. para. 6.68.

[13] DWP (2008) No-One Written Off: Reforming Welfare to Reward Responsibility, DWP. para. 2.70–1.

[14] DWP (2007) Ready for Work: Full Employment in Our Generation, DWP. pp. 32–3.

[15] DWP (2007) Ready for Work: Full Employment in Our Generation, DWP. p. 40.

[16] DWP (2007) Ready for Work: Full Employment in Our Generation, DWP. p. 42.

[17] DWP (2007) Ready for Work: Full Employment in Our Generation, DWP. p. 35.

[18] DWP (2007) Ready for Work: Full Employment in Our Generation, DWP. p. 40.

[19] DWP (2007) Ready for Work: Full Employment in Our Generation, DWP. p. 42.

[20] DWP (2007) Ready for Work: Full Employment in Our Generation, DWP. p. 46.

[21] DWP Provider Guidance ch. 13: 'New Deal for Lone Parents', para. 1 http://www.dwp.gov.uk/supplyingdwp/what_we_buy/pg_chapter_13.pdf Accessed 26 January 2009.

[22] DWP (2007) Ready for Work: Full Employment in Our Generation, DWP. p. 44. 23http://www.jobcentreplus.gov.uk/JCP/Customers/outofworkhelplookingforwork/ Getting_job_ready/Programmes_to_get_you_ready/New_Deal/New_Deal_for_ Lone_Parents/index.html Accessed on 4 March 2009.

[24] Refugee Council, Refugee Council Information p. 6. http://www.refugeecouncil.
org.uk/Resources/Refugee%20Council/downloads/practice/advice_guides/
AsylumSupport_Apr07.pdf Accessed 26 January 2009.

[25] DWP (2007) Ready for Work: Full Employment in Our Generation, DWP. p. 45.

[26] DWP (2007) Ready for Work: Full Employment in Our Generation, DWP. p. 46.

[27] DWP Provider Guidance ch. 13: 'New Deal for Lone Parents', para. 1.
http://www.dwp.gov.uk/supplyingdwp/what_we_buy/pg_chapter_13.pdf Accessed
26 January 2009

[28] Find a definitive source to verify this. (http://www.dwp.gov.uk/asd/asd5/
rports2007-2008/rrep499.pdf not authoritative enough?)

[29] DWP (2007) Ready for Work: Full Employment in Our Generation, DWP. p. 46.

[30] NHS, Returning to the NHS.
http://www.nhscareers.nhs.uk/explore_returning.shtml Accessed on 21 January
2009.

[31] DWP (2007) Ready for Work: Full Employment in Our Generation, DWP. p. 45.

[32] Jenkins, S. (2008) Extension of the New Deal Plus for Lone Parents Pilot to
Scotland and Wales: Qualitative Evaluation
http://www.dwp.gov.uk/asd/asd5/rports2007-2008/rrep499.pdf Accessed on 22
January 2009.

5 Out of work with a health condition or disability

Benefits for workless people with disability or ill health and their carers

If your illness or disability means that you are unable to work, you should be able to get one or more benefits. The benefit you receive will normally depend on whether you are employed, have paid National Insurance (NI) contributions, or fulfil certain other conditions. You could get:

- Employment and Support Allowance (ESA), or
- Statutory Sick Pay (SSP) or
- Incapacity Benefit plus
- Disability Living Allowance (DLA), or
- Attendance Allowance (AA), and
- benefits for work-related accidents and diseases.

You may also be able to receive means-tested benefits (such as Council Tax benefit and Housing Benefit (HB)), either on top of another benefit or as an alternative source of income.

If you care for someone with ill health or a disability, you may be entitled to Carer's Allowance (CA).

Incapacity Benefit, Income Support and Severe Disablement Allowance

Before 27 October 2008, people who were unable to work because of physical or mental health problems or disabilities received Incapacity Benefit (IB) or Income IS. It has not been possible to make a new claim for these benefits since then. New claims for Severe Disablement Allowance (SDA) stopped in April 2001.

If you currently get any of these benefits, they will carry on for as long as you are ill, unless you leave the benefit for 12 or more weeks. In certain situations, if you leave the benefit because of paid work or training, you have up to 104 weeks to return to the benefit. However, all IB, IS and SDA payments will stop whenever the government decides to move people over to ESA over the next few years. The current plan is to make the change by 2013, though the new medical assessments will apply to people aged under 25 from 2010.

Employment and Support Allowance

Customer journey for Employment and Support Allowance

1. The first step

You'll need a medical certificate to make your claim. If you don't already have one of these, see your doctor.

↓

2. Chat to Jobcentre Plus

Call 0800 055 6688 to start your claim (use a claim form online). If you have speech or hearing difficulties, you can contact Jobcentre Plus using a textphone on 0800 023 4888. They'll ask you some questions about your circumstances and you'll need to provide them with ID (such as your National Insurance number). You may need to send them documents to confirm what you have told them. They'll also tell you about what to expect in the coming weeks.

↓

3. Next, a letter

Jobcentre Plus will put a letter in the post asking you to check all the details of your claim. You only need to tell them if you spot anything that needs to be changed. A few days after they receive any documents they have asked you for, Jobcentre Plus will confirm your Employment and Support Allowance payments (see page 189).

4. Work Capability Assessment

You will usually have to complete an ESA 50 form asking for details of your health/ disability and may also be asked to attend an assessment with a doctor or nurse. They'll look at how your illness or disability affects your ability to carry out day-to-day activities. Seek advice about the ESA 50 (see page 187).

5. Some decisions

Based on the results of your assessment, Jobcentre Plus will decide whether you can continue to receive Employment and Support Allowance, and how much you'll receive. You'll be placed in either the Work-Related Activity Group (where you'll be expected to prepare for work), or the Support Group (see page 189).

6. Your personal adviser

From around this stage, if you are in the Work-Related Activity Group you will be expected to attend up to six sessions with a personal adviser, who will talk with you about tailored support and help you move into suitable work (see page 189).

7. Ongoing help

Finding a job isn't the end of the story. You will be offered ongoing help once you're in work (such as coaching, mentoring and financial support) to help you stay in employment and make the most of your abilities (see page 193).

Material adapted from DWP publication 'Employment and Support Allowance. The Way to Work'. http://www.dwp.gov.uk/esa/pdfs/journey.pdf Crown copyright

The following table sets out what ESA claimants can expect to get at different stages of their ESA claim, what they will be required to do, and the employment programmes they can choose to take part in.

Claiming ESA

	Start ESA claim	Week 8	By Week 13	After Work Capability Assessment
What ESA claimants can get	Basic rate of ESA (see page 346)	Basic rate of ESA (see page 346)	After your Work Capability Assessment, you will be placed in either the Support Group or the Work-Related Activity Group (see page 189). The amount of your allowance will depend on which group you are in (see page 346).	If you are in the Support Group, you will get the highest rate of ESA If you are in the Work-Related Activity Group, you will get a lower rate See page 346 for ESA rates
What ESA claimants must do	Show limited capability for work through medical certificates (see page 187)	Work Focused Interview (see page 148)	Fill out form ESA50 Work Capability Assessment (may happen before Week 13, or after it) (see page 187) Limited Capability for Work Related Activity Test (see page 318)	If you are in the Work-Related Activity Group: • Monthly Work Focused Interviews, for five months • Agree an Action Plan with your personal adviser • A Work Focused Health-Related Assessment (see page 189)
Optional programmes			New Deal for Disabled People (see page 210) Pathways to Work (see page 207) Workstep (if you are in the ESA Support Group) (see page 216)	New Deal for Disabled People (see page 210) Pathways to Work (see page 207) Workstep (if you are in the ESA Support Group) (see page 216)

Day 1 of your Employment and Support Allowance claim

To claim ESA, you will have to meet certain basic eligibility rules:

- You must be aged 16 or older
- You must have Limited Capability for Work, and
- You must not be getting or able to get Jobseeker's Allowance (JSA), SSP, or IS (for example, as a carer).

In addition, to qualify for ESA, you must either have a low income now, or have paid enough NI contributions in the past. If you qualify because of your NI record, then it doesn't matter whether you have a partner or not, what they earn, or what savings you have. However, you cannot get Income-Related ESA at all. Any earnings they have from work of fewer than 24 hours, or if they are getting other benefits for themselves such as JSA, will affect how much ESA you get. See page 62, for more information on the NI contribution rules.

You are allowed to do a limited amount of work while claiming ESA, but you cannot do any government-funded training. See page 192 for more details.

If you think you may be eligible for ESA, your first step is to phone Jobcentre Plus. They will ask you questions on the phone and fill out a claim form for you. If you don't want to make your claim on the phone, ask Jobcentre Plus to send you the claim forms so you can fill them out and return them yourself.

In the first two weeks of your Employment and Support Allowance claim

Within about two weeks of making your ESA claim, Jobcentre Plus will send you a letter to confirm what you said on the phone. You should check this letter carefully and make sure that what it says about you is true.

Weeks 1–13 of your Employment and Support Allowance claim: the Assessment Phase[1]

The first 13 weeks of your claim for ESA is called the Assessment Phase, and during this phase you are paid the basic rate of ESA. To get your payments, you must show that you have Limited Capability for Work (LCW), and you will show this through medical certificates (Med 3 or Med 5). At about Week 8 of your ESA claim, you will have a Work Focused Interview, unless the interview is deferred. You must attend this interview (and any others) and you must participate in the interviews by giving details of your qualifications, education, plans for work, and so on.

As part of the Assessment Phase, you will have a Work Capability Assessment. First, the Department for Work and Pensions (DWP) will usually ask you to fill out Form ESA50. Your answers may show that you have LCW but, if there is doubt, you will have a medical examination with a healthcare professional. It is very important to fill in the ESA50 form carefully, and preferably with independent help. You must send the form back to Jobcentre Plus within four weeks, and you should take your copy of the form to your health assessment. If you miss the assessment, you have five days to contact Jobcentre Plus and explain why. If you do not contact the Jobcentre, or you do not have a very good reason for missing the assessment, your benefit may be cut.

After the Work Capability Assessment, you will have a Limited Capability for Work Related Activity test. This will determine whether you qualify for the Support Component or the Work Related Activity Component of ESA.

The Assessment Phase ends when the Work Capability Assessment is complete. If the assessment has not been completed within 13 weeks (for example, because of DWP delay or non-attendance by you), then your Assessment Phase may continue beyond 13 weeks.

The Work Capability Assessment[2]

The Work Capability Assessment uses a points system to decide whether or not you have LCW. To count as having LCW, you must score at least 15 points on the assessment. The points system is given on page 318.

The following people are automatically treated as having LCW, and will not have a Work Capability Assessment:[3]

* hospital inpatients
* people suffering from a progressive disease where death within six months can reasonably be expected

- people being treated by intravenous, intraperitoneal or intrathecal chemotherapy (there are other forms of delivering chemotherapy that do not qualify)
- people refraining from work because they carry, or have been in contact with, an infectious disease
- pregnant women, where there is a serious risk to the health of the mother or the child if the woman does not refrain from work, and
- women who are pregnant or have recently given birth but are not entitled to maternity allowance or statutory maternity pay, from six weeks before the baby is due to two weeks after the birth.

Overall, many more people will be found 'fit to work' under the Work Capability Assessment compared with the old medical assessment used for IB.

If you do not pass the assessment, even if you don't score enough points to have Limited Capability for Work you can still be treated as having LCW if the healthcare professional can give evidence that:

- you are suffering from a severe life threatening disease, and there is medical evidence that the disease is uncontrollable, or uncontrolled, by a recognised therapeutic procedure (in the case of a disease that is uncontrolled, there must be a reasonable cause for the disease to be uncontrolled by a recognised therapeutic procedure), or
- you suffer from a specific disease, bodily or mental disablement, and there is a substantial risk to the mental or physical health of any person if you are found not to have LCW.

The last category is a very important safeguard for many people who fail the Work Capability Assessment. It takes into account the range of work you can do, along with things such as getting ready for work, travel to and from work, and the broad results of being found as not having LCW.[4] 'Substantial risk' means that there is a risk of serious harm, even though it may be unlikely to happen.[5]

Limited Capability for Work Related Activity Test[6]

As well as doing a Work Capability Assessment, you also have to do a test to decide whether you have Limited Capability for Work Related Activity (LCWRA). This test will decide whether you get the Support Component of ESA, or the Work Related Activity Component. The LCWRA test will apply unless you are terminally ill or you have other proof that you can't do Work Related Activity (for example, you are on the kind of chemotherapy, or you have the kind of pregnancy described in the previous section). The LCWRA test has 46 descriptors, and if you satisfy at least one, you will qualify for the Support Component of ESA.

Week 14 and onwards of your Employment and Support Allowance claim: Support Group and Work Related Activity Group

If you pass the LCWRA test, you will get the highest rate of ESA (including the Support Component) and you will not have to participate in Work Related Activity. You will be in what is commonly called the 'Support Group'. If you are in this group, you can still look for work, and you can volunteer for Work Related Activity, but you will be under no pressure from Jobcentre Plus while your health stays the same.

If you do not pass the LCWRA test, but you do have LCW, then you will get ESA at a lower rate (but you can add on the Work Related Activity Component to your basic rate of ESA), and you have to participate in Work Related Activity. You will be in what is commonly called the 'Work Related Activity Group'.

Work Related Activity Group

If you are awarded ESA but you are not put in the Support Group, then you will go into the Work Related Activity Group instead and get ESA at a lower rate than those in the support group. You will have to participate in Work Related Activity.

You will have a Work Focused Health Related Assessment. This checks the barriers to paid work and how these might be managed or reduced. The assessment also asks for your views on your situation and your aspirations. These will go into a capability report to be given to you and your Jobcentre Plus personal adviser.

You will have a further five Work Focused Interviews with your personal adviser. The interviews will usually be held monthly, unless there is a reason for them to be deferred (you have no right to appeal a decision not to defer a WFI, though you could use the DWP's complaints procedure and take judicial review or ombudsman action).

You must attend and participate in the WFIs, which means that you must give details of your qualifications, education, plans for work, and so on, and also agree to an Action Plan. The Action Plan lists the jobsearch and training activities you are willing to do, and anything else that is relevant to finding or staying in work. This could include drawing up a CV, taking steps to improve your health, doing some voluntary work or training, and looking for suitable jobs.

Even though you have to agree to the Action Plan, at present you are not required to carry out anything specific in the plan (though this will change in the future). The plan must be in writing and a copy of the plan must be given to you.

If you fail to attend or participate in a WFI, or to draw up an Action Plan, and you do not tell the DWP within five working days that you had 'good cause' for not attending or participating, then your ESA will be sanctioned. This means that the Work Related Activity component you get for being in that group is reduced by 50 per cent for four weeks and then by 100 per cent until you either attend and participate in WFIs or qualify for the Support Component. As soon as you either attend and participate in WFIs, or qualify for the Support Component, the sanction will be lifted but not backdated. The basic rate of ESA (which is the same as JSA) cannot be sanctioned.

When deciding whether or not you have good cause for not attending or participating in a WFI, the DWP must take a number of things into account.[7] You can have good cause if you:

- did not understand the need to take part in the WFI because of learning, language or literacy difficulties, or because you were given misleading information by government staff

- had transport difficulties, and no reasonable alternative was available
- were attending an interview with an employer
- were following up employment opportunities as a self-employed earner
- were attending a medical or dental appointment, and it was unreasonable in the circumstances to change the appointment
- were accompanying someone for whom you have caring responsibilities to a medical or dental appointment, and it was unreasonable for that person to change their appointment
- had an accident, sudden illness or relapse of a physical or mental condition, or your dependant or someone you care for had an accident, sudden illness or relapse of a physical or mental condition
- were attending the funeral of a relative or close friend on the day of your WFI
- have a physical or mental condition which made it impossible to attend at the time and place fixed for the interview, or
- the established customs and practices of your religion stopped you attending on that day or at that time.

The DWP will also take into account anything else that it deems appropriate.

The DWP has set up many safeguards to help you avoid sanctions. These include contacting you before the WFI to remind you to attend, offering alternative times, dates and venues for the WFI, visiting you at home when there has been no verbal contact before the WFI, and visiting you at home if you have a mental health problem or learning disability.

Personal advisers' work will usually be done by organisations under contract to DWP (including private companies). These companies do not have the power to sanction you, but they will pass on information about sanctions to DWP Decision Makers.

Employment and Support Allowance benefit rules

National Insurance contributions

You must have paid enough NI contributions in order to qualify for ESA through the contributions route. That normally means having worked and paid NI during the past couple of years. However, if you are under the age of 20 (or 25 in some cases) you may qualify for ESA (called 'ESA in Youth') without having paid NI contributions.[8]

You may qualify for ESA in Youth if you are:[9]

- aged under 20, or
- aged under 19 and in education for 21 or more hours per week, not counting education that is not suitable for someone of the same age who does not have a disability, or
- aged 20 to 24 and have been on a course of full-time education or training in the three months before age 20, no longer attending the course and stopped attending some time after the last two tax years before the calendar year when ESA is claimed. (Training should be sponsored by the government and funded through the Learning and Skills Council, in England)

Once awarded, ESA in Youth may continue to be paid beyond the age of 25.

Working while on Employment and Support Allowance

You can do a limited amount of work while you get ESA. The same rules about work apply to both contributory ESA and Income-Related ESA.

You are allowed to do:[10]

- work for which the earnings in any week are less than £20, or
- work for which the earnings in any week are less than £93, and which is:
    - part of a treatment programme under medical supervision, or
    - done while you are a hospital inpatient or outpatient, or
    - supervised by someone from a public, local authority or voluntary body involved in providing work for people who have a disability, or

- work for fewer than 16 hours per week (on average), where your earnings in any week are less than £93, and where you do not do this work for more than 52 weeks (if you have done this kind of work before while you were on ESA, and you want to do the work again, you must either wait 52 weeks from the last period of work, or stop claiming ESA for at least 12 weeks), or
- work for fewer than 16 hours per week (on average), where your earnings in any week are less than £93, if you are in the ESA Support Group, or
- work while self-employed under an approved training programme, or
- voluntary or unpaid work where it is reasonable to work without pay (you can be paid out-of-pocket expenses), or
- work on an unpaid work placement approved in advance by the DWP, or
- domestic tasks carried out for a relative or in your own home, or
- work in an emergency to protect people, property or livestock.

If you do any other work (paid or unpaid), or if you exceed the earnings limit or the working hours limit in any week, you will be disqualified from ESA for that week because you will not count as having LCW.[11]

Don't forget that, even though you can earn up to £93 and still get ESA, earnings above £20 will usually affect any housing or council tax benefit that you get unless you qualify for Income-Related ESA.

Going into work or training

If you work for 16 or more hours per week (including breaks at work), or if you join government-funded training, you cannot get ESA (but you may qualify for in-work benefits such as Working Tax Credit or HB). You can return to your ESA if you leave the benefit but reclaim it within 12 weeks.

If you are working for at least 16 hours per week, or if you are on government-funded training, you will be classed as a 'work or training beneficiary'. This means that you can return to your ESA within 104 benefit weeks, if you reclaim the benefit straight after you leave the work or training.[12]

To be classed as a work or training beneficiary, you must also:

- start the work within one month of being in receipt of ESA (or within eight weeks, if you go into training)
- not have a decision to stop your ESA because you do not have LCW
- be paid Working Tax Credit and/or Child Tax Credit on the day before you stop work (the Child Tax Credit must be paid at more than the family rate of £547.50 per year)
- have LCW when you reclaim ESA.

Even though the rules say you can return to your old benefit rate (increased to cover any annual increases), there is still a risk that a DWP official may send you for another medical examination, because questions about your LCW may arise if you have been in work or training.

Studying while receiving ESA

If you are aged under 19, see *Inclusion's* Young Person's Handbook.

You can study part-time while receiving Income-Related ESA. You can study full-time if you receive Disability Living Allowance or Contributions ESA. If you are receiving Income-Related ESA, fees for non-advanced further education should be remitted.

If you do not receive Disability Living Allowance, you should seek advice before you start your course.

Switching from Jobseeker's Allowance to Employment and Support Allowance during illness

If you are claiming JSA and you are sick for more than two weeks, or if you expect your sickness to last for more than two weeks, you will have to make a claim for ESA instead.

You should notify Jobcentre Plus as soon as you are sick because you can continue to claim JSA for up to two weeks, despite being unfit for work.[13] If you are unable to visit Jobcentre Plus to sign on because of your sickness, you should also tell them straight away so that your payments aren't disrupted. The Jobcentre should then send you a form so that you can notify them about your sickness. You must complete and return this form to safeguard your benefit. You can receive JSA while sick for up to two fortnights out of every 12 months that you claim the benefit.

If you fail to sign on at Jobcentre Plus on the right day, you have five working days to sign a written declaration stating that you had good cause for not signing-on on your normal day. Good cause might include a few days of sickness. Your JSA claim should not be stopped because you could not sign on due to sickness (but payment of your benefit will be delayed).[14]

Employment and Support Allowance amounts

Contributory ESA and Income-Related ESA are paid at the same basic rate. During the Assessment Phase, ESA is paid at the same age-related rates as IS and JSA.

Like IS, Income-Related ESA can be increased to include premiums (for example, if you are a carer) and housing costs for owner-occupiers. There is no disability premium in Income-Related ESA but there are severe disability and enhanced disability premiums (see page 344).

Income is assessed for Income-Related ESA in the same way it is assessed for IS. See page 271.

There is no special rate for couples who are claiming the Work Related Activity Component or the Support Component. If both members of a couple qualify for ESA, double amounts of the components are paid.

The ESA rates are given on page 346.

Statutory Sick Pay[15]

SSP is the legal minimum that is paid by employers to their staff, for a maximum of 28 weeks. It is not a means-tested benefit, but it counts as income for means-tested benefits. SSP is not paid for the first three days of your absence from work (unless you have been getting SSP within the last eight weeks). Some employers have occupational sick pay schemes, and these may be more generous and last for more than 28 weeks. Employers with employees off sick for long periods may reclaim their spending on SSP from HM Revenue and Customs (HMRC).[16]

Who is entitled to Statutory Sick Pay?

You can receive SSP if:

- your average gross earnings are more than the lower earnings limit for NI (£95 per week)
- you are incapable of work
- you have been incapable of work for at least four days (unless you have been ill within the last eight weeks)
- you are within a 'period of entitlement', and
- you have notified your employer of your sickness.

SSP is only paid for days you would normally work ('qualifying days').[17] There are special rules for when normal working patterns change, and you may need to seek advice if this applies to you.

Who is an 'employee'?

'Employee'[18] includes people who are employed by an employment agency, certain office-holders and people on temporary contracts, as well as people on permanent contracts. You do not need to have a written contract of employment to count as an employee. Generally, whoever deducts NI for you is considered to be your employer.

Some employers try to avoid taking responsibility for employee rights by classing their workers as self-employed or sub-contractors. You may be able to challenge their classification, and you should seek advice on employment law in such cases.[19]

There are no rules about the number of hours you must work to qualify for SSP, and it is possible to get SSP from more than one employer (for example, if you have two part-time jobs). You can also be unfit for one type of employment but fit for another type, and so receive SSP from one job and earnings from the other job.

Notification of sickness

You should notify your employer of your sickness as soon as possible. Your method of notification needs to be approved by your employer.

For the first seven days of sickness, you should personally vouch for your sickness. After that, you should give a medical certificate (a Med 3, or a Med 5 if you are proving a past sickness). People other than a doctor can give medical evidence for SSP and ESA. A community nurse, a physiotherapist or a social worker can give proof of sickness, if it is reasonable in the circumstances (for example, if you don't have a GP).[20] Extra proof from other professionals can also help in borderline or unusual situations.

Period of entitlement

An employer who lays off an employee mainly to avoid paying SSP is still liable to pay SSP during the period of entitlement, or until the contract of employment is due to end.[21] This may also count as unfair dismissal and/or discrimination, and you should seek employment law advice. If your employer fails to pay SSP, it is also worth telling HMRC, who can enforce payment of SSP. If your employer refuses to pay SSP, you can ask HMRC to make a decision[22] which then binds the employer, and which you can also appeal against if you feel it is wrong.

What happens when my claim to Statutory Sick Pay ends?

After 28 weeks of SSP, your employer must send you a notice (called SSP1) telling you that you have had the maximum amount of SSP.[23] You should complete the SSP1 notice and send it with a medical certificate to Jobcentre Plus. Jobcentre Plus will use the notice as a claim for ESA. Your employer must also send a SSP1 notice if you are not entitled to SSP from the start, so that you can use the notice to claim ESA instead. If your employer fails to keep adequate records or fails to notify you correctly about your SSP, HMRC can make them pay a penalty of up to £300, plus a daily penalty, or up to £3,000 in more serious cases.[24]

People on work-based training

Trainees who are employed will normally qualify for SSP. Trainees who are not employees will usually qualify for ESA instead.

Disability Living Allowance

What is Disability Living Allowance?

Disability Living Allowance (DLA) is for people who have a physical or mental disability (including mental illness, learning disability and behavioural problems). It is paid to people who need help looking after themselves, or who need someone on hand in case of danger, and/or to people who find it difficult to walk or get around. It can be given to children or adults, but you must claim the benefit before you turn 65 years old. DLA is not means-tested, is tax-free and is paid on top of other social security benefits. It has two components: one for care, and the other for mobility. There are three care component rates and two mobility component rates.

DLA is based on your mobility needs and/or your need to be helped or watched because you can't do certain everyday personal tasks, so you can claim the benefit whether or not you are in work. Taking on a job or voluntary work while you get DLA does not give the DWP legal grounds to review your DLA[25] but, in practice, the DWP will often look into your entitlement if you take on any work or increase your hours. This is because the DWP assumes that you may be starting work because your disabilities have reduced.

DLA can help you to claim higher amounts of benefits such as Working Tax Credit, HB and IS.

Who is entitled to Disability Living Allowance?

To claim DLA, you must be aged:

- 0 to 65 years for the care component, and
- three to 65 years for the mobility component (or five years or over to claim the lower mobility component rate). If you get the mobility component, you will still be paid after the age of 65, as long as you continue to meet the rules for receiving the benefit.

Also, to claim either component, you must:

- have needed help or had mobility problems for at least three months, and
- your condition must be likely to last for at least six months (unless you have a terminal illness).

The three rates of the care component[26]

Low rate

To receive the low rate, you must:

- need attention in connection with your bodily functions for a large part of the day, or
- be unable to prepare a cooked meal from ingredients you have on hand (if you are aged 16 or over).

Middle rate

To receive the middle rate, during the day you must:

- need frequent attention in connection with your bodily functions, or
- constant supervision to avoid substantial danger to yourself or other people.

Or, during the night you must:

- need frequent or prolonged attention in connection with your bodily functions, or
- need someone to be awake for a prolonged period or at frequent intervals to watch over you.

High rate

To receive the high rate, you must satisfy both the night and the day rules for the middle rate.

The two rates of the mobility component[27]

Low rate

To receive the low rate, you must need guidance or supervision from another person most of the time when you walk in unfamiliar places. You do not need to be physically disabled to qualify for the low rate, and people with visual impairments or chronic anxiety problems can often make a claim.

High rate

To receive the high rate, you must be physically disabled and one of the following must apply to you:

- you are unable to walk, or
- your ability to walk outdoors is so limited that:
    - you can only walk a short distance, or
    - you can only walk at a slow speed, or
    - walking takes a long time, or
    - you can only walk in an unusual manner so that you are virtually unable to walk
- the effort of walking outdoors could affect your health or cause it to worsen.

You can also get the higher rate if:

- you are both blind and deaf (the government has announced that from April 2010 this will include people with a severe visual impairment)
- you are severely mentally impaired with severe behavioural problems and you also qualify for the high-rate care component of DLA, or
- you have had both legs amputated.

Children

To claim DLA, as well as meeting the usual rules of entitlement, children aged under 16 must show that they have substantially more needs than other children in normal health. Quality and quantity of care are important. Children under 16 cannot use the 'cooking test' to claim the low-rate care component.

Hospitals and care homes

If you live in certain types of publicly funded accommodation (for example, local authority-funded care or a NHS hospital), it may affect your DLA. Speak to a social worker if this applies to you and get specialist advice.

How to claim Disability Living Allowance

You can claim DLA by phoning the DWP on 0800 882200 and asking for a DLA claim pack to be sent to you. You can also print out a claim form from the DWP website (www.dwp.gov.uk) or claim online at www.directgov.uk. You cannot backdate your DLA claim unless your claim is lost in the post, so do not delay in making a claim. You may be asked questions about your health when you try to get a claim form. This is a new tactic by the DWP to stop people making claims that are unlikely to succeed. Don't be put off by the questions, even if the person on the phone tells you that your claim probably won't succeed – tell them you want the claim form anyway so that a proper assessment is done.

Further points

Keep these things in mind when you apply for DLA:

- You will not be called for a Work Focused Interview, if you claim DLA on its own.
- It is important to fill out the claim form as fully as possible because many claims are denied when people don't spell out their needs in detail.
- Your entitlement is based on the help you need – not the help you receive.
- It's not just about being unable to do things – you might be able to get dressed by yourself, for example, but it takes you a lot longer than most other people.
- If you can do things for yourself but need someone to motivate you, supervise you or persuade you, then put that on the claim form too.

- Help with things such as gardening or housework won't normally qualify but, sometimes, extra help with laundry (for example, because of soiling) may qualify.
- There is no set list of disabilities that qualify for DLA. Any type of long-term illness or disability may create needs that entitle you to the benefit.
- If your claim is refused or you are paid at a rate that is too low, you can challenge this with a good chance of success, but you should get independent advice.
- You can claim and receive DLA if you are working.

Attendance Allowance

What is Attendance Allowance?

Attendance Allowance (AA) is for people who make their first claim after age 65. It only has one component: a care component. The care component of AA is paid at the same rate, and for the same reasons, as the middle rate or the upper rate of the DLA care component. There is no mobility component for AA and no equivalent of the lower-rate care component.

Who is entitled to Attendance Allowance?

To claim AA, you must:

- be aged 65 or older, and
- show that you need help with personal care and/or supervision to avoid danger to yourself or others, and
- have needed help or supervision for at least six months (this rule is different from DLA).

How to claim Attendance Allowance

You can claim AA by phoning the DWP on 0800 882200 and asking for an AA claim pack to be sent to you. You can also print out a claim form from the DWP website (www.dwp.gov.uk) or claim online at www.directgov.uk. You cannot backdate your AA claim unless your claim is lost in the post, so do not delay in making a claim.

Further points

Keep these things in mind when you apply for AA:

- It is important to fill out the claim form as fully as possible because many claims are denied when people don't spell out their needs in detail.
- Your entitlement is based on the help you need – not the help you receive.
- Help with things like gardening or housework won't normally qualify, but sometimes, extra help with laundry (for example, because of soiling) may qualify.
- There is no set list of disabilities that qualify for AA. Any type of long-term illness or disability may create needs that entitle you to the benefit.
- If your claim is refused or you are paid at a rate that is too low, you can challenge this with a good chance of success, but you should get independent advice.

Carer's Allowance

What is Carer's Allowance?

Carer's Allowance (CA) is a benefit for carers. It is not means-tested, but your pay can affect your entitlement because there is a maximum amount you can earn while claiming CA (currently £95 per week).

CA can increase your entitlement to means-tested benefits because extra amounts for carers are included when calculating these benefits.

Who is entitled to Carer's Allowance?

To claim CA, you must:

- spend at least 35 hours per week looking after someone who claims either AA or the middle- or high-rate care component of DLA, and
- not be in education that has 21 or more hours of supervised study or teaching each week.[28]

If you are working part-time while receiving CA, you can offset certain costs against your earnings when calculating whether or not your earnings are less than the £95 earnings limit. You can offset the following from your gross earnings:

- Income Tax and NI
- Half of any contributions to a personal or occupational pension scheme
- The cost of paying a carer (who is not a close relative) to look after children or the person you care for while you are at work (up to half of your net earnings can be offset by these care expenses)[29]

How to claim Carer's Allowance

You make a claim for CA by filling out form DS700, which you can get by phoning the DWP on 0800 882200 (textphone 0800 243355). You can also print out a claim form from the DWP website, or claim this benefit online at www.directgov.uk

Further points

Keep these things in mind when you are making a claim for CA:

- You can't claim CA if you also receive another non-means-tested benefit that pays the same or more than your CA (for example, Contributory ESA, IB, ESA [contributions] or Retirement Pension). However, you should still make a claim so that you have 'underlying entitlement' to CA, because then you will qualify for higher amounts of means-tested benefits.
- People who receive CA are also credited with NI contributions.
- If you claim CA, you will not have a Work Focused Interview (see page 150) unless you choose to have one or also receive IS.
- CA is given to a carer who looks after a named individual. This means that a couple can have two carers who receive CA.
- If a carer receives CA, it may affect the means-tested benefits that are paid to the person they care for. Seek advice to check this before making a claim.
- Your CA will be affected if the person you care for goes into hospital or publicly-funded care and their AA or DLA stops.

- CA was known as Invalid Care Allowance until April 2003, and people aged 65 or over were not entitled to start a new claim for it until October 2002.

Benefits for work related accidents and diseases

What are the benefits for work related accidents and diseases?

There are a number of benefits for people who have ill health or disability because of their employment. These are:

- Disablement Benefit
- Reduced Earnings Allowance
- Retirement Allowance
- Constant Attendance Allowance.

These benefits are often called industrial injury benefits, and they are paid to people who have a disability or health problem because of an accident at work or a prescribed industrial disease. These benefits are non-taxable, non-contributory, and they can be paid whether or not you are working and regardless of your income or capital. They do not affect any tax credits you may get.

Because of this, these benefits can help you go back into paid work, maybe for reduced hours or on lower pay than before you had the accident or disease.

You do not have to prove that your employer was negligent, and you can receive these benefits whether or not your employer has paid you compensation.

Who is entitled?[30]

To claim a benefit for a work related accident or disease, you must:

- be an employed earner (self-employed people do not count), and
- have had an accident caused by and during your work, or have a prescribed industrial disease that has caused a loss of faculty assessed as a disability of at least 14 per cent (one per cent for Reduced Earnings Allowance), and

- have had the accident or caught the disease at least 90 days before your claim, and still have a disability or ill health.

For Reduced Earnings Allowance, your accident or disease must have happened before 10 October 1990, and you must be unable to follow your regular occupation or do work of an equal standard.

How to claim

You can get claim forms from a Jobcentre Plus office, or you can print them from the DWP website (www.dwp.gov.uk).

Further points

Keep these things in mind when you claim for a work-related accident or disease:

- These benefits are not means-tested (though Reduced Earnings Allowance depends on your earnings), but they do count as income for means-tested benefits. They are ignored as income for tax credits, so they are particularly helpful if you are in work.
- These benefits are not affected if you receive compensation for an injury, but the amount of compensation you receive from legal action can be affected if you are paid benefits.
- You will not be asked to have a Work Focused Interview if you make a claim.
- You need to have a medical examination to decide the degree of your disability.
- Different amounts of Disablement Benefit are paid according to the degree of your disability.
- It is important to register any accident or incident at work so that you have proof if you have to make a claim later on.
- If you are injured or catch a prescribed industrial disease while you are an unwaged trainee on Work Based Training, you may be able to claim similar benefits under the Analogous Industrial Injuries Scheme. You can get more information about the scheme by contacting Jobcentre Plus on 0800 055 6688.

- The full list of Prescribed Industrial Diseases is set out in Schedule 1 of the Social Security (Industrial Injuries) (Prescribed Diseases) Regulations 1985. It has been heavily changed over the years and there is a summary of the current amounts in the Welfare Benefits and Tax Credits Handbook published by the Child Poverty Action Group.

Pathways to Work

What is Pathways to Work?

Pathways to Work Is a programme aimed at helping disabled people and people with health conditions claiming certain benefits to start or return to work.

Who is eligible for Pathways to Work?[31]

You are eligible for help from Pathways to Work if you are entitled to receive certain benefits because of your disability or health condition. You will automatically be considered for Pathways to Work if you are claiming any of the following benefits for the first time, or claiming again after a break in receiving benefit:

- ESA
- IB
- IS, on the grounds of incapacity
- IS, being received during an appeal against a decision that you are capable of work
- SDA.

Programme elements

The Pathways to Work programme gives you access to a wide range of personalised support.

Mandatory Work Focused Interviews

You will usually be invited to six Work Focused Interviews during the first seven months of your claim for any of the benefits listed above. These are likely to be with the same adviser at monthly intervals. You must attend these interviews, unless they are waived because it is not appropriate, or will not be of help due to the nature of your illness or disability.

Warning: if you fail to attend the interviews, the amount of benefit you receive might be reduced.

The interviews will be with a personal adviser who will help you to identify future life and work goals, and any barriers to achieving them, and will support you in overcoming these barriers. The adviser will also help you to focus on your ability to work and discuss job opportunities with you. You will agree an Action Plan with your adviser that outlines the activities you will undertake. This will be reviewed at each meeting.

The Condition Management Programme

The Condition Management Programme aims to help you understand and manage your disability or health condition so that you can function better. The programme is delivered by healthcare professionals and is tailored to meet your personal needs.

Return to Work Credit

Return to Work Credit is a tax-free payment of £40 per week. You can receive this credit for up 52 weeks and is on top of tax credits as long as:

- you are working over 16 hours a week on average
- your job is expected to last at least five weeks
- you earn less than £15,000 per year
- you are earning at least the National Minimum Wage
- you have been receiving benefits on the grounds of disability or ill health for at least 13 weeks.

Other elements

If you are a new or existing customer, you may also be entitled to the following support:

- a job preparation premium of £20 per week for a maximum of 26 weeks if you agree an Action Plan and participate in activity that supports a return to work
- access to existing training, employment programmes and financial help,
- access to the New Deal for Disabled People (see page 214).

Leaving the programme and sanctions

The only part of Pathways that is mandatory is the standard series of interviews with a personal adviser. The sanctions for non-attendance and the rules that apply are the same as those for Work Focused Interviews (see page 150).

You may leave the opportunities such as the Condition Management Programme or the New Deal for Disabled People at any time, because these elements are voluntary. If you stop claiming a benefit that makes you eligible for the programme, you will no longer be required to attend the mandatory Work Focused Interviews.

Programme coverage and delivery

Since April 2008, the Pathways to Work programme has been available throughout Great Britain.

The areas where Pathways to Work is delivered by Jobcentre Plus are:

- Ayrshire, Dumfries, Galloway and Inverclyde
- Cumbria and Lancashire
- Cheshire, Halton and Warrington (partial district coverage)
- Derbyshire
- Dorset and Somerset
- Essex

- Glasgow
- Greater Manchester Central
- Highland, Islands, Clyde Coast and Grampian
- Lanarkshire and East Dumbartonshire
- Merseyside
- Northumbria
- South Tyne and Wear Valley
- South Wales Valleys
- South West Wales
- South Yorkshire
- Staffordshire
- Tees Valley

The remaining areas in England, Scotland and Wales have the Pathways to Work service delivered mainly by the private and voluntary sector.

The Pathways to Work programme focuses on new claimants, although existing claimants can voluntarily join the programme.

New Deal for Disabled People

What is New Deal for Disabled People?

The New Deal for Disabled People (NDDP)[32] is a voluntary programme designed to help people receiving a disability or health related benefit to prepare for, find, and sustain paid work. NDDP Job Brokers will provide help with looking for a job and any support or training that is needed (see page 000). NDDP is a voluntary programme, so your benefits will not be affected if you choose not to participate.

Who is eligible for New Deal for Disabled People?

To participate in NDDP you must want to find a job, be between the age of 18 and pensionable age (60 or 65), and be in direct receipt of one or more of the following[33] (to find out if you are eligible for these benefits, see page 000):

- ESA
- IB
- A benefit equivalent to IS from an European Union (EU) member country
- NI Credits on the grounds of incapacity (which may be awarded on their own, or in addition to payments of income related benefits – IS, HB, Council Tax Benefit, or War Pension)
- IS with a disability premium (replaced by ESA for new claims)
- IS, because your IB has been stopped and you are appealing against the decision
- SDA
- DLA, provided you are not receiving JSA, and you are not in paid work of 16 hours or more per week
- HB with a disability premium, provided you are not in receipt of JSA, and you are not in paid work of 16 hours or more per week
- Council Tax Benefit with a disability premium, provided you are not in receipt of JSA, and you are not in paid work of 16 hours or more per week
- Industrial Injuries Disablement Benefit with an Unemployability Supplement.

Note: If you are between 16 and 20 and have a claim for one of the benefits above, you are eligible for NDDP. In some other circumstances, you may be entitled to participate if you are 16 or 17, or beyond state retirement age.

Programme elements

Once you have registered with a Job Broker, you will have regular and direct contact with them regarding your search for work. The services they offer may include:

- offering careers advice
- assessing how taking a job would affect you financially, including information about in-work benefits
- offering basic training (for example, on interview technique)
- matching you to employers, by looking at your skills, interests and experience
- helping and advising on adaptations (such as special chairs or computer equipment) and how to fund them
- an in-work support service for you and your employer to make sure the first few months in the job go smoothly.

Job Brokers have access to other Jobcentre Plus services and may refer you to another programme if you meet the eligibility criteria.

New Deal for Disabled People Job Brokers

Jobcentre Plus contracts a range of organisations to be Job Brokers. You need to register with a Job Broker to receive their services. It is up to you to choose a Job Broker. You can only register with one Broker at a time, and their services vary, so it is advisable to find out about all the different Brokers in your area and what services they offer before choosing one.

Jobcentre Plus advisers can inform you about all the Job Brokers in your local area and the services they offer. This should happen at your initial Work Focused Interview (see page 148), if you are making a claim for a disability or health related benefit. There is no formal referral to a Job Broker, but after the interview, you may be contacted to check whether you have registered with a Job Broker. If you have decided not to, the adviser may offer you the opportunity for further interviews or referral to a Disability Employment Adviser.

You can find out which Job Brokers are in your area either by ringing the NDDP Helpline on 0800 137 177 (or textphone 0800 435 550), or by visiting www.jobbrokersearch.gov.uk

Note: Once you have registered with a Job Broker, if you feel you are not progressing, or you are unhappy with the service they are offering, you may de-register and then re-register with a different Job Broker.

Disability Employment Advisers

Disability Employment Advisers (DEAs) are usually based in Jobcentre Plus offices, and provide specialist help with employment issues. If you are already in work, they can help you with issues relating to your current job. For example, if you think you might lose your job because of a disability or health problem, they can work with you and your employer, giving advice and exploring practical solutions to help you keep your job.

If you are looking for work, your adviser can plan your return to work with you by drawing up an action plan, helping you find a job that is suitable and using Jobcentre Plus's links with employers.[34]

Leaving the programme

There is no time limit for your participation on NDDP – you can continue to access support for as long as you want.

As NDDP is a voluntary programme, you may choose to leave it at any time without it affecting your benefit. You are however encouraged to discuss any concerns with your Job Broker before you de-register.

Other programmes to help disabled people into work

Access to Work

What is Access to Work?

The Access to Work (AtW)[35] programme can help you if you have a disability or health condition that makes it difficult for you to do your job.

The programme can provide you and your employer with advice, as well as practical and financial support.

Who is eligible for Access to Work?

You may be able to take part in the AtW programme if:

- you are employed or self-employed, whether on a part-time, full-time, permanent or temporary basis, or
- you are unemployed and about to start a job, and
- you have a disability or health condition likely to last for at least 12 months that affects your ability to do your job or certain parts of it. Even if your disability causes only small problems at work, you may be able get help from AtW.

Programme Elements

AtW can help you in a number of ways. It can give you and your employer advice and support, and can help pay towards extra costs that may arise because of your disability or health condition. For example, AtW can help cover the cost of:

- special equipment and changes to work premises (for example, wheelchair access)
- communication support at job interviews (for example, a communicator if you are hearing impaired)
- employing support workers to help you at a job interview, or while you are travelling to work
- travelling to work, if your disability or health condition prevents you from using public transport.

Practical help and advice is tailored so that it suits your individual needs for a period of three years. After three years, your case will be reviewed.

How to apply for Access to Work – the process

If you have a disability or health condition that is likely to last for at least 12 months, and you feel it affects your ability to do your job, get in touch with your regional AtW contact centre to see if you can get support through AtW. Alternatively, you can speak to the DEA at your local Jobcentre about AtW and whether you are eligible to receive support.

If you are likely to be eligible to receive help through AtW, you will be sent an application form, which you need to fill in and return. An AtW adviser will then contact you and speak to you and your employer about what support you should receive. This can be done over the telephone, and in person if necessary. Your adviser will decide what kind of help you need at work, and can even send out an assessor to your workplace to decide your level of need, if appropriate. Your adviser will seek formal approval for their recommendations from Jobcentre Plus. You, as well as your employer, will then be sent a letter informing you of the level of support approved and the grant available to pay for it. It is your employer's responsibility (or your own responsibility, if you are self- employed) to buy the approved support, and then claim back the agreed costs from AtW.

Access to Work Grants

The amount your employer (or you, if you are self-employed) can claim back depends on what kind of support you need, whether you are self-employed, and how long you have been employed for.

AtW will pay grants of up to 100 per cent if:

- you are unemployed and about to start a job
- you are self-employed
- you have been working for your present employer for less than six weeks when you first apply for AtW.

AtW will also pay grants of up to 100 per cent, whether you are employed, self-employed or about to start work, to cover the cost of:

- support workers
- additional travel costs while going to and from work, and also while carrying out your work
- communication support at interview.

AtW will share the cost with your employer if:

- you are employed and have been in your job for at least six weeks, and
- you require changes to premises and special equipment.

Work Preparation

What is Work Preparation?

Work Preparation is a flexible programme, offering a short period of unpaid work experience with a local employer to help you get ready for work. You can be given a range of support to help you find work and stay in it. Work Preparation can last from a few hours to a number of weeks, but on average most people are involved for between six and 13 weeks. Work Preparation will be replaced by Work Choice in October 2010.

Who is eligible for Work Preparation?

If you are considering going back to work after a long period of sickness or unemployment, you may be suitable for Work Preparation. Your DEA at Jobcentre Plus will discuss Work Preparation with you further.

WORKSTEP

What is WORKSTEP?

WORKSTEP,[36] previously known as the Supported Employment Scheme, is a programme for disabled people facing complex barriers to getting and keeping a job because of their disability. If you are eligible, WORKSTEP could help you to reach your potential and to progress in your job. It provides individually tailored and flexible support to you and your employer to make sure needs are met. WORKSTEP will be replaced by Work Choice in October 2010.

Who is eligible for WORKSTEP?

You may be eligible to receive help through WORKSTEP if you are disabled and your disability creates significant and complex barriers to working for which other forms of support are considered inappropriate, and you:

- are receiving ESA
- are receiving IB and/or NI Credit (including SDA and IS)
- are receiving JSA and/or NI Credits only for six months or more
- are receiving JSA and/or NI Credits for less than six months but are on IB before claiming JSA, or
- have been supported before and need to return to the programme within two years.

Contact your DEA, usually based at your local Jobcentre Plus office, to find out whether you are eligible to receive help through WORKSTEP and to discuss whether it is the best option for you.

Programme Features

WORKSTEP can provide tailored support to you and your employer for almost any kind of job. It offers a range of support, including practical help such as job training, job coaching, and advice. It also offers awareness support for your employer and colleagues. WORKSTEP can also help you to keep your job if you would otherwise lose it and AtW (see page 213) is not enough on its own to help you keep it.

Local Employment Partnerships

If you are disabled, or have been out of work because of a long-term illness, you could get training through a Local Employment Partnership. See page 115 for more information.

Employability Skills Programme (England)

You can take part in the Employability Skills Programme if you are aged 18 or over, have a literacy, language or numeracy need at Level 1 or below on the National Qualifications Framework (see page 119), and are getting benefit payments, credits, or a New Deal training allowance.

However, if you are eligible for Pathways to Work at the same time as you are eligible for an Employability Skills Programme, you will have to do Pathways to Work, where appropriate. See page 122, for detailed information on the Employability Skills Programme.

Endnotes

1 Regs 4–7 Employment and Support Allowance Regulations 2008 (ESA Regs).

2 Regs 19–21 ESA Regs.

3 Regs 32–3 ESA Regs.

4 CIB/26/2004 and CSIB/33/2004.

5 CIB/3519/2002.

6 Regs 34–6 ESA Regs.

7 Reg. 61(3) ESA Regs.

8 Para 4, sched. 1 Welfare Reform Act 2007.

9 Regs 8–13 ESA Regs.

10 Reg. 45 ESA Regs.

11 Reg. 40 (1) ESA Regs.

12 Reg. 148 ESA Regs.

13 Reg. 55 Jobseeker's Allowance Regulations 1996.

14 Reg. 24 Jobseeker's Allowance Regulations 1996.

15 Ss 151–5 and schs 11 and 12 Social Security Contributions and Benefits Act 1995.

16 Sect. 159A Social Security Contributions and Benefits Act 1992 (SSCB Act).

17 Sect. 154 SSCB Act and Reg. 5 Statutory Sick Pay (General) Regulations 1982.

18 Reg. 16 Statutory Sick Pay (General) Regulations 1982.

19 Sect. 151 SSCB Act.

20 Reg. 2(1) (d) Social Security (Medical Evidence) Regulations 1976.

21 Reg. 4 Statutory Sick Pay (General) Regulations 1982.

22 Sect. 8 Social Security Contributions (Transfer of Functions etc) Act 1999.

23 Regs 15 and 16 Statutory Sick Pay (General) Regulations 1982.

24 HMRC Employer helpsheet E14 supplement.

25 See Social Security and Child Support Commissioners' decisions CSA/114/1990 and CDLA/2160/2003.

26 Sect. 72 SSCB Act.

27 S73 SSCB Act & reg 12 Social Security (Disability Living Allowance) Regulations 1991.

28 Sect. 70 SSCB Act.

29 Reg. 10(3) Social Security Benefit (Computation of Earnings) Regulations 1996.

[30] Ss 94–120 SSCB Act.

[31] WP (2004) 'Pathways to Work' Touchbase 36, (September), 17 and DWP 'Pathways to Work' (2005) Touchbase 39, (June), 10.

[32] DWP. 'New Deal for Disabled People'. In Jobcentre Plus New Deals, /www.jobcentreplus.gov.uk/JCP/Customers/outofworkhelplookingforwork/Getting_job_ready/Programmes_to_get_you_ready/New_Deal/New_Deal_for_Disabled_People/index.html Accessed on 20 January 2009.

[33] Directgov. 'New Deal for Disabled People'. In Directgov Disabled People, www.direct.gov.uk/DisabledPeople/Employment/WorkSchemesAndProgrammes/WorkSchemesArticles/fs/en?CONTENT_ID=4001963&chk=cV3TWD Accessed on 20 January 2009.

[34] http://www.jobcentreplus.gov.uk/JCP/Customers/Disabled_People_and_Carers/Dev_015099.xml.html

[35] Directgov, 'Access to Work – Practical Help at Work', www.direct.gov.uk/en/DisabledPeople/Employmentsupport/WorkSchemesAndProgrammes/DG_4000347 Accessed on 21 January 2009.

[36] Directgov, 'WORKSTEP – Supported Employment', www.direct.gov.uk/en/DisabledPeople/Employmentsupport/WorkSchemesAndProgrammes/DG_4001973 Accessed on 21 January 2009.

6 People affected by drug and alcohol misuse, homelessness, and people with an offending background

Increased obligations for problem drug users

Overview of changes to benefits for problem drug users

Over the next few years, the government will be bringing in a new treatment and employment programme for problem drug users. A 'problem drug user' is someone who uses opiates or crack cocaine. Jobcentre Plus will have new ways to work out which benefit claimants are problem drug users, and these claimants will have to take part in a support programme until they are ready to move onto mainstream benefit programmes. If claimants fail to engage with the support programme, their benefit could be sanctioned.

If you have a substance misuse problem, you may qualify for Disability Living Allowance.

Timetable of changes

Currently, the government has not set out a time-frame for introducing the changes to benefits for problem drug users. It has said that developing and rolling out the changes will be a slow process.[1] The first step was to create drug co-ordinator posts in Jobcentre Plus offices. These posts started in England from April 2009, and will be evaluated before they are rolled out across the nation.[2]

In time, the new support programme may be extended to people who use cannabis and/or powder cocaine, and people with an alcohol addiction.[3]

Identifying problem drug users

The government plans to identify possible problem drug users in the following ways:

- If you make a new claim for Employment and Support Allowance (ESA), your drug problem will most likely be identified during your Work Focused Health-Related Assessment.[4]

- If you are making a claim for Jobseeker's Allowance (JSA) and a Jobcentre Plus adviser suspects that you have a drug problem, they can ask you whether current or recent use of crack cocaine or heroin is stopping you from working.[5]

- The government may bring in legislation so that Jobcentre Plus can identify problem drug users by getting data from criminal justice agencies. This data would include details of people who have left prison, and people who have been given a Drug Rehabilitation Requirement by the courts. Jobcentre Plus would safeguard the shared information and only use it in connection with benefits and the new support programme.[6]

Health assessment

If the government (or Jobcentre Plus) thinks you could be a problem drug user, you will be referred for a health assessment with a healthcare professional. The healthcare professional will decide whether you have a heroin or crack cocaine problem, and whether you should go on the new programme for problem drug users.[7]

Support programme

If you are identified as a problem drug user and you are claiming ESA or JSA, you will have to go on a programme of personalised support to help you overcome your problem and move into work. The programme will include:[8]

- support to stabilise your drug problem
- support to build self-esteem and confidence
- steps to address barriers to work (such as housing and debt), and
- support to gain skills and get ready for work.

You may have to attend an interview with a drug treatment provider, who will let the government know what kind of special help you need.[9]

Jobcentre Plus will get regular feedback on your progress, and you will stay on the support programme until you are ready to move onto mainstream benefits (such as Flexible New Deal or Pathways to Work).[10]

Rehabilitation plan

As part of the support programme, you will have to agree to a rehabilitation plan.[11] The details of this are still a little unclear, but you may have to draw up your plan with a specialist employment provider.[12] The plan will set out your steps to:

- stabilise your drug dependency
- move towards recovery
- tackle any problems you face, and
- get into work.

Treatment Allowance

While you are on the support programme, you will receive a Treatment Allowance instead of ESA or JSA. However, your Treatment Allowance will still be paid under either the ESA or the JSA framework.

The rules for your Treatment Allowance will be different from the normal rules for claiming ESA or JSA. They will be more tailored and appropriate for helping a recovering drug user. So, for example, if you get Treatment Allowance under the JSA framework, you will not have to follow the normal JSA rules about signing on at the Jobcentre and looking for work, but you will have to engage with and follow your rehabilitation plan.[13]

Sanctions

To get your Treatment Allowance, you must agree to a rehabilitation plan and make real efforts towards progress. If you fail to engage properly with the support programme, and you do not have good cause for failing to engage with the programme, then your benefit could be sanctioned. Treatment Allowance sanctions will be based on the normal sanction amounts for ESA or JSA.[14]

The government is bringing in legislation that will allow personal advisers to direct you to take part in appropriate activities. So, if your personal adviser decides that an activity is appropriate for you, you will have to take part in it. The government is still working out the sanctions for failing to take part in an appropriate activity without good cause.[15]

National Treatment Agency

If you are suffering from problem drug or alcohol use and you would like to enter treatment, you can access help by referring yourself directly to the National Treatment Agency (NTA) (Head Office: 020 7972 1999). You can also approach your Jobcentre Plus drugs coordinator, GP, local NHS services, social worker or local hospital and they can put you in touch. Depending on your personal situation and where you live, The NTA's services are provided by a range of professionals and organisations from GP surgeries and specialist clinics to charities and voluntary organisations in both the community and at home. Services are also provided in prisons and by private organisations.

The NTA offers a range of services through these providers including advice and information on reducing drug intake and giving up, advice on injecting safely, needle exchange services, administration of heroin substitutes, advice on how to prevent blood borne infections, vaccination against and testing for Hepatitis A, B and C, testing for HIV infection and advice on preventing overdose. You can also access counselling regarding both your drug use and any health problems arising from it. Help and advice can also be offered to your partners and families.

A care plan is devised for you when you seek treatment and your individual care needs and situation are taken into account. The care plan is a written agreement between you and your key worker (your contact at the drug treatment service) which outlines the goals to be achieved during treatment and the timeframe in which to achieve them. Your care plan may involve several forms of treatment at the same time, such as counselling to go alongside the prescription of substitute drugs, or it may involve a sequence of treatments such as a period in a rehab clinic after time as an inpatient in a hospital. Regular reviews of the plan ensure maximum benefit to you. Not everyone who uses treatment services will necessarily be going through a detox program; they may be seeking harm reduction care such as those outlined above like needle exchanges services, for example.

Progress2Work

What is Progress2Work?

Progress2Work (P2W) is a programme that helps people with a history of drug misuse to get back into work. Through specialist and personalised support, the programme aims to help drug misusers to join mainstream programmes (such as New Deal), and to find and stay in employment.

P2W is usually run by specialist providers on behalf of Jobcentre Plus. Jobcentre Plus staff receive awareness training so they are better able to identify and refer appropriate customers to the programme.

Who is eligible for Progress2Work?

P2W is a voluntary programme. Taking part in P2W will not affect your benefits.

You are eligible[16] for P2W if you are disadvantaged in finding a job because of drug misuse, but have made enough progress in your recovery to be drug-free or stabilised. You can join the programme if you have finished a drug treatment programme, are still undergoing a drug treatment programme, or are identified by Jobcentre Plus as a recovering drug misuser.

To join P2W, you must also be claiming one of the following benefits:

- Jobseeker's Allowance
- Employment and Support Allowance)
- Income Support)
- Incapacity Benefit
- Severe Disability Allowance
- Disability Living Allowance
- Pension Credit.

In exceptional cases, you may be able to join P2W even if you are not claiming any benefits.

Programme elements

Employment Support Worker

If you join P2W, you will be given an employment support worker. The support worker will prepare you to join mainstream programmes (such as New Deal) by:

- consulting other support agencies with whom you are already involved
- assessing your employment and drug-related history, and any other factors that could affect your chance of finding and staying in work
- working with you to draw up an individual action plan, which will be reviewed regularly

- helping you to overcome any personal barriers to work (by providing, for example, training in confidence-building, assertiveness and life skills)
- helping you to access specialist agencies to address anything else that is acting as a barrier to work (such as debt, housing, health and criminal justice issues).

Individual Action Plan

The individual action plan that you draw up with your support worker will include steps to move into work, along with any necessary extra activities. The action plan will vary from person to person, but could include:

- gaining access to jobsearch training and resources
- developing your 'soft skills'
- identifying suitable work
- accessing work-tasters or work experience
- learning how to cope with any drug testing required by employers
- learning the best way to disclose your drug and/or criminal history to employers
- developing a way to cope with the move to employment and a wage
- learning how to manage any benefit problems that arise during your move to employment.

When you're ready to join mainstream employment programmes

When you're ready to join mainstream programmes (such as New Deal), your support worker will talk to Jobcentre Plus to make sure that the content and pace of your programme are suitable. Your support worker will continue to help you to complete the mainstream programme. Where your original action plan is not working out, your support worker will help to revise your plan.

Your support worker will continue to support you for up to 13 weeks after you have started work.

Leaving the programme

There is no fixed time for participation in P2W. Your support worker will assess your progress and your provider of P2W will then take appropriate decisions about your continuation with the programme. P2W is a voluntary programme, so you can drop out at any time without your benefits changing.

Progress2Work-LinkUP

What is Progress2Work-LinkUP?

Progress2Work-LinkUP (P2W-LinkUP) is basically the same as P2W, but it is designed for people who are disadvantaged by homelessness, alcohol misuse and/or an offending background.

Who is eligible for Progress2Work-LinkUP?

The homeless and alcohol misusers

You are eligible[17] to join P2W-LinkUP if you:

- are wholly unemployed, and
- your homelessness or alcohol misuse significantly contributes to your employment disadvantage, and
- you are claiming one of the following benefits:
    - Jobseeker's Allowance
    - Employment and Support Allowance
    - Income Support
    - Incapacity Benefit
    - Severe Disability Allowance
    - Disability Living Allowance
    - Pension Credit.

People with an offending background

You have an offending background, if you:[18]

- are on final release, or
- you have served a custodial sentence within the last 12 months, or
- you are serving a non-custodial sentence supervised by the probation service.

You are eligible[19] to join P2W-LinkUP, if you:

- are wholly unemployed, and
- you have an offending background, and
- you are claiming one of the following benefits:
    - Jobseeker's Allowance
    - Employment and Support Allowance
    - Income Support
    - Incapacity Benefit
    - Severe Disability Allowance
    - Disability Living Allowance
    - Pension Credit.

Exceptions

In exceptional cases, people who are not claiming benefit, and are aged 16 to 17 and have a claim to Jobseeker's Allowance, Employment and Support Allowance or Incapacity Benefit are also eligible to join P2W-LinkUP.[20]

Programme Availability

P2W-LinkUP is a pilot programme that currently operates in the following areas:

- London South
- Liverpool
- Tayside
- Fife
- Bridgend Rhondda Cynon Taff
- Rotherham/Barnsley
- Bristol

- Bradford
- Manchester
- Lancashire West
- Berkshire
- Birmingham and Solihull
- Sheffield
- Greater Nottingham
- Gateshead and South Tyneside
- Eastern Valleys
- Glasgow
- Wakefield
- Lancashire East
- Knowsley and Sefton
- Leicester
- Sussex.

Other programmes to help people affected by drug and alcohol misuse, homelessness, or an offending background back into work

Local Employment Partnerships

If you are a former offender, or have very low qualifications, you could get training and skills help through a Local Employment Partnership. See page 117, for more information about the programme.

Skills for Life (England)

If you are a prisoner, or are supervised in the community, you could get help with basic skills through Skills for Life. See page 119, for detailed information about the programme.

Employability Skills Programme (England)

If you are aged 18 or over; have a literacy, language or numeracy need at Level 1 or below on the National Qualifications Framework; and are getting benefit payments, credits or a New Deal training allowance, you could take part in the Employability Skills Programme.

Your training provider should try to fit your Employability Skills Programme around your recovery programme (if you are taking part in one), and they should take into account complex circumstances such as homelessness when arranging your course. See page 123, for programme information.

Working for Families (Scotland)

If you are a parent or carer who has stresses in the household that make it difficult to find or stay in work or training (including problems with disability, mental health, drug, alcohol and debt), you could get help with childcare through Working for Families.

Endnotes

[1] DWP (2008) No-One Written Off: Reforming Welfare to Reward Responsibility, DWP. para. 2.47.

[2] DWP (2008) Raising Expectations and Increasing Support: Reforming Welfare for the Future, DWP. para. 6.44.

[3] DWP (2008) No-One Written Off: Reforming Welfare to Reward Responsibility, DWP. para. 2.48.

[4] DWP (2008) Raising Expectations and Increasing Support: Reforming Welfare for the Future, DWP. para. 6.37.

[5] DWP (2008) Raising Expectations and Increasing Support: Reforming Welfare for the Future, DWP. para. 6.37.

[6] DWP (2008) Raising Expectations and Increasing Support: Reforming Welfare for the Future, DWP. para. 6.38.

[7] DWP (2008) Raising Expectations and Increasing Support: Reforming Welfare for the Future, DWP. paras 5.34 and 6.40.

[8] DWP (2008) Raising Expectations and Increasing Support: Reforming Welfare for the Future, DWP. para. 6.39.

[9] DWP (2008) Raising Expectations and Increasing Support: Reforming Welfare for the Future, DWP. para. 5.29.

[10] DWP (2008) Raising Expectations and Increasing Support: Reforming Welfare for the Future, DWP. para. 6.41.

[11] DWP (2008) Raising Expectations and Increasing Support: Reforming Welfare for the Future, DWP. para. 6.42.

[12] DWP (2008) No-One Written Off: Reforming Welfare to Reward Responsibility, DWP. para. 2.41.

[13] DWP (2008) Raising Expectations and Increasing Support: Reforming Welfare for the Future, DWP. para. 6.42.

[14] DWP (2008) Raising Expectations and Increasing Support: Reforming Welfare for the Future, DWP. paras 6.43 and 6.36.

[15] DWP (2008) Raising Expectations and Increasing Support: Reforming Welfare for the Future, DWP. paras 5.31 and 5.29.

[16] DWP, Provider Led Pathways to Work Guidance, sect. 13: 'Other Provisions' http://www.dwp.gov.uk/supplyingdwp/what_we_buy/plp_section13.pdf Accessed 23 January 2009.

17 DWP, Provider Led Pathways to Work Guidance, sect. 13: 'Other Provisions' http://www.dwp.gov.uk/supplyingdwp/what_we_buy/plp_section13.pdf Accessed 23 January 2009.

18 DWP, Provider Led Pathways to Work Guidance, sect. 13: 'Other Provisions' http://www.dwp.gov.uk/supplyingdwp/what_we_buy/plp_section13.pdf Accessed 23 January 2009.

19 DWP, Provider Led Pathways to Work Guidance, sect. 13: 'Other Provisions' http://www.dwp.gov.uk/supplyingdwp/what_we_buy/plp_section13.pdf Accessed 23 January 2009.

20 DWP, Provider Led Pathways to Work Guidance, sect. 13: 'Other Provisions' http://www.dwp.gov.uk/supplyingdwp/what_we_buy/plp_section13.pdf Accessed 23 January 2009.

People affected by drug and alcohol misuse, homelessness, and people with an offending background

6

7 Partners

New Deal for Partners

What is New Deal for Partners?

New Deal for Partners (NDP)[1] is for partners of those claiming certain benefits. It is a voluntary programme designed to get one member of the household into work. It gives you access to a personal adviser who can help you look for work or move towards work, and a range of support tailored to meet your needs.

Who is eligible for New Deal for Partners?

You are eligible[2] for NDP if you are not working, or are working fewer than 16 hours per week, and your partner is claiming one of the following benefits:

- Jobseeker's Allowance
- Income Support
- Employment and Support Allowance, or Incapacity Benefit
- Carer's Allowance
- Severe Disablement Benefit
- Pension Credit.

You may also join NDP if:

- your partner gets Pension Credit, and you are working for fewer than 24 hours per week, or
- you or your partner gets Working Tax Credit, and you are working for fewer than 16 hours per week.[3]

You count as a partner if you are married or living together (as though you are married) and your partner is claiming a dependant's addition to their benefit for you.[4]

If your partner is on New Deal, Training for Work, or Employment Zones, and you meet the other criteria, you can still join NDP.

You cannot join NDP, if you are claiming Jobseeker's Allowance (JSA) in your own right, or if you are making a Joint Claim for JSA.

Programme elements

NDP can offer a range of support to help you move into work. You can get advice and help from a personal adviser through a series of interviews, if you choose. Your personal adviser is a central part of the NDP, and will offer a package of advice and support, including:

- advice about job vacancies, finding jobs, writing applications and CVs, and interview techniques
- advice about the benefits and incentives that are available to you when you start work (such as the Childcare Subsidy)
- advice on local childcare (your adviser should have links to the local Sure Start)
- a calculation of how much better off you and your family might be if you start work (your partner may have to agree to their benefit details being used for this)
- drawing up an Action Plan to check your progress and record your actions
- the chance to do training courses (such as a Level 2 National Vocational Qualification) to update and learn skills

- a weekly Training Premium, if you take part in NDP approved training for at least two hours per week
- an opportunity to gain work experience by taking part in one of the phases of Flexible New Deal),[5] and
- an in-work support service.

Training

If you take part in NDP, you will be expected to attend at least 16 hours of training per week. These hours can be split between training and jobsearch, according to your needs.

While on NDP, you will have access to a range of training. This includes:[6]

- training available through Training for Work in Scotland (except employed-status Training for Work)[7] (see page 130)
- Work Trials and work experience (as part of an approved training course) (see page 158)
- the full-time education and training, Environmental Task Force, and voluntary sector options of New Deal for Young People
- the Intense Activity Period education and training for New Deal for 25 Plus
- the self-employment advice and training for New Deal for 25 Plus (including drawing up a business plan, and doing 26 weeks of test-trading)
- training through a New Deal music industry consultant and Music Open Learning provider
- New Deal Basic Skills training (except short intensive Basic Skills courses), and
- education through the further education system.

If you are thinking about doing paid training, you should be aware that you or the main benefit claimant (your partner) may no longer be entitled to passported benefits.

Help with costs

When you attend an interview with a personal adviser or an employer, you are can get help with the costs you incur. These include childcare and travel costs. You may also qualify for help with travel costs, if you are attending approved training and other activities.

Training

If you do approved training for at least two hours per week, you could get the Training Premium. This is a sum of about £15, which is paid weekly in arrears.

If you get a Training Premium, it is your responsibility to tell the Inland Revenue that you are getting NDP funding and the Training Premium.

Childcare

You can also get funding for childcare while you attend approved activities or interviews, so long as the childcare is:

- provided by carers registered with Ofsted (payment for childcare provided by friends or family members cannot be authorised, unless your friends or family members are registered childminders)
- run on school premises, or
- run by the local authority.

Childcare costs can be paid until the first Tuesday in the September following your child's 15th birthday.[8] The maximum amount of funding you can get for childcare costs depends on the amount of time you spend attending approved activity or training, and how many children you have.

In-work support

If you move into work, you may still get some support through the Childcare Subsidy and In Work Credit.

Childcare Subsidy

You can get the Childcare Subsidy if you move into part-time work of up to 16 hours per week. This helps with the cost of childcare while you are working. You can get the Childcare Subsidy for a one-off period of 42 weeks. You cannot get help with travel costs when you are working part-time.

In Work Credit

In Work Credit is usually available only to lone parents, but parents who are a couple (couple parents) and who are taking part in New Deal Plus for Lone Parents in a pilot district (see the list at the end of this chapter) may also get help through In Work Credit.[9] You could get a tax-free payment of £40 per week, or £60 per week if you live in London, if you or your partner starts work of at least 16 hours per week and meet the conditions required of lone parents (see page 259).

In Work Credit is paid for a period of 12 months from the time your partner starts work. The credit will stop if your partner stops working for more than five weeks.

Additional courses

If you are a healthcare professional, you may be able to go on an NHS-funded return to practice course. These courses are aimed at encouraging former healthcare professionals to return to the NHS, and course availability varies according to your location, profession and how long you've been away from work. These courses are often funded by the NHS, depending on your local trust and their workforce needs.[10]

Leaving the programme

Since NDP is voluntary, you can leave at any time and your benefits will not be affected.

New Deal Plus for Partners

Partners may be able to get extra support through New Deal Plus for Lone Parents (NDLP+). NDLP+ has been extended to cover couple parents, not just lone parents, so you may be able to access help through NDLP+ if you:

- live in an area where NDLP+ runs, and
- have a dependant child living in your household, and
- your partner is claiming one of the following benefits:
    - Income Support
    - Jobseeker's Allowance
    - Incapacity Benefit
    - Severe Disablement Allowance
    - Carer's Allowance.

For NDLP+, a 'dependant child' is defined in the same way as for Child Tax Credit (see page 250).

NDLP+ can offer partners of benefit claimants the following things:

- Access to Discovery Events (three-days events where you can explore different career paths and boost your self-confidence and motivation)
- Access to the In Work Emergency Discretion Fund (which helps parents to overcome barriers that make it difficult to stay in their first 26 weeks of work)
- Access to the Flexible Provision Fund (a fund that can be used to buy training courses or similar things that are not already available, or that cannot be paid for through another source)
- More voluntary contact (this gives you extra contact with your personal adviser)
- In Work Advisory Support (this gives you extra advice during your first 26 weeks of work)
- Help through Childcare Assist (if you're starting work of eight hours per week or more, you can claim up to five days' worth of childcare expenses in the week before you start work).

The districts in which NDLP+ is available are:

- Leicestershire
- North and North East London
- South London
- Central London
- West London
- City and East London
- Lambeth, Southwark and Wandsworth
- Edinburgh and Lothian and Borders
- South West Wales (in Cardiff and Vale only)
- Black Country (in Dudley and Sandwell only)
- West Yorkshire (Bradford only).

7

Endnotes

[1] http://www.dwp.gov.uk/supplyingdwp/what_we_buy/pg_chapter_14.0.pdf Accessed on 22 January 2009.

[2] DWP (2004) 'New Deal for Partners – New Eligibility Rules' Touchbase 36, (September), p. 9.
3www.jobcentreplus.gov.uk/JCP/Customers/outofworkhelplookingforwork/Getting_job_ready/Programmes_to_get_you_ready/New_Deal/New_Deal_for_Partners/ Accessed on 23 January 2009.

[4] Reg. 2(1) Social Security (Jobcentre Plus Interviews for Partners) Regulation 2003.

[5] http://www.delni.gov.uk/index/finding-employment-finding-staff/fe-fs-help-to-find-employment/newdeal/new-deal-for-partners.htm Accessed 23 January 2009.

[6] Jobcentre Plus Provider Guidance, ch. 13, paras 1 and 14; ch. 14, paras 2 and 19.

[7] www.hie.co.uk/trainingforwork.htm Accessed on 23 January 2009.

[8] http://www.dsdni.gov.uk/childcare_subsidy_for_lone_parents_working_pt.htm Accessed on 23 January 2009.

[9] http://research.dwp.gov.uk/welfarereform/parents.asp Accessed on 7 July 2009.

[10] NHS, Returning to the NHS. http://www.nhscareers.nhs.uk/explore_returning.shtml Accessed on 21 January 2009.

8 People in work: making work pay

Tax Credits

There are two Tax Credits:

- Working Tax Credit, and
- Child Tax Credit.

There are three additional 'credits' that can also be paid when people start employment but they are not part of the tax credits system:

- Return to Work Credit
- Self-Employment Credit, and
- In Work Credit.

Working Tax Credit

What is Working Tax Credit?

Working Tax Credit (WTC) is a regular payment made by Her Majesty's Revenue and Customs (HMRC) to people doing paid work who have a low family income.

Who can get Working Tax Credit?

You can qualify for WTC if:[1]

- you (or your partner) are aged 25 or over and normally work for at least 30 hours per week or
- you are aged 16 or over and either you or your partner normally work for 16 or more hours per week, and you either have a dependent child, or

- you have a physical or mental disability that puts you at a disadvantage in gaining work. The person in paid work must also either currently receive a benefit for disability or incapacity for work, or have received either Employment and Support Allowance (ESA), Incapacity Benefit (IB) (the long-term rate or higher short-term rate), Severe Disablement Allowance (SDA), or a means-tested benefit disability premium at some time in the 182 days before making a claim or a benefit for incapacity for work (including Income Support (IS), Occupational Sick Pay (OSP) and Statutory Sick Pay (SSP) for at least 20 weeks within 56 days of making a tax credit claim.
- you (or your partner) meet the rules for the 50-Plus element of WTC (this is paid for one year only).

Rules about income

When assessing your claim for WTC, HMRC will take your annual income from the following sources into account:[2]

- Your gross earnings, and your partner's (if you have one)
- Pensions
- Profits from self-employment
- Most social security benefits, except:
    - Disability Living Allowance
    - Income Support
    - Income-Related Jobseeker's Allowance
    - Income-Based Jobseeker's Allowance
    - Housing Benefit
    - Council Tax Benefit
    - Child Benefit
    - Guardian's Allowance
    - Maternity Allowance
    - the lower rate of short-term Incapacity Benefit
    - Severe Disablement Allowance, and
    - benefits paid because of a work-related accident or disease.

Income that is free of Income Tax is not included as annual income.

Some of your earnings may not count as income, including:

- up to £100 per week of Statutory Maternity Pay, Statutory Adoption Pay, or Statutory Paternity Pay
- Statutory Sick Pay
- money reimbursed for expenses that are wholly, exclusively and necessarily incurred in your job (for example, travel expenses), and
- contributions to an approved personal or occupational pension scheme.

If you are self-employed, HMRC will look at your profits from the most recent Income Tax assessment period to decide your eligibility for WTC.

If you are receiving maintenance payments, these will not count as income for tax credits. For lone parents, especially those in full-time paid work, this rule about maintenance payments gives them a major incentive to make sure they are getting as much in maintenance as possible.

Rules about capital

When applying for WTC, income from capital is treated like any other sort of income. This means that there is no capital cut-off point for WTC claims. However, HMRC will not count the first £300 per year of income from taxable savings and private or occupational pensions. HMRC will also ignore any income from tax-free savings.

Exceptions to eligibility criteria

Even if you are not in work, you will be treated as if you are in full-time work, if:[3]

- you are not at work because of ordinary sick, maternity or paternity leave and you are getting one of the statutory benefits for your leave, or
- you are on strike, or
- you were in full-time paid work within the last seven days, or
- you are employed, but you have been suspended from work for disciplinary reasons.

Qualifying for Income Support, Employment and Support Allowance or Jobseeker's Allowance along with Working Tax Credit

Sometimes you may qualify for both WTC and Income Support (IS) or ESA, or for both WTC and Income-Based Jobseeker's Allowance (IBJSA). This could be the case if you:

- receive WTC but you are off sick from your job, or
- are a term-time worker, or
- have a disability which reduces your pay or working hours to 75 per cent or less than the pay or working hours of people who are not disabled, or
- are a childminder.

In such cases, it is very important to get independent advice about which benefit would be best for you.

Qualifying for Working Tax Credit run-on

You could be paid WTC as a run-on for four weeks after you leave a paid job (in this case, your WTC will count as income for means-tested benefits, so when your WTC stops, you should tell the office where you claimed the benefit).

How is Working Tax Credit calculated?[4]

If you earn less than the income threshold (which is £6,420 per year), you will be eligible for the maximum amount of WTC. For every £1 you earn above the threshold, your WTC will drop by 39 pence, until your WTC entitlement falls to nothing.

Maximum WTC is made up of the following elements (see Appendix 1 for amounts):

- Basic element
- Couple element (you can claim this if you have a partner, unless you are using the 50x-Plus element to qualify for WTC and neither of you work for 30 or more hours per week)

- Lone parent element
- Disability element (you can get this if you (or your partner) meet the disability benefit conditions and have a physical or mental disability that puts you (or your partner) at a disadvantage in getting a job. If you are a couple and both of you meet this rule, then you will get two disability elements)
- 30-hour element (you can get this if you (or your partner) do paid work for at least 30 hours per week. If you (or your partner) are responsible for a child or young person, then you can get the 30-hour element if your combined working time is 30 or more hours per week)
- Severe disability element (you can get this if you receive the high rate of either the Disability Living Allowance Care Component, or Attendance Allowance (see page 202). If you have a partner and you are both severely disabled, then you will get two severe disability elements.)
- 50-Plus element (this is paid for one year if you are aged 50 or over and you have just returned to work after being on benefits. If you are working less than 30 hours per week, you will get £1,300 in WTC, and if you are working 30 or more hours per week, you will get £1,935 in WTC)
- Childcare element (this pays 80 per cent of your eligible childcare costs, up to a maximum of £175 per week for one child or £300 per week for more than one child)

Disadvantage test for people who want to claim the disability element[5]

There are 21 criteria in this test, and you must meet only one of them to prove that you are disadvantaged in getting a job. HMRC may ask you to name a professional who is involved in your care (for example, an occupational therapist, nurse or doctor), and who can confirm how your mental or physical disability affects you.

Examples of the criteria in the test include:

- inability to balance without support
- being registered blind or partially sighted, in a register compiled by a local authority
- having trouble with hearing, and
- having a mental illness for which you get regular treatment supervised by a medically qualified person.

Eligible childcare costs for the childcare element[6]

To get help with childcare costs, you must use registered childcare for children aged under 15, or registered childcare for disabled children aged under 16 (the meaning of 'disabled' is based on the rules for the disability element of Child Tax Credit, see page 251).

You can get help with childcare that is provided by:

- nurseries
- registered childminders
- certain types of approved childcare in your home
- other accredited providers, and
- an out-of-hours or breakfast club run by a school or local authority.

You cannot get help with childcare provided by close relatives, unless your relatives:

- are caring for your child outside your home, and
- are registered childminders, and
- care for at least one other child who is not your child.

Can couples qualify for the childcare element?

You will usually need to be a lone parent to qualify for help with childcare, but couples can qualify if:

- you both work for 16 or more hours per week, or
- one of you works for 16 or more hours per week and the other receives one of the following disability benefits:
  - Short-term Incapacity Benefit at the higher rate
  - Long-term Incapacity Benefit
  - Employment and Support Allowance
  - Attendance Allowance
  - Severe Disablement Allowance
  - Disability Living Allowance
  - Industrial Injuries Disablement Benefit with Constant Attendance Allowance.

Child Tax Credit

What is Child Tax Credit?

Child Tax Credit (CTC) is a regular payment made by HMRC to help you with the costs of bringing up children.

Who is entitled to Child Tax Credit?[7]

You can get CTC if you are:

- responsible for a dependent child or young person (in most cases, this means that the child or young person normally lives with you), and
- aged 16 or over, and
- not subject to immigration restrictions.

In addition, when you claim CTC, the dependent child or young person must be:

- aged under 16, or
- aged between 16 and 21 and in full-time, non-advanced education (that is, in education that is equal to or below A-level or Scottish Higher, or on an unwaged training scheme that is funded by the

government). If the young person is aged 20 or over, they must have started their course or training before their 20th birthday.[8]

Your eligibility for CTC will be decided at the same time that your eligibility for WTC is decided. So, you don't need to claim separately for each tax credit.

Income and Capital

The rules about income and capital for CTC are the same as the rules about income and capital for WTC (see page 248).

How is Child Tax Credit calculated?

If your income is less than the threshold amount (which is £16,040 per year), you can get the maximum amount of CTC. For every £1 you earn above the threshold, your CTC will drop by 39 pence, until all that remains is the family element. All families with an income of less than £50,000 per year can claim the full family element. If your family's income is more than £50,000 per year, then for every £15 you earn above £50,000, the family element amount will drop by £1, until you are not entitled to anything. These rules mean that 80 per cent of families are entitled to some CTC.

Maximum CTC is made up of the following elements
(see Appendix 2 for amounts):[9]

- Family element (this is paid to all eligible families)
- Family element baby addition (this is paid on top of the family element, for one year after a child's birth)
- Child element (this is paid for each child in the family, including those aged under one year)
- Disabled child element (this is paid for each child in the family who is registered blind or qualifies for Disability Living Allowance)
- Severely disabled child element (this is paid for each child in the family who qualifies for the high-rate care component of Disability Living Allowance).

What happens if your circumstances change while claiming tax credits?

HMRC does a provisional calculation at the beginning of your claim for tax credits, and makes a final decision about how much you are entitled to at the end of each tax year, when your benefit is checked against your actual income. You don't have to tell HMRC if your income changes during the year but it's best to, so that you don't end up being underpaid or paid too much at the end of the year.

There are some changes in circumstance that you have to tell HMRC about within one month. These changes in circumstance include:

- changing your employer
- having someone join or leave your family (for example, you separate or get a new partner, or your child leaves home)
- varying your hours of work so that they go above or drop below the 16- or 30-hour thresholds
- stopping work altogether, and
- changing your childcare costs by £10 or more per week for more than four weeks.

You risk a £300 penalty if you do not tell HMRC about changes to your circumstances.

If you become part of a couple, or if you stop being part of a couple, you will need to make a new claim for tax credits. Telling HMRC about these changes too late commonly causes overpayments.

If you have a change of circumstances that increases your entitlement to tax credits (for example, you have new baby or your hours of work reduce), the increase in your tax credits can be backdated for no more than 12 weeks. So, if you wait too long to tell HMRC about your change in circumstance, you will lose out.

How do tax credits affect other benefits?

The amount of tax credit you get is taken into account for Housing and Council Tax Benefits (unless you receive IS, Income-Based Jobseeker's Allowance (IBJSA) or Income-Related Jobseeker's Allowance (IRJSA). If you are already getting CTC, you cannot get benefit add-ons to other benefits for having dependent children.

If you have been receiving tax credits you are not entitled to, these credits will not count as income for means-tested benefits.[10]

Any CTC you get is ignored when claiming IS, Income-Related ESA or IBJSA, but WTC still counts as income when claiming these benefits. The Department for Work and Pensions and HMRC plan to move all people who have children and receive IS or IBJSA onto CTC, but no firm date has been set.

Tax credit overpayments

Overpayments of tax credits are common, and many people have their current tax credits reduced to make up for past overpayments. This can cause difficulty. HMRC usually notices overpayments, when looking at the amount of tax credits you were paid in the previous tax year and also when working out your entitlement for the current tax year.

Overpayments may be caused by many things, including errors by HMRC, or changes in your income or household that you did not tell HMRC about. Overpayments are very likely to happen in a system that is based on annual income from the year before.

If your income increases, HMRC will ignore it if the increase is for less than £25,000 per year. However, the following year, they will use the new income figure when working out future payments of tax credits.

HMRC must write and tell you if you have been overpaid, and they must tell you by how much they will reduce your tax credits to cover your repayments.[11]

If you receive IS, Income-Related ESA or IBJSA, and your tax credits are reduced to cover an overpayment, your other benefit will not be increased to make up for the change to your tax credits. However, if you get Housing and/or Council Tax Benefits (without IS, Income-Related ESA or IBJSA), then your Housing and/or Council Tax Benefits will be based on the tax credits you are actually paid, so they will reflect any reduction to your tax credits.

You can appeal the amount of an overpayment if you think it is wrong, but you can't appeal against HMRC's decision that you must repay money. However, the law gives HMRC a wide discretion when recovering overpayments,[12] and you can ask them to waive the recovery of your overpayment. HMRC policy[13] is to waive recovery if:

- the overpayment was caused by HMRC's error, or
- recovering the overpayment would cause you hardship.

HMRC will also usually waive the recovery of small overpayments (up to £300).

Because HMRC has a wide discretion, the above situations are not the only times when HMRC could legally waive a recovery.

If repayment is causing you hardship, you can reduce the amount that you repay (you can do this by making top-up payments, which spreads your repayments over a longer period). HMRC will also stop their recovery action, if you dispute the amount of the overpayment.

You can write and ask HMRC to waive recovery. If you do this, it is important to give full details of your circumstances, especially if you are asking them to waive recovery on the grounds of hardship. You may find that they refuse to waive recovery when you first ask. If this happens, you can ask the HMRC Adjudicator or the Parliamentary Ombudsman (whom you contact through your local MP) to look at your case. Sometimes HMRC staff may not seem to understand the rules about waiving or reducing an overpayment to take account of hardship.

In cases where HMRC have behaved unreasonably or very inflexibly, you may be able to take a type of legal action called 'judicial review'.

Financial help after moving into paid work

Better off in work credit

In the December 2009 white paper 'Building Britain's recovery: achieving full employment', the government announced its intention to develop a national back to work credit. This is intended to be an enhanced credit which will guarantee that people who have been unemployed for six months or more are at least £40 a week better off in work. The government will start rolling out this credit nationally from October 2010, and hope it to be available nationally from January 2011.

Payments for starting work

Job Grant

What is a Job Grant?

A Job Grant is a £100 tax-free payment (£250 if you have a child or children) for people entering full-time paid work (work of 16 or more hours per week). People whose partner moves into work of 24 or more hours per week can also get a Job Grant. It does not count as income or capital for means-tested benefits.

The Job Grant Fund aims to help people to overcome barriers to starting work.

Who is entitled to a Job Grant?

You can claim Job Grant if:

- you are aged 25 or over, and
- you have received IS, JSA, ESA, IB, SDA, or a combination of these benefits for at least 26 weeks (if you have been on a New Deal or Employment Zone scheme, this counts towards the 26 weeks, as long as you were receiving JSA at the time), and
- the full-time work is expected to last five weeks or more.

If you are working part-time and the hours you are working increase to 16 or more per week, then you may also qualify for a Job Grant. In the same way, if you start full-time work that is self-employed, you may be able to qualify for a Job Grant.

Jobcentre Plus should automatically pay a Job Grant, so long as you tell them that you have started work.

Please note that you can only receive one Job Grant during any 52-week period.

Travel to Interview Scheme

The Travel to Interview Scheme (TIS) can help to pay the cost of travel and some other costs of job interviews.

The TIS will refund the cost of travel to a job interview and the cost of one or two unavoidable overnight stays. If you travel by car, you will normally be paid the cost of public transport (or the equivalent amount) and you will receive a refund after the interview.

In order to qualify for the TIS, you must be receiving one of the following:

- Income support
- Jobseeker's Allowance
- Employment and Support Allowance
- Incapacity Benefit
- Carer's Allowance
- Maternity Allowance
- Bereavement benefits
- a Training Allowance
- National Insurance credits (for example, because you are unemployed or incapable of work)

You must also meet the following conditions:

- You must have a definite job interview for a specific job. The job must be for at least 16 hours per week and expected to last for at least three months.

- You must have been living in your current home area for at least four weeks.
- The interview must be beyond 'normal daily travelling distance' (this distance varies from area to area and you will need to ask your local Jobcentre Plus office).
- You must apply for the TIS before you go to the interview.

If the employer offers to reimburse your costs, you cannot get help from Jobcentre Plus. Jobcentre Plus will confirm with the employer that you have an interview and will also check that you attended.

For more information, see the Jobcentre Plus leaflet Travel to Interview Scheme.

Benefit Run-ons

What are Benefit Run-ons?
Benefit Run-ons are periods when you still receive your benefit after you have started paid work of at least 16 hours per week (or when your partner has started paid work of at least 24 hours per week). This helps to ease the change from welfare to work.

There are three Benefit Run-ons:

- Mortgage Interest Run-on
- Extended Payment of Housing Benefit
- Extended Payment of Council Tax Benefit.

Who is entitled to Benefit Run-ons?
You can claim a Benefit Run-on if you:[14]

- have been receiving IS, IBJSA, ESA, IB or SDA for 26 weeks or more (this does not include any period of Mortgage Interest Run-on that you may have received in the past), and

- tell your local Jobcentre Plus office (or your local authority, for Extended Payment of Housing/Council Tax Benefit) within four weeks of starting or increasing hours that you are working full-time (which means you are working for 16 hours or more per week or your partner is working for 24 hours or more per week), and
- have a job that is expected to last for five or more weeks.

If you have been receiving JSA, it is important to tell Jobcentre Plus (or your local authority, for Extended Housing/Council Tax Benefit) that you have started work, so that any run-on can be paid. If you just stop signing on at the Jobcentre, the run-on will not be paid.

Mortgage Interest Run-on

Mortgage Interest Run-on means that you continue receiving IS, IBJSA, or Income-Related ESA to cover some of your mortgage or housing loan interest for up to four weeks after you start full-time work.

Housing Benefit Extended Payment

Housing Benefit Extended Payment means that you continue receiving maximum Housing Benefit for up to four weeks after you have started full-time work. You receive Housing Benefit at the same rate as when you were on IS, IBJSA, ESA, IB or SDA.

After the four-week extension period, you may be able to keep on claiming Housing Benefit when you are in full-time work. This will be a new claim and will be assessed on:

- the rent you are paying or the level of the Local Housing Allowance if you are a private tenant
- your income
- your savings and capital, and
- your personal or family circumstances.

If you start a claim for Housing Benefit or Council Tax Benefit, and you have received Extended Housing Benefit or Extended Council Tax Benefit in the past, then your new claim should be fast-tracked and processed within seven days.

Extended Council Tax Benefit

The rules for Extended Council Tax Benefit are the same as the rules for Extended Housing Benefit.

For more details about Housing and Council Tax Benefits, see pages 281 and 291.

In Work Credits

What are In Work Credits?

These are additional tax-free payments for people who enter low-paid work. In Work Credits should not be confused with Tax Credits, which are different. In Work Credits and Tax Credits may both be paid at the same time.

Who is entitled to In Work Credits?

There are three In Work Credits:

- Return to Work Credit is paid at a rate of £40 per week for up to 52 weeks. It is for people who move from IB, ESA, SDA, or IS (paid because of incapacity for work) into paid work of at least 16 hours per week. To claim Return to Work Credit, you must earn less than £15,000 per year before tax and National Insurance deductions. Your job must be expected to last for least 5 weeks.
- Self-Employment Credit is a payment of £50 per week for up to 16 weeks. You can claim Self-Employment Credit if you have been unemployed and claiming JSA for six months or more and you move into self-employed work of at least 16 hours per week. To get the credit, you must show that your self-employment will last for at least five weeks, register with HMRC as self-employed, and not be claiming any other In Work Credits. Self-Employment Credit has been available since April 2009.

- In Work Credit is a payment of £40 per week (£60 in London) for lone parents who have been receiving either IS or JSA for at least 52 weeks, and who are starting a job of at least 16 hours per week.

In London, couples with children also qualify for In Work Credit, and the time on benefits can also include those for which Return to Work Credit is paid, (so, for example, you could have been receiving ESA for 26 weeks and then JSA for 26 weeks).

You must complete and return an In Work Credit claim form to your Jobcentre Plus office within five weeks of starting work.

Training programmes after moving into paid work

Train to Gain

What is Train to Gain?[15]

Train to Gain (TtG) is a programme that aims to improve employee skills in the workplace. Your employer is responsible for choosing whether or not their business will take part in TtG. If their business is involved in TtG, you will be able to access individual advice and in-work support, and you will also have the chance to grow valuable skills. Improving your skills can help your future in many ways. Skills can add to your salary, or open up opportunities for promotions, new career directions and new experiences.

How does Train to Gain work?[16]

TtG is run through the Learning and Skills Council (LSC). Employers are responsible for choosing whether or not their business will get involved in TtG. If employers are interested in TtG, they will get in touch with either a TtG skills broker, or a college or training provider that is linked to the programme. Skills brokers, colleges and training providers help employers by finding good-quality training courses, scheduling courses, and giving advice on the funding and subsidies available for training. Getting advice from a skills broker does not cost money. If your employer is not already taking part in TtG, you could tell them about the programme.

Who can take part in Train to Gain?

TtG runs in England only. It works with a wide range of people, including:[17]

- contracted employees (full-time and part-time)
- self-employed people
- volunteers, and
- employment agency workers.

In 2008, the government announced plans to extend TtG, to offer training and support programmes to people who are facing redundancy. These programmes aim to help those facing redundancy to develop the skills they need to move into a new job easily, either in the field in which they already work, or in a new sector.[18]

What qualifications can you get through Train to Gain?[19]

TtG works with colleges and training providers of all kinds, including universities, private training companies and business experts. It will only use colleges and training providers that have been approved by the LSC.

There are a wide range of qualifications and skills you could get through TtG. You can access:

- National Vocational Qualifications (NVQs)
- Level 2 and Level 3 qualifications
- apprenticeships
- leadership and management training
- courses tailored to your needs
- basic skills courses (such as Skills for Life qualifications), and
- training for sector-specific skills.

Funding for Level 2 qualifications

If you do not already have academic or vocational qualifications equal to Level 2 (that is, equal to five GCSEs at grade A–C, or equal to a Level 2 NVQ), then TtG will offer your employer free training for you to achieve a Level 2 qualification. If you need to improve your literacy, numeracy or English language skills, TtG will give funding for this, along with funding to help you get your first Level 2 qualification. You may be able to get funding for more than one Level 2 qualification.

Funding for Level 3 qualifications

TtG will contribute to the cost of getting a Level 3 qualification, if you already have a Level 2 qualification.

TtG will cover the full cost of getting a Level 3 qualification, if you:

- don't already have a Level 2 qualification, but have the skills to go straight to a Level 3 qualification, or
- are aged 19 to 25.

If you already have a Level 3 qualification or above, and you want to get an extra Level 3 qualification, TtG may be able to help with the costs.

Funding for apprenticeships

Funding for apprenticeships and Advanced Apprenticeships is available through TtG.

What should you do if you want to get training, but your employer doesn't want to take part in Train to Gain?[20]

If you want to increase your skills, but your employer is not interested in joining TtC, you may be able to get help from the LSC's 'In Our Hands' campaign. The campaign can help you to assess your skills and gain more skills to further your career. It can help you to get involved in training schemes such as:

- apprenticeships
- Entry to Employment (a work focused course for young people)
- Get On courses (which help to improve your maths, literacy and language skills), and
- Nextstep (which gives face-to-face advice on learning and careers).

You can contact the campaign for advice on 0800 100 900, or you can ask an adviser for help by visiting http://inourhands.lsc.gov.uk

Skills for Life (England)

If you are aged 16 or over, are employed, and do not have an up-to-date English or maths qualification at Level 2 on the National Qualifications Framework, you can get help through Skills for Life. See page 118, for more information.

Employability Skills Programme (England)

The Employability Skills Programme is a course of learning that leads to basic skills qualifications and employability qualifications. You can take part in the programme if you are aged 18 or over; have a literacy, language or numeracy need at Level 1 or below on the National Qualifications Framework; and are getting tax credits, benefit payments or a New Deal Training Allowance. See page 122, for more details.

Working for Families (Scotland)

If you are a parent or carer living in a low-income household, and you are having trouble taking up training opportunities because of childcare problems, you could get support through Working for Families.

Endnotes

[1] Reg. 4 Working Tax Credit (Entitlement and Maximum Rate) Regulations 2002.

[2] Tax Credits (Definition and Calculation of Income) Regulations 2002.

[3] Regs 5-8 Working Tax Credit (Entitlement and Maximum Rate) Regulations 2002.

[4] Tax Credits (Income Thresholds and Determination of Rates) Regulations 2002 and Tax Credits (Entitlement and Maximum Rate) Regulations 2002.

[5] Regs 9-9B and sched. 1 Working Tax Credit (Entitlement and Maximum Rate) Regulations 2002.

[6] Regs 13-16 Working Tax Credit (Entitlement and Maximum Rate) Regulations 2002.

[7] Ss 3(3), (7), 8 and 42 Tax Credits Act 2002 and Regs 3-5 Child Tax Credit Regulations 2002.

[8] Sect. 8(4) Tax Credits Act 2002 and Regs 2 and 5(1)-(3A) Child Tax Credit Regulations 2002.

[9] Regs 7 and 8 Child Tax Credit Regulations 2002.

[10] CIS 1813/2007 and DMG Memo 07/08.

[11] Sect. 28 Tax Credits Act 2002.

[12] Ss 28 and 29 Tax Credits Act 2002 – see use of words 'may' and 'recoverable'.

[13] HMRC leaflet COP 26: What Happens If We Have Paid You Too Much Tax Credit? Available on: http://www.hmrc.gov.uk

[14] Reg. 72 and sched. 7 Housing Benefit Regulations 2006; Reg. 60 and sched. 6 Council Tax Benefit Regulations 2006.

[15] www.traintogain.gov.uk Accessed on 18 March 2009.

[16] www.traintogain.gov.uk Accessed on 18 March 2009.

[17] www.traintogain.gov.uk Accessed on 18 March 2009.

[18] This information appeared in the UKCES Commentary. I'm not sure how/if to reference this.

[19] www.traintogain.gov.uk Accessed on 18 March 2009.

[20] www.traintogain.gov.uk Accessed on 18 March 2009.

9 Benefits for people in specific circumstances

This chapter covers the benefits that are open to a wide range of people. It gives information about:

- Income Support
- benefits for maternity, adoption and paternity
- Child Benefit
- help with housing costs (including rent, taxes and mortgages), and
- the Social Fund (which includes bereavement benefits).

Income Support

What is Income Support?

Income Support (IS) is a means-tested benefit for a person on a low income who is working fewer than 16 hours per week, or whose partner is working fewer than 24 hours per week. IS makes up the difference between your actual income and your applicable amount (what the government thinks you need to live on). To claim IS, you (and any partner) must have less than £16,000 in capital.

Who is entitled to Income Support?

You can get IS if you are:

- aged 16 or over, and
- not in full-time, non-advanced education (though there are exceptions), and
- not working, or working for fewer than 16 hours per week (there are a few exceptions). If you have a partner, they must be working fewer than 24 hours per week.

If you are part of a couple, whether you are married or not, the government will look at your combined circumstances, income and savings when working out your eligibility for IS.

To qualify for IS, you must also be in a certain group. The most common groups are:[1]

- those caring for a disabled person who has claimed, or who receives, Disability Living Allowance (DLA) or Attendance Allowance (AA)
- lone parents responsible for looking after a child aged under 12, and
- those expecting a baby (or those whose partner is expecting a baby), and those taking paternity or adoption leave.

Before 27 October 2008, you could claim IS on the grounds of being unable to work because of illness or disability. This has now changed for new claims. To get IS on these grounds, you must have made your claim before 27 October 2008, or be covered by the linking rules.

Before 24 November 2008, you could claim IS on the basis of being a lone parent, until your child turned 16. That age limit was reduced to 12, and further reduced to 10 from 29 October 2009. The limit will be reduced to seven from 25 October 2010. However, the new rules about the age limit don't apply to foster carers or parents of disabled children.

Students

Provided you satisfy the rules about income, capital and work hours, you can get IS while in full-time education or training, if you:

- are under 21 and in full-time non-advanced education, and you have to live away from your parents or anyone acting in their place for various reasons (this is known as 'estrangement' – see *Inclusion's* The Young Person's Handbook for more details)
- are aged 24 or younger and attending a course provided by the Learning and Skills Council, or its equivalent in Wales or Scotland
- have been granted refugee status and are attending an English course for more than 15 hours per week during your first year in the UK
- are a lone parent
- are sick or disabled, and started your IS claim before 27 October 2008 (after this date, you would be claiming Employment and Support Allowance (ESA) instead), or
- are aged 16 to 20, are in non-advanced education, and are an orphan.

Carers

You may get IS as a carer, if you are:

- caring for another person, and either:
  - you receive Carer's Allowance, or
  - the person you are caring for gets AA, the middle or higher rate of the Disability Living Allowance Care Component, or Constant Attendance Allowance paid under the Industrial Disablement Benefit or War Disablement Pension rules
- caring for someone who has applied for one of the above benefits, but their claim has not yet been processed (you will be able to claim IS for up to 26 weeks while you are waiting), or
- looking after a family member who is temporarily ill, as long as they are part of your family for IS purposes.

Caring for a child or children

You may get IS as a carer for children if you:

- are a lone parent responsible for a child aged under 12 (this age limit will be reduced to 10 from 25 October 2010 – see page 168 for details)
- are a lone parent or part of a couple, and you have to take unpaid statutory parental leave to look after a dependent child, and you are entitled to Housing Benefit (HB) or Council Tax Benefit (CTB), WTC with a disability or a severe disability element, or Child Tax Credit (CTC) at a rate above the family element
- are single or a lone parent and are fostering a child aged under 16 through a local authority or voluntary organisation
- are looking after a child aged under 16 because the child's usual guardian is ill or temporarily away, or
- your partner is temporarily abroad and you are responsible for a dependent child.

Maternity, adoption and paternity

You may get IS if you (or your partner) are expecting a baby (you can claim IS from 11 weeks before the baby is expected until 15 weeks after it is born). You may also get IS if you are taking paternity or adoption leave.

Others

You may also get IS if you:

- qualify for IS urgent case payments as a person subject to immigration control
- have started work and are eligible for the first four weeks of Mortgage Interest Run-on
- have to attend court as a Justice of the Peace, juror, witness, defendant or plaintiff
- are remanded in custody for trial or sentencing (if this is the case, you can only get certain help with housing costs), or
- are involved in a trade dispute.

Working

If you work for more than 16 hours per week, you may be able to get IS if you fall into any of the eligible groups listed above, and if you are:

- mentally or physically disabled, and your hours of work or your earnings are 75 per cent or less than the hours or earnings of someone without your disability who does the same work as you
- living in a care home and working (if you need personal care because of a disability, a past or present dependence on alcohol or drugs, a past or present mental disorder, or a terminal illness)
- a volunteer, or working for a charity or voluntary organisation, and you only get help with expenses
- a carer who looks after someone regularly and at length
- a foster parent paid by a health body, local authority or voluntary organisation to provide care in your own home
- a childminder working in your own home
- on a training course and getting a Training Allowance
- involved in a trade dispute, and you have stopped work for more than seven days
- working more than 16 hours per week, but fewer than 24 hours per week, and you are still covered by the transitional protection you were awarded in 1991, or
- on statutory maternity, paternity or adoption leave.

This is not an exhaustive list.

Some foster carers and childminders can choose whether to claim IS or Working Tax Credit (WTC), because HM Revenue and Customs considers caring and childminding as 'working.' Each case will be different and should be assessed by a benefits expert to decide the best option.

People who may have problems claiming Income Support (L4)

Depending on your circumstances, you may have trouble getting IS because you fall into a group that is usually excluded from the benefit, you cannot meet the benefit conditions, or you have problems proving your identity. You should seek advice, if you are:

- 16 or 17 years old
- on strike
- from overseas
- suspected of living with a partner (this applies to lesbian and gay partners as well as heterosexual partners)
- living in a care home or a hostel, or
- homeless.

How is Income Support calculated?

Earnings

IS is a means-tested benefit, so your earnings will be used to work out your eligibility.

Earnings do not include:

- payments in kind
- periodic payments (for example, payments because employment has ended through redundancy)
- payments made when an employee is on maternity leave
- sick pay
- occupational pensions, and
- payments for work-related expenses (for example, specialist clothing, travel expenses, or telephone calls made entirely for work purposes).

Along with these exceptions, between £5 and £20 of your income does not count as earnings, depending on which group you fit into.

Other income

Almost all other income will be used to work out your eligibility for IS, but some is ignored. For example, income from these sources is ignored:

- Disability Living Allowance
- Attendance Allowance
- Child Benefit (if you also get CTC or Guardian's Allowance)
- your children's earnings
- payments made for you by a third party (unless the payments are for everyday food, fuel, clothing and sometimes housing)
- payments for volunteers' expenses
- Education Maintenance Allowances
- fostering allowances
- £20 a week of child maintenance, and
- voluntary and charitable payments.[2]

If in doubt, seek advice.

If you get income from CTC, this will be ignored along with your Child Benefit. However, the IS calculation will not take into account any children that you have, unless you have been claiming IS continuously since before April 2004 and you do not receive CTC.

Capital

To get IS, you must have less than £16,000 in capital or savings. If you have capital between £6,000 and £16,000, then you will count as having £1 of 'tariff income' for every £250 of capital that is above £6,000. If you live in a care home, you can have up to £10,000 in savings before the tariff income rule is applied.

If you have capital assets outside the United Kingdom, these will count as capital for IS.[3]

If you deliberately get rid of capital to bring your capital down to the level where you can get extra benefit, you may still count as having the extra capital. The Department for Work and Pensions will try to guess your intentions from a one-off expenditure that is unusually high.[4] Seek advice if you are unsure about this, or if you are affected by it.

Applicable amount

Your applicable amount is the minimum amount the government thinks you need to live on. If your income is less than your applicable amount, you will normally receive IS to bring your income up to that level.

The applicable amount is made up of a weekly personal allowance for you and your partner, weekly premiums (paid if you are disabled or a carer), plus housing costs for such things as interest on mortgages, loans for repairs and improvements, and service charges. This means that your applicable amount may vary to take into account some of your circumstances. The cost of rent is not included in your applicable amount,so, if you are renting, you should claim Housing Benefit (HB).

Some people with children do not get CTC, but instead receive IS, which includes amounts for children. The government currently has plans eventually to move all people in this situation onto CTC. Most people will see no difference in the amount of money they get – some will gain, and a few will lost. Get advice if you are affected by this.

For more information on how to calculate IS, (and other means-tested benefits), see Welfare Benefits and Tax Credits Handbook by the Child Poverty Action Group.

Attending Work Focused Interviews during your Income Support claim

When you claim IS, you will usually be asked to attend a Work Focused Interview, unless an interview would not be appropriate or would not help you. If you miss the interview without good cause, your IS claim will lapse. You can appeal, if you feel that you had a good reason for not attending.

Benefits for maternity, adoption and paternity

What are the benefits for maternity, adoption and paternity?

There are four benefits for maternity, adoption and paternity. Women who stop work to have a baby may be able to claim one of the following:

- Statutory Maternity Pay – a benefit that employers pay for up to 39 weeks to female employees who stop work to have a baby (this benefit may be paid in conjunction with your employment-based maternity pay)
- MA – which is paid for up to 39 weeks to women who have worked continuously for 26 of the 66 weeks immediately before their baby was due
- Statutory Adoption Pay – a benefit paid for up to 39 weeks when a child aged under 18 is placed for adoption, and the adoptive parent has worked continuously for 26 of the 66 weeks immediately before the child is placed (members of a couple can choose which person will take the Statutory Adoption Pay and the leave entitlement that goes with it). Statutory Adoption Pay is paid at the same rate and in the same way as Statutory Maternity Pay.
- Statutory Paternity Pay – which is for people (not just fathers) who take up to two weeks of paternity leave within 56 days of the birth of a child. In the case of an adoption, members of a couple can choose which partner takes paternity leave, Statutory Paternity Pay and Statutory Adoption Pay.

Statutory Maternity Pay

Statutory Maternity Pay (SMP) is paid weekly by an employer to women who have a baby. It is paid for up to 39 weeks and is taxable. SMP is not means-tested but it counts as income for means-tested benefits. The first £100 per week of SMP does not count as income for Tax Credits.

Who is entitled to Statutory Maternity Pay?

To claim SMP, you must:

- be employed in the 25th week of the pregnancy (the qualifying week), and
- have worked for the same employer for at least 26 weeks by the qualifying week, and
- earn more than the National Insurance (NI) lower earnings limit (£95 per week).

SMP is paid at two rates. The higher rate pays 90 per cent of your average earnings. The average is based on the eight weeks of earning immediately before the 16th week of your pregnancy. The higher rate is paid for the first six weeks after the baby is born, to all women who qualify. The standard rate (£123.06 or 90 per cent of your average weekly earnings, whichever is less) is then paid for the next 33 weeks.

If you choose to work up to the week when the baby is due, you will still be entitled to 39 weeks of SMP. If you don't intend to return to work, you are still entitled to 39 weeks of SMP. The earliest date that you can receive SMP is the 11th week before your baby is due. You can return to work for up to ten 'keeping in touch' days without this affecting your benefit.

How to claim

You should be given the form MATB1 by your GP, clinic or midwife at least 28 days before you intend to stop work. You should also ask your employer to pay SMP from the time when you stop work. For Statutory Adoption Pay, this time limit does not apply.

Maternity Allowance

You can claim Maternity Allowance (MA) if you:

- have worked as an employed or self-employed earner for 26 of the 66 weeks immediately before your baby is due, and
- have average weekly earnings above the MA Threshold (£30), and
- are not entitled to SMP for the same week in respect of the same pregnancy.

You can claim MA from the 11th week before the week that your baby is due, and the benefit is paid for 39 weeks. If you have average weekly earnings of £95 or more, you will be paid a standard rate of £123.06 per week. If your earnings average £30 to £94.99 per week, you will be paid 90 per cent of your average earnings. You may work for up to ten 'keeping in touch' days without affecting your benefit.

How to claim

You can claim MA by filling out form MA1, which you can get from Jobcentre Plus offices or on the DWP website (www.dwp.gov.uk). This form should be handed in with the maternity certificate (MATB1) at 26 weeks in the pregnancy.

Further points

Keep these things in mind, if you are claiming maternity, adoption or paternity benefits:

- If you are not entitled to SMP, your employer should give you form SMP1, which you can then use to claim MA. If you are not entitled to MA, Jobcentre Plus should automatically consider a claim for Incapacity Benefit (IB), aiming to award it from six weeks before the birth and for up to two weeks after, provided that you have enough NI contributions or credits. You do not need to give medical evidence of incapacity for work.

- If you are not entitled to maternity-related benefits, you may qualify for ESA on the grounds of pregnancy or illness. If you qualify for IS, you may also use this benefit to top up maternity benefits.

- If you are receiving CTC, your benefit can be increased as soon as your baby is born, rather than at the end of the award period. You can also receive extra amounts of HB and Council Tax Benefit (CTB) while your baby is aged under one. People who have been claiming IS or Jobseeker's Allowance (JSA) non-stop since before April 2004 can get extra payments of these benefits.

- When you are on maternity leave, you count as being in paid work if you or your partner makes a Tax Credit claim.

See page 298, for details of maternity grants

Child Benefit

What is Child Benefit?

Child Benefit is a tax-free benefit for people who have a dependent child or children. Eighty per cent of those who can claim Child Benefit can also claim CTC (see page 254).

Child Benefit is not based on your assets, income or savings, and receiving Child Benefit does not affect your entitlement to WTC or CTC.

Child Benefit is a very important benefit for people who go into work, because it helps to reduce the poverty-trap effect. The poverty-trap effect is when someone takes on a job and finds that they are either not better off, or only a little better off, than when they were unemployed and getting benefits.

Dependent Children

A dependent child is someone who is:[5]

- under the age of 16, or
- under the age of 21 and studying for A-levels, a Level 3 National Vocational Qualification or equivalent, or doing unpaid training that is funded by the government (such as Entry to Employment), so long as their course started before the age of 19, and
- studying for more than 12 hours per week at school or college (not including homework, private study, unsupervised study or meal breaks).

A child stops being dependent when they:

- get married, or
- get certain benefits in their own right (for example, IS, Income-Based Jobseeker's Allowance (IBJSA), Income-Related Employment and Support Allowance (IRESA), or IB), or
- have employed trainee status, or
- are in custody, or

- are in care for more than eight weeks (unless they come home for at least two nights per week or a whole week), or
- are aged 16 or over and work for 24 hours or more per week.

Once any of these events happens, you can no longer claim Child Benefit and you should tell the Child Benefit office to avoid being overpaid.

The terminal date

If your child reaches age 16 and they decide to leave school, your Child Benefit (and CTC) will be paid until the 'terminal date'. The terminal date is the last day of February, May, August or November, depending on when your child leaves education or training (see the chart about terminal dates).[6] If your child has not found a job or training place after the terminal date, you can apply to have Child Benefit (and CTC) paid for up to another 20 weeks, counted from the date they left education, so long as your child has registered with the Careers Service or Connexions.

Child Benefit terminal dates

Date of leaving education or unwaged training	Date Child Benefit stops (terminal date)	Date Child Benefit Extension Period (CBEP) starts	Date Child Benefit Extension Period stops
December–February	Last day in February	First Monday after leaving education or training	20 weeks after start of CBEP
March–May	Last day in May	First Monday after leaving education or training	20 weeks after start of CBEP
June–August	Last day in August	First Monday after leaving education or training	20 weeks after start of CBEP
September–November	Last day in November	First Monday after leaving education or training	20 weeks after start of CBEP

If your child decides to stay in or return to education or training, you should tell the Child Benefit office (and the Tax Credit office) so that they can pay you.

Who receives Child Benefit?

The person who is responsible for the child should always make the claim. This person must normally be living with or supporting the child through maintenance. Child Benefit for an individual child (and other benefits and tax credits) can't be shared between a separated couple. If a separated couple share the care for two or more children, Child Benefit can be shared by paying one parent for the care of one child, and the other parent for the care of the other child, and so on.[7]

If you get Child Benefit for a full tax year for a child aged under 16, you are entitled to Home Responsibilities Protection. This protects the amount of Retirement Pension and/or bereavement benefits you can claim at a later date. In April 2010, this protection will be renamed as a Carer's Credit, but it will have the same effect.

If your partner is working and paying NI but you are not, make sure that you are the person who claims Child Benefit if you have a child aged under 16. If you are claiming Child Benefit, you should get Home Responsibilities Protection automatically – you don't need to make a separate claim.[8]

Home Responsibilities Protection will not affect your right to benefits such as JSA and IB so, if you cannot work because of unemployment or incapacity, you should think about claiming these benefits in order to get a full NI contribution credit.

How to claim

You can claim online at www.direct.gov.uk, or by phoning 0845 302 1444 (Great Britain) or 0845 603 2000 (Northern Ireland). Many parents of new babies receive a 'Bounty Pack' in hospital. This pack may contain a Child Benefit claim form. You will need to register the child's birth so that you can claim any benefits or tax credits for him or her.

There is no lower or upper age limit for a parent or carer to qualify for Child Benefit.

You should register the birth and make your claim as soon as possible after the child is born, because Child Benefit can only be backdated three months from the date your claim is received.

How is Child Benefit calculated?

See page 350, for Child Benefit rates.

A higher award is made for the first child and a lower award for the second and every later child.

Child Trust Fund

Child Trust Funds help children to build up savings that they can draw on when they are aged 18 or over.

The government gives every newborn child a voucher worth £250, so long as a Child Benefit claim has been made (you do not need to make a separate claim for a Child Trust Fund payment). To receive the voucher, the child must live in the UK once they are born. Vouchers are paid into special accounts which can't be touched until the child reaches 18.

Those who are entitled to maximum CTC (that is, people who have an annual income less than £16,040) will receive a voucher worth £500.

Parents, family and friends can add to a Child Trust Fund by making annual payments of up to £1,200. When the child reaches the age of seven, the government will make a further payment. The value of a Child Trust Fund is ignored for any benefit or tax credit claims, and will also be tax-free.

Help with Housing Costs

Help with rent: Housing Benefit

What is Housing Benefit?

Housing Benefit (HB) is a means-tested benefit that helps people on a low income to pay their rent.[9] You may be able to claim it if you pay rent on the home you usually live in. It does not normally matter what type of rent you pay because HB can be claimed by licensees or tenants alike.

You can claim HB if you are working or out of work. In each case, your income from work benefits or tax credits is taken into account in deciding how much you get.

Who is entitled to Housing Benefit?

You may qualify for HB if:

- you are liable to pay rent on a home that you usually live in, and
- you are resident in Great Britain and you are not subject to an immigration restriction, and
- your capital is not more than £16,000 (unless you also receive the guarantee credit part of Pension Credit, which has no capital limit). Any savings over £6,000 reduce the amount of weekly benefit you can claim.

The amount of HB you get depends on:

- whether you are liable to pay rent or other charges for your accommodation
- the amount of rent you are liable to pay
- your income and capital, and
- the number of people you are able to claim for.

If you are buying a share of your council or housing association home, but you still pay rent on the other part (called 'shared ownership'), you can get HB for the rent part, and you may also be able to get IS, IBJSA or IRESA for your mortgage interest on the other part.

Liability for rent

To be able to claim HB, you must be liable to pay rent or similar housing costs on your home.[10] A written agreement is not necessary, but having a proper written agreement, such as a tenancy or licence agreement, will avoid problems and give you clearer housing rights.

The home you usually live in

To be eligible for HB, the home you are claiming HB for must be the home you and your family usually live in.

There are exceptions to this rule. You can get HB while you live away from home, as long as:[11]

- you do not live away from home for longer than 13 weeks, and
  - you intend to return to your home
  - you do not sub-let the property.

If your absence is likely to last more than 13 weeks, you will lose all of your benefit, unless you meet the rules to get HB for up to 52 weeks. You must return home to keep your benefit, but there is no rule about how long you must stay when you return. However, if you just come home to collect post, for example, this will not count as 'returning home.'

You can also get HB for up to 52 weeks, if:

- you are on a training course, either in the UK or abroad
- you are a hospital inpatient or in a registered care home
- you have health-related problems (you will need to seek advice about this), or
- you are being held in prison on remand, or are awaiting sentence.

Moving from one home to another

There are special rules about getting HB when you move from one home to another:

- You can make a claim for HB up to 13 weeks before you are liable to pay rent.[12]

- In certain situations, when you move from one rented home to another, you may get HB for both homes for up to four weeks (if you have actually moved into the new home but you are still liable to pay rent on the old home), or for up to 52 weeks if you had to move because of a fear of violence.[13]

- If the rent payments for your new home start before you actually move in, you may be able to get HB for up to four weeks before you move, but this rule only applies in certain circumstances.

Seek advice, if you think that any of these circumstances apply to you.

How is Housing Benefit calculated?

Means test

You can only receive maximum HB if:

- you receive IS, or
- you receive IBJSA, or
- you receive IRESA, or
- you receive the guarantee credit part of Pension Credit, or
- your income is below the applicable amount.

If none of the above applies to you, then the amount of HB you receive will be reduced – the higher your income is, the less HB you will be paid.

If your income is above your applicable amount (the income the government decides you need to live on), then your HB per week will be calculated as:

- your weekly eligible rent, minus
  - any amounts for non-dependants, minus
  - 65 per cent of your excess income.

Any income over your applicable amount is called 'excess income'. In effect, you lose 65 pence for every £1 you earn over your applicable amount. This means that if you receive HB while in work and your pay increases, you will lose most of your pay increase through the reduction of your HB.

If you have between £6,000.00 and £16,000 in savings and capital, the amount of your HB will be calculated based on an 'assumed' income. For most people aged under 60, the assumed income is £1 per week for every £250 they have above the £6,000-limit. For most people aged over 60, the assumed income is £1 for every £500 they have above the £6,000-limit. Some examples of savings and capital include cash, money in a bank, building society or Post Office accounts, investments (such as stocks, shares, bonds and unit trusts), and other property or land you own.

Eligible rent

'Eligible rent' is used to work out your maximum HB.

Not all of your rent will be eligible for HB, and some payments you make to your landlord will be excluded. These include:

- some service charges
- charges for light and heating
- charges for water, and
- charges for meals.[14]

This applies whether you are in work or unemployed.

Reductions to your eligible rent

The amount of HB you receive can be reduced, if:

- your rent is unreasonably expensive or your accommodation is unreasonably large[15]
- you live in privately rented housing and the rent is more than the Local Housing Allowance for your area, or
- you are under 25 and living alone, in which case your eligible rent may be reduced to the average rent for a room in shared accommodation in your area.

If there is a chance that any of these rules applies to you, you should get further information or advice because there are many exceptions.

You can find out about the rent levels paid by your local HB authority by:

- looking at the Rent Service LHA Direct website https://lha-direct. therentservice.gov.uk, and
- asking HB officers or an advice centre about the rent levels that are paid in the area.

The rent restrictions listed above do not apply to some people who have been claiming HB since before 1 January 1996.

You might be able to keep your protection from rent restrictions, if:

- you do not stop claiming HB for more than 52 weeks, and
- you or your partner are:
  - unable to work because of ill-health or disability, or
  - responsible for a child or dependent young person.[16]

If you wish to keep your protection from rent reductions, but you do not fit the above criteria, then you must not have a gap of more than four weeks in your claim for HB.

If you wish to remain exempt from the HB reduction, it is best to seek advice and further information, especially if you are thinking of moving home.

Who can you claim Housing Benefit for?

Your claim can include your partner (also a same-sex partner, if you live together as a couple), children under the age of 16 who live with you, and young people aged 16 to 21 who live with you and who are either in full-time education (doing a course up to A-level or Scottish Highers standard) or in unwaged training that is funded by the government, such as Entry to Employment.

Other people who live with you may be classed as 'non-dependants', which may affect the amount of HB you get.

Non-dependants

A non-dependant is someone who lives with you but does not count as part of your family for benefit purposes (for example, a relative, friend, or grown-up child who is no longer a dependant). Your HB and/or CTB will be reduced if you have any non-dependants, because it is assumed that non-dependants contribute towards your rent and/or council tax. However, if you are a private tenant with HB based on a Local Housing Allowance, you will be allowed a higher rent because of the extra bedroom your non-dependant needs.

The following are not classed as non-dependants:

- boarders, sub-tenants and joint tenants (that is, people who are also liable to pay rent to your landlord) although income from them will be taken into account when deciding how much HB you get)
- certain types of carers provided by charities
- children under 16 or aged 16 to 20 who are in full-time education or unwaged training
- a landlord and any of their family members.[17]

Even if you have non-dependants living with you, there will be no deductions from your HB, if you or your partner:

- are registered as blind, or ceased to be registered as blind within the last 28 weeks

- receive the Care Component of Disability Living Allowance (paid at any of the three rates)
- receive Attendance Allowance
- receive Constant Attendance Allowance.[18]

Similarly, there will be no deductions, if the non-dependant:

- receives a Training Allowance as part of work-based training for young people
- is a full-time student (but it will only be reduced during their summer vacation, if they are not in work, unless you or your partner are aged 65 or older)
- is aged under 18
- is aged under 25 and receives IS, IBJSA or IRESA
- receives Pension Credit
- has been in hospital for more than 52 weeks
- is in prison, or
- does not normally live with you.[19]

Reductions for non-dependants can be very high and errors are common. The amount of reduction can also depend on whether the non-dependant is in full-time paid work and, if so, how much they earn. There are six bands of non-dependant reductions, which are based on the non-dependant's earnings. If the non-dependant doesn't tell you their income, you will lose the highest rate of deduction from your HB.

Sometimes, in cases where there is no deduction for a non-dependant, another part of your HB calculation may be affected. This is particularly true where you or your partner (or both) are disabled. Seek advice, if this applies to you.

Working and receiving Housing Benefit

If you start working full time (16 or more hours per week), then for the first four weeks of your employment you may be able to get HB at the same rate as you received when you were claiming IS, IBJSA, IB, Severe

Disablement Allowance, or IRESA. This is known as Extended Payments (see page 291).

To be eligible you have to have been receiving one of the benefits below for 26 weeks before starting work:

- Income Support
- Income-based Jobseeker's Allowance
- Income-related or contributory Employment and Support Allowance
- Incapacity Benefit
- Severe Disablement Allowance.

You do not need to make a new claim for HB each time you return to work. You need only report changes in your circumstances to the local authority, the DWP, or both. This can be done by phone, but you should always confirm changes in writing. If you report a change of circumstance by phone, you should make a note of who you spoke to and when. If you are entitled to Extended Payments, you will get the higher rate of HB for four weeks, and after that, the amount of your HB will depend on your new income.

It is important to notify the local authority of changes in your circumstances, such as starting work or increasing your hours of work, so that you can qualify for Extended Payments. You will also avoid being overpaid and having action taken against you as a result.

You may be able to work full time and receive HB. The amount you get will depend on:

- your income, and
- your applicable amount (see page 287), and
- the amount of rent you have to pay.

Keep in mind that the rules for HB are different for lone parents. Lone parents are allowed to earn £25 per week before their income is counted. Other people who are working are allowed to keep between £5 and £20 per week before their earnings count as income, depending on their circumstances. Parents can also keep all of the child maintenance they receive from a former partner who is the parent of their child. If you have a dependent child and you are getting child maintenance but the maintenance is not for that child, only the first £15 per week will not count as income. If you are getting child maintenance but do not have a dependent child, all of the maintenance counts as income.

On top of these normal disregarded amounts, an extra £16.85 per week of earnings is disregarded for some tenants who work 16 or more hours per week. This includes lone parents, some people with disabilities, and couples with children where one partner is unable to work because of disability or incapacity. In other cases, the extra £16.85 will only be disregarded if the tenant works for 30 or more hours per week. This includes single people and non-disabled couples without children.

You may also offset your childcare costs by up to £175 per week for one child or £300 per week for two children if you:

- are a lone parent who works 16 or more hours per week
- are a couple and both of you work 16 or more hours per week, or
- one of you works 16 or more hours a week and the other is either unable to work because of ill health or disability, or they receive a disability or ill-health benefit.

The childcare must be for a child aged under 15 (or 16 if the child is disabled) and should also be formally provided by a nursery, after-school club or a registered childminder.[20]

New Deal and Housing Benefit

If you want to know how New Deal and HB fit together, the rules are that:

- if you are on a New Deal scheme and you are employed, then you will count as being in paid work
- if you are paid a Training Allowance, this will count as income/ earnings unless you are a trainee (this is because the training allowance includes an IBJSA payment of 10 pence).
- if you are on a New Deal scheme and still receive benefit, then Housing Benefit is unaffected by your being on the New Deal.

Any awards made by Jobcentre Plus do not count as capital for 52 weeks. The following awards do not count:

- training premiums
- any childcare costs that are reimbursed to a New Deal participant, and
- childcare payments made as a lump sum.

Your HB should not be affected, if:

- you are receiving IBJSA or
- you are on a paid work placement for a subsidised job.

The Employment Zone weekly payments do not count as income, and any arrears will be treated as capital and ignored for 52 weeks.

For young people who are trainees or trainee employees, the rules are:

- if you are an employee, the normal earnings rules apply
- if you are a trainee, you will receive a Training Allowance from which no tax or NI contributions are deducted.

If you are a trainee, your Training Allowances count as income other than earnings. However, you do not have to count any reimbursed travelling expenses or training premiums.

Where and how can you claim Housing Benefit?

You can claim HB at your local council, or at the Department for Work and Pensions. Your claim must normally be made in writing, on the HB claim form. Some councils will accept claims by phone.

If you contact your council or the DWP to claim HB, and you submit your claim forms within one month of making contact, the start-date of your claim will usually be recognised as the day you first made contact.

Help with taxes: Council Tax Benefit

CTB helps people on a low income to pay their Council Tax. There are two types of CTB:

- CTB (the main source of help)
- Second adult rebate (formally known as Alternative Maximum CTB).

You can qualify for either of these benefits whether you are in full-time work, part-time work or if you are unemployed.

Who is entitled to Council Tax Benefit?

CTB is a means-tested benefit. The means test rules are the same as those for HB.

People who cannot claim CTB are:

- those subject to immigration control or classed as a person from abroad, and
- most full-time students.

Many of the rules for CTB are similar to those for HB. For example, you can get CTB during a temporary absence from your home, but you can only claim CTB on one home.

You may be able to get help under the second adult rebate scheme, if:

- you are responsible for Council Tax,
- you are single (or your partner is not liable for Council Tax – for example, because they are a student)
- your income is too high for CTB, and
- there is someone living in your property who is on a low income or is claiming IS, IBJSA or IRESA.

You should get further advice.

Council Tax Benefit restrictions

There are restrictions on the amount of CTB you can claim. Apart from the means test, the calculation is based on your weekly eligible Council Tax.

CTB is based on the amount of Council Tax you are liable to pay after you have been awarded any reductions (for example, because of a disability or for certain types of carer).

How is Council Tax Benefit calculated?

CTB is calculated in a similar way to HB.

If your income is above the applicable amount, your CTB is reduced by 20 per cent. In other words, you lose 20 pence for every £1 you earn over your applicable amount.

Help with Council Tax costs

You can reduce the cost of Council Tax by making sure you are receiving any deductions applicable to you. Deductions might apply if:

- you are single or treated as being single (your Council Tax can be reduced by 25 per cent in these circumstances, whatever your income)
- you have a disability that requires your home to be adapted or for a special room to be set aside for your needs (you might be able to have your Council Tax reduced into a different valuation band)
- an adult living in your home is a carer, a full-time student, severely mentally impaired or in one of the other groups of people who are not liable to pay Council Tax.

You should get advice or ask at the Council Tax office.

Help with mortgages and homeowner housing costs

There is a limited amount of help available with mortgage costs. You can only get help with mortgages, if:

- you receive the guarantee credit part of Pension Credit, or
- you receive IS, IBJSA or IRESA.

You can only receive help with the interest on a mortgage or loan for repairs and improvements of no more than £200,000. The help you receive is calculated using a standard interest rate. Capital, endowment and insurance payments are excluded. You can also get help with the cost of service charges, if you are a long-leaseholder.

The applicable amount calculation for IS, IBJSA or Pension Credit includes the amount of help you qualify for with mortgage and leasehold costs. This means that, if your income is otherwise too high for one of these benefits, you may qualify for the benefit after your housing costs have been included in your applicable amount calculation.

If you or your partner are aged under 60, you will usually have to wait for 13 weeks until you receive any help. You will be paid a standard interest rate, which is currently 6.08 per cent. Whether the rate on your mortgage is higher or lower than 6.08 per cent, the standard rate is paid.

If you get help with your housing costs through IBJSA, you will only get this help for a maximum of 104 weeks. If you want to calculate your 104-week period, ignore any time before 5 January 2009, any time when IBJSA has more than a 12-week gap between different claims, and any time when your mortgage capital was £100,000 or less.[22]

If you stop receiving IS, IBJSA, IRESA or Pension Credit and you then have to claim again, there are rules that allow some people to be off benefit for 12 weeks and others for 104 weeks without having to wait to receive help again. These are known as linking periods. It is very important to think about linking periods if you are planning to take a temporary job, and you should get advice to find out which linking period you qualify for.

Help with your mortgage interest is usually paid directly to your lender every four weeks. It is very important to discuss your circumstances with your lender, if you have to claim IS, IBJSA, IRESA or Pension Credit.

Your mortgage interest will still be paid for up to four weeks after you start work (see page 258).

As with HB, mortgage interest help can be reduced in some cases, if:

- your home is too big or too expensive, or
- you have non-dependants living with you, or
- your loan is for certain types of repairs and improvements that don't qualify.

If any of these circumstances might apply to you, seek further advice and information.

The Social Fund

What is the Social Fund?

The Social Fund is a one-off social security payment towards the cost of a particular need.

There are two parts to the Social Fund:

1 The regulated Social Fund – this helps with expenses that arise for a specific reason. This includes maternity expenses, funeral expenses, cold weather payments and winter fuel payments.

2 The discretionary Social Fund – this gives grants and loans to meet a range of other needs, such as clothing or furniture.

To get help from the Social Fund, you have to meet criteria such as being in receipt of certain benefits. Getting help from the discretionary Social Fund is very complex, and you will need to persevere.

The regulated Social Fund

Maternity Expenses[23]

You can claim the Sure Start Maternity Grant (up to £500 for each qualifying child), if:

- you are claiming:
    - IS
    - IBJSA
    - IRESA or WTC with a disability or severe disability element, or
    - CTC or Pension Credit at a rate which is higher than the family element of £545 per year (£1,095 if you have a child aged under one), and
- you:
    - or your partner are pregnant and within 11 weeks of giving birth, or have given birth in the last three months, or
    - have adopted a child under the age of one, or
    - have a Residence Order under the Children Act (or under equivalent Scots or Northern Irish legislation) for a child under the age of one,[24] or
    - have been granted a parental order for a child born to a surrogate mother, and
    - have advice on the health of your baby from a healthcare professional.

As well as the Sure Start Maternity Grant, there is a Health in Pregnancy Grant that is paid to all pregnant women, not just those who are on a low income.

The Health in Pregnancy Grant (HPG) is a scheme that started on 6 April 2009. Under the scheme, £190 is paid to any pregnant woman of any age who has reached 25 weeks' pregnancy and attended ante-natal appointments with a healthcare professional (that is, a midwife, obstetrician or general practitioner). The HPG is not means-tested and you don't need to be on benefits or a low income to qualify. The HPG should be claimed from Her Majesty's Revenue and Customs within 31 days of the healthcare professional counter-signing your claim form.[25]

A Sure Start Maternity Grant can be paid on top of the HPG.

Funeral Payment

You will be eligible to claim a Funeral Payment, if:[26]

- you or your partner are responsible for the cost of a funeral that takes place in the UK (if you are a worker from a European Economic Area (EEA) country, a family member of an EEA worker, or you have the right to reside in the UK under EC law, you may get help with the cost of a funeral that is held outside the UK but still in an EEA country),[27] and
- the deceased was ordinarily a resident in the UK at the time of death, and
- you or your partner are receiving IS, IBJSA, IRESA, Pension Credit, WTC with a disability or a severe disability element, CTC that is paid above the family element, HB or CTB, and
- you make a claim for a Funeral Payment within three months of the funeral.

Cold Weather Payment

You are automatically eligible for the Cold Weather Payment if you:

- receive IS, or IBJSA, IRESA or Pension Credit, and you are responsible for a child aged under five, or
- are aged 60 or over, or
- receive a disability premium for IS or IBJSA, or
- receive CTC that includes a disability or severe disability element, and
- the outside temperature in your area is zero degrees centigrade or less for seven days. You don't have to make a claim – the money will be added to your weekly benefit.

Winter Fuel Payment[28]

The Winter Fuel Payment is for people who are aged 60 or over in the week following on from the third Monday in September. It is normally paid automatically to people who are receiving Retirement Pension during this qualifying week. Those aged 60 or over who are not receiving Retirement Pension will need to make a claim. Payment is made between mid-November and Christmas.

The discretionary Social Fund

Community Care Grant

Community Care Grants help those on IS, IBJSA, IRESA or Pension Credit to meet certain costs. In particular, the grants are supposed to:

- assist you to live in the community after being in institutional care
- help to reduce the chance that you will go into institutional care
- ease exceptional pressure on you and your family
- help you to set up home as part of a programme of resettlement after an unsettled way of life
- allow you to care for a prisoner on temporary release, or
- help with certain travel expenses within the UK.[29]

Budgeting Loan

Budgeting Loans are interest-free loans to help people who have been on IS, IRESA or IBJSA for 26 weeks or more to buy a specific item.

The loan should be for:

- furniture and household equipment
- clothing or footwear
- rent in advance and/or removal expenses for new accommodation
- improvement, maintenance and security of your home
- travel costs
- expenses for seeking or starting work
- hire purchase or other debts, for the above.[30]

The maximum loan that can be given is £1,500 and the minimum loan is £100. In all cases, the loan should be repaid within 104 weeks. Your local Jobcentre Plus will reduce your weekly benefit by up to 20 per cent so that the loan is repaid. Because Budgeting Loans reduce your income, you should always apply for a Community Care Grant instead, if you feel that you qualify.

If you need help with the costs of finding work or taking a job, you may be able to get a grant that you don't have to repay from the Adviser Discretion Fund. As from April 2009, every jobseeker has been able to apply for a grant from the Adviser Discretion Fund, not just those people who have been unemployed for over six months.

Crisis Loan

The Crisis Loan is an interest-free loan for people who are unable to meet a short-term need, or for people who need money in an emergency or because of a disaster.[31]

To claim a Crisis Loan:

- you must be aged 16 or over
- the item you apply for must be included in the Crisis Loan scheme
- the loan must not be more than you can afford to repay.
- you must need the loan because of an emergency, and
- you must not have any other source of income or savings to cover the costs for which you are claiming the loan (this includes your wages and borrowing from your employer, but does not include HB, other Social Fund payments, business assets, or personal possessions).

Because repaying the Crisis Loan will reduce your benefits, you should always apply for a Community Care Grant instead, if you feel that you qualify.

You can also apply for a Crisis Loan if you are a lone parent who has been receiving IS and the DWP has transferred you to JSA, creating a gap in your payment.

If you have applied for a benefit and you are waiting for a decision or payment to be made, you may also qualify for a Crisis Loan. The DWP should not put you off or decide that you don't qualify for a Crisis Loan until your benefit application is approved. See page 20, for details of what to do about delays in deciding your benefit entitlement.

You can apply to have Social Fund loan repayments rescheduled (reduced, but spread over a longer period) and the Secretary of State has the power to decide that you do not need to repay the loan. Seek advice, if refused.

Bereavement benefits

What are bereavement benefits?

There are three benefits available for people who were legally married or had a Registered Civil Partnership with their partner at the time their partner died. The benefits are contributory (they are paid at a lower rate if you have not made enough NI contributions in the past). They count as income for means-tested benefits (but £300 per year of Widowed Mother's and Widowed Parent's Allowances are ignored for Tax Credits). It is not possible to claim a bereavement benefit and another contributory benefit at the same time – the other benefit will usually be increased to the bereavement benefit level. Some bereavement benefits are taxable.

The three bereavement benefits are:

- Bereavement Payment (a one-off lump sum)
- Widowed Parent's Allowance (some people may still be receiving Widowed Mother's Allowance, if they started their claim before 9 April 2001)
- Bereavement Allowance

Who is entitled to bereavement benefits?[32]

Bereavement Payment

This is a tax-free lump sum of £2,000, which does not count as capital for means-tested benefits. As the surviving spouse or civil partner, you must be under pensionable age (60 for women and 65 for men, but increasing for women from April 2010 onwards) when your spouse or civil partner dies. If you are over the pension age, you may still be able to claim the benefit, if your late spouse or civil partner was not receiving a Category A Retirement Pension. If your spouse or civil partner died from a work-related accident or a prescribed industrial disease, the NI contribution conditions for Bereavement Payment are waived. You must normally claim the benefit within 12 months of your spouse or civil partner's death – it is not paid automatically.

Widowed Parent's Allowance

This is for parents who were widowed on or after 9 April 2001. To claim the benefit, you must have a dependent child or children (that is, you should qualify to receive Child Benefit for at least one child).

Bereavement Allowance

This benefit is taxable and is paid for 52 weeks from the date of your spouse or civil partner's death, provided the death happened on or after 9 April 2001. Because you cannot receive both the Bereavement Allowance and the Widowed Parent's Allowance at the same time, the Bereavement Allowance serves as a benefit for people without dependent children. If you were aged between 45 and 54 on the date that your spouse or civil partner died, you can claim an extra age allowance. Bereavement Allowance is based on your late spouse or civil partner's NI record.

How to claim

To claim any of the three bereavement benefits, fill out a claim form from a Jobcentre Plus office, or print a form from the Direct Gov website (www.direct.gov.uk).

Further points

Keep these things in mind, when you claim a bereavement benefit:

- You will be asked to have a Work Focused Interview if you make a claim and you are not working for 16 or more hours per week. However, the interview will normally be postponed for at least three months after bereavement.
- You cannot claim these benefits if:
    - you and your partner never married or entered a civil partnership, or
    - you are divorced (if you are separated and do not have a decree absolute, you count as still being married), or
    - your civil partnership has been dissolved.

- However, sometimes long-standing relationships celebrated by a customary ceremony may qualify and, in Scotland, you can be classed as married if you and your partner live together in a stable way over a long period of time.
- Women who were widowed before 9 April 2001 are covered by the old Widow's Pension and Widowed Mother's Allowance.
- Bereavement Allowance and Widowed Parent's Allowance both stop if a widow or widower starts to live as a couple with another man or woman, or if the widow or widower re-marries or enters a civil partnership. You cannot get Bereavement Payment, if you are living as a part of a couple at the time of your claim.
- Surviving partners who receive IS, IBJSA, Pension Credit, Tax Credits with income below a set amount, HB or CTB may also qualify for a Social Fund payment toward funeral costs.
- DWP leaflet D49 What to do After a Death contains a lot of useful information. There is a separate version of this leaflet for those living in Scotland.
- You may get financial help from the deceased's occupational or personal pension scheme, trade union, or trade or professional body. It is worth finding out the deceased's work history to see whether you can get any help from their past work or activities.

Endnotes

[1] Sched. 1B Income Support (General) Regulations 1987.

[2] Sched. 9 Income Support (General) Regulations 1987.

[3] Reg. 50 Income Support (General) Regulations 1987.

[4] Reg. 51 Income Support (General) Regulations 1987.

[5] Sect. 142(2) Social Security Contributions and Benefits Act 1992; Regs 2–7 Child Benefit (General) Regulations 2006.

[6] Reg. 7(2) Child Benefit (General) Regulations 2006.

[7] R v Board of Inland Revenue ex p Ford [2005] EWHC 1109. 19 May 2005.

[8] Reg. 2(5) Social Security Pensions (Home Responsibilities) Regulations 1994.

[9] Housing Benefit Regulations 2006 ('HB Regs'); Housing Benefit (Persons who have obtained the qualifying age for State Pension Credit) Regulations 2006 ('HB(PC) Regs').

[10] Regs 11 and 13 HB Regs.

[11] Reg 7 HB Regs.

[12] Reg. 83 HB Regs.

[13] Reg. 7 HB Regs.

[14] Reg. 12(3)(b) HB Regs; Reg. 12(3) HB(PC) Regs.

[15] Reg. 12 HB Regs.

[16] Sched. 3 paras 4(1) (a), (3) and (4) Housing Benefit and Council Tax Benefit (Consequential Provisions) Regulations 2006.

[17] Reg. 3 HB Regs; Reg. 3 Council Tax Benefit Regulations 2006.

[18] Regs 2(1) and 74(6) HB Regs; Regs 2(1) and 55(6) HB(PC) Regs.

[19] Regs 2 (1) and 74 HB Regs; Regs 2(1) and 55 HB(PC) Regs.

[20] Regs 27(1) (c) and 28 (6)–(8) HB Regs.

[21] Sched. 5 paras 13 HB Regs.

[22] The SS (Housing Costs Special Arrangements) (Amendment and Modification) Regulations 2008 (SI 2008 No. 3195) Reg 11(b), JSA Regs, sched. 2 para. 4A.

[23] Reg. 5(1) Social Fund Maternity and Funeral Expenses General Regulations 1987.

[24] Francis v Secretary of State for Work and Pensions [2005] EWCA Civ 13033.

[25] Health in Pregnancy Grant (Entitlement and Amount) Regulations 2008.

[26] Reg. 7 Social Fund Maternity and Funeral Expenses General Regulations 1987.

[27] Reg. 7(1A) Social Fund Maternity and Funeral Expenses General Regulations 1987.

[28] Social Fund Winter Fuel Payment Regulations 2000.

[29] Dir. 4 Social Fund Directions.

[30] Dir. 2 Social Fund Directions.

[31] Dir. 3 Social Fund Directions.

[32] Ss 36–9 SSCB Act.

10 Decisions and appeals about benefits and tax credits

Decision Makers

Decision Makers are responsible for making decisions about your benefits and tax credits. They work in several different government departments and offices, depending on the type of benefit or credit, as follows:

- Decision Makers in the Department for Work and Pensions (DWP) are responsible for making choices about your entitlement to benefits
- Decision Makers acting on behalf of Her Majesty's Revenue and Customs (HMRC) make decisions about tax credits
- Staff who work for local authorities make decisions about Housing Benefit and Council Tax Benefit.

You are entitled to get a written explanation of any decision, so long as you ask for the explanation within one month of the decision. The Decision Maker or local authority must send you the explanation within 14 days of your request.[1] After receiving the explanation, you then have one month to take matters further. However, you can challenge the decision without asking for an explanation in the first place.

Appeals

You are able to appeal against almost all decisions, on matters such as:

- whether you are entitled to a benefit or tax credits
- how your benefit or tax credit has been worked out
- whether your claim for Jobseeker's Allowance should be stopped or sanctioned, and for how long, and
- whether you have been overpaid.

However, you cannot appeal against decisions on matters such as:

- whether or not the government has set benefit amounts high enough to live on, and
- how and on what day of the week a benefit or tax credit should be paid.

You must make your appeal in writing, and the relevant department or office must receive it within one month of the date when they first made their decision (and not one month from the date when you received the decision).[2] The date when the department or office made their decision will be shown on the letter they sent to tell you about the decision. You should normally use form GL24 to make your appeal, and you can get this form from the DWP (or online at www.dwp.gov.uk). If you're making an appeal about tax credits, you should use Form TC62[3], which you can get online at www.hmrc.gov.uk. Your appeal will be passed on to the Tribunals Service, which is in charge of appeal tribunals.

If you appeal after the one-month deadline, the tribunal may still hear your case if you can show that:

- there is a reasonable chance that your appeal will succeed, and
- it is in the interests of justice that your appeal be heard, and
- special circumstances meant that it was not practical for you to appeal within the normal time limit.[3]

You can also ask for a revision or supersession (see p. 307).

Appeal Tribunal

Appeals are heard by First Tier Tribunals, which are run by the Tribunals Service. Tribunals are independent of the DWP, HMRC and local authorities, and can change the decisions that were made by each of these departments or authorities. A tribunal is normally made up of one legally qualified Judge, who can ask other experts to hear the appeal. Tribunals that hear appeals about Employment and Support Allowance always include a doctor, and tribunals for Disability Living Allowance and Attendance Allowance include both a doctor and someone who has personal or professional experience of disabilities.

Sometime after you have sent your appeal letter, the Tribunals Service will send you a letter asking whether or not you still want your appeal to go ahead. It is very important to reply to this letter within 14 days because, if you don't, your appeal may not go ahead.

If there is a long delay in dealing with your appeal case, you can write and ask a tribunal Judge to give a Direction to the DWP, HMRC or local authority to prepare their paperwork quickly for the appeal.[4]

You do not have to attend the tribunal, if you'd prefer the panel to reach a decision using only documents. However, it is far better to attend, because you can explain any facts that are not clear from your documents, and you also have a much better chance of winning your appeal. Remember, you can bring someone to support you, if you are not confident enough to go to the tribunal on your own. Ideally, an adviser who understands social security law should represent you at your tribunal (this could be someone from an advice agency or a welfare rights service). No matter what you choose to do about representation, it is still very important to get independent advice before your appeal hearing.

If the tribunal is made up of more than one person, the panel will try to reach a unanimous decision. If they cannot, the Judge has the power to make the final decision. A decision will usually be made on the day of your hearing. You will normally hear the decision in person, and then later you will be given or sent a short written summary. You can write and ask for a more detailed summary.

You can get help with some travel costs to and from the appeal hearing. You may also be able to claim for loss of earnings, or for childcare costs. You must have receipts for all of the costs that you want to claim.

Revisions

If you have no right to appeal a decision, you can ask for a revision. You must ask for a decision to be revised within one month of the date when the decision was sent to you. If you have received a written explanation of the reasons for the decision, then you must ask for a revision within 14 days of the date when the letter was sent. You can also ask for a revision when you do have a right of appeal,[5] and the DWP, HMRC or local authority should think about revising their decision if you request an appeal.

If you ask for a revision less than one month after the decision was sent to you (or less than 14 days after the reasons for the decision were sent to you), you do not have to give any reasons for your request. If more than one month, but less than 13 months has passed since the date of the decision, you will need to show that you have good reasons for applying late.[6]

The Secretary of State can revise a decision at any time without a request from you. This may happen if, for example, a decision was based on an official error or a factual mistake. You can also ask for a benefit decision to be revised at any time (even years later), if there was an official error (for example, you were paid the wrong amount of benefit, or some evidence was overlooked).[7]

Revisions usually take effect from the date the decision was revised.

Appeals against revisions

In most cases, if a decision is not revised in your favour you can appeal to a tribunal. You should appeal against the Secretary of State's revised decision within one month of the revision.

Supersessions

Supersessions are another way that a benefit decision can be changed. However, a supersession will usually only take effect from the date when the DWP, HMRC or local authority receives the request for the supersession.[8]

The main grounds for requesting a supersession are:

- there has been a change of circumstances
- there was a mistake about, or ignorance of, a material fact
- a decision was wrong in law
- you have been given a benefit (known as a 'qualifying benefit') that affects your entitlement to other benefits.

The Secretary of State can supersede a decision, and must do this in certain situations. The Secretary can either enforce or change decisions to do the following things:

- apply a sanction to your Jobseeker's Allowance
- stop your benefit because it is felt that you are no longer incapable of work
- decide that you have been overpaid a social security benefit.

Appeals to the Upper Tier Tribunal

If a First Tier Tribunal makes a decision on a point of law and you disagree with the decision, you may be able to appeal to the Upper Tier Tribunal. It is very important to get independent advice before appealing to the Upper Tier Tribunal, particularly if your case might set a bad pattern for similar cases.

To follow this course of action, you must apply to the First Tier Tribunal Judge in writing. See www.tribunals.gov.uk, for more details and advice.

Complaints

If you do not agree with the way a local council made a decision, you can complain to the council's Monitoring Officer and to the Local Government Ombudsman (visit www.lgo.org.uk to find out who the ombudsman is). Before you can go to the ombudsman, you will have to use the council's internal complaints procedure (there are normally three stages in the procedure).

If you have a complaint against the DWP, you can contact your Member of Parliament and ask them to take up your case. Alternatively, each DWP office has a customer services manager who can handle your complaint.

Endnotes

[1] Reg. 28 Social Security and Child Support (Decisions and Appeals Regulations 1999 (D&A Regs).

[2] Reg. 31 D&A Regs.

[3] Reg. 32 D&A Regs.

[4] Reg. 38(2) D&A Regs.

[5] Reg. 3 D&A Regs.

[6] Reg. 4 D&A Regs.

[7] Reg. 3(5)(a) D&A Regs.

[8] Regs. 6 & 7 D&A Regs.

10

11 Useful Contacts

Useful books about benefit rights

Welfare Benefits and Tax Credits Handbook 2009–10 (Child Poverty Action Group)

Disability Rights Handbook 2009–10 (Disability Alliance)

Help with finding work

Department for Work and Pensions (DWP)

There is a comprehensive list of government helpline and contact numbers on the DWP website: www.dwp.gov.uk

Directgov

This website offers help and advice for anyone who is in work or looking for work and training, information about benefits and tax credits, as well as claim forms: www.direct.gov.uk

Jobcentre Plus

Details of all local Jobcentre Plus offices can be found on the Jobcentre Plus website: www.jobcentreplus.gov.uk

If you need to make a claim for benefit, call 0800 055 6688 or textphone 0800 023 4888. If you are searching for work, call 0845 6060 234 or textphone 0845 6055 255.

Jobseeker Direct helpline

This helpline provides information about the latest job vacancies, training and childcare and help finding the job that is right for you.

Tel: 0845 60 60 234
Textphone: 0845 60 55 255
Or online at: www.jobseekers.direct.gov.uk

Children and Young People

Connexions Service

The Connexions Service is for those who are 13–19 years old, living in England and seeking practical help or confidential advice on a wide range of topics. It also provides support for those up to the age of 25 who have learning difficulties or disabilities.

Tel: 080 800 13 2 19
Website: www.connexions-direct.com

Child Poverty Action Group (CPAG)

CPAG promotes action for the relief of poverty among children and families with children. It works to ensure that those on low incomes get their full entitlement to welfare benefits. CPAG publishes several books detailing information on welfare rights and social policy issues.

Address: 94 White Lion Street, London N1 9PF
Tel: 020 7837 7979
Fax: 020 7837 6414
Email: staff@cpag.co.uk
Website: www.cpag.org.uk

CPAG in Scotland

Address: Unit 09 Ladywell, 94 Duke Street, Glasgow G4 0UW
Tel: 0141 552 3303
Email: staff@cpagscotland.org.uk
Website: www.cpag.org.uk

Child Support Agency

The Child Support Agency ensures that, where an application for child maintenance has been made, parents who live apart make financial contributions to the upkeep of their children.

Tel: 08457 133 133
Textphone: 08457 138 924
Website: www.csa.gov.uk

The Prince's Trust

The Prince's Trust offers a range of services to young people aged 18–30. Services focus on helping educational underachievers, refugees and asylum seekers, the unemployed, and those in/leaving care.

Tel: 0800 842 842
Email: webinfops@princes-trust.org.uk
Website: www.princes-trust.org.uk

Child Benefit Enquiry Line

The Child Benefit Enquiry Line provides advice and information on Child Benefit and Guardian's Allowance.

Tel: 0845 302 1444
Textphone: 0845 302 1474
Website: www.hmrc.gov.uk/childbenefit

Lone Parents

One Parent Families

Gingerbread supports one-parent families through local contact groups and a helpline.

Tel: 0800 018 5026
Website: www.oneparentfamilies.org.uk

One Parent Families Scotland

One Parent Families Scotland runs the Lone Parent Helpline for single parents in Scotland.

Tel: 0808 801 0323

Equality

Equality and Human Rights Commission

The Equality and Human Rights Commission is supported by public funds, but is independent of government. The Commission promotes a number of aspects of equality: race, opportunity, disability, age, sexual orientation and religion or belief, as well as human rights.

Tel: 0845 604 6610 (England)
0845 604 5510 (Scotland)
0845 604 8810 (Wales)

Textphone: 0845 604 6620 (England)
0845 604 5520 (Scotland)
0845 604 8820 (Wales)

Email: info@equalityhumanrights.com
Website: www.equalityhumanrights.com

Age Concern

Age concern promotes the welfare of all older people. It offers detailed information to older people and their families on a range of issues and benefits, care and housing.

Tel: 0800 00 99 66
Website: www.ageconcern.org.uk

Employment Relations

Advisory, Conciliation and Arbitration Service (ACAS)

ACAS is the employment relations expert. It offers free impartial help and information to people experiencing problems with employment issues. ACAS has an office base in seven regions of England, with its head office in London.

Address: Brandon House, 180 Borough High Street, London SE1 1LW
Tel: 08457 47 47 47

Health and Safety Executive (HSE)

The HSE ensures that risks to health and safety from work activities are properly controlled.

Tel: 0845 345 0055
Website: www.hse.gov.uk

Trades Union Congress (TUC)

The TUC is the voice of Britain at work. Their 71 affiliated unions campaign for a fair deal at work and for social justice at home and abroad.

Address: Congress House, Great Russell Street, London WC1B 3LS
Tel: 020 7636 4030
Website: www.tuc.org.uk

Training

Department for Children, Schools and Families (DCSF)

The DCSF aims to secure integrated services and educational excellence for children. It is responsible for improving all aspects of policy affecting children and young people.

Tel: 0870 000 2288
Textphone: 01928 794274
Email: info@dcsf.gsi.gov.uk

Learning and Skills Council (LSC)

The LSC is responsible for funding and planning education and training for everyone in England other than those in university, until August 2010.

Tel: 0870 900 6800
Email: info@lsc.gov.uk
Website: www.lsc.gov.uk

In August 2010, the Skills Funding Agency, the Young People's Learning Agency and local authorities, will take over these responsibilities. Further details can be found at: www.dius.gov.uk/further_education/fe_reform/skills-funding-agency-transition and www.dcsf.gov.uk

Other

Citizens Advice Bureau (CAB)

The CAB helps people to resolve legal, money and other problems by providing free advice and information. A directory of local telephone numbers is on their website at: www.citizensadvice.org.uk.

Refugee Council

If you are a migrant, seek advice from a professional. Initial help for refugees, asylum seekers, and those with Exceptional Leave to Remain or Humanitarian Protection can be found from the Refugee Council.

Tel: 020 7346 6700
Website: www.refugeecouncil.org.uk.

Shelter

If you need housing advice, particularly if you are without a home, Shelter is able to help.

Tel: 0808 800 4444
Website: www.shelter.org.uk

12 Appendix 1

Test for whether you have Limited Capability for Work

This is the scoring system for Employment and Support Allowance. Choose the highest descriptor for each activity, and add up the points to get your overall score. You must score at least 15 points to have Limited Capability for Work; or, you must be in an exempt group, or count as having Limited Capability for Work because of exceptional circumstances.

Part One: Physical disabilities

Activity	Descriptors		Points
1. Walking with a walking stick or other aid, if such aid is normally used	1 (a)	Cannot walk at all	15
	1 (b)	Cannot walk more than 50 metres on level ground without repeatedly stopping or feeling severe discomfort	15
	1 (c)	Cannot walk up or down two steps, even with the support of a handrail	15
	1 (d)	Cannot walk more than 100 metres on level ground without stopping or feeling severe discomfort	9

Activity	Descriptors		Points
	1 (e)	Cannot walk more than 200 metres on level ground without stopping or feeling severe discomfort	6
	1 (f)	None of the above apply	0
2. Standing and sitting	2 (a)	Cannot stand for more than 10 minutes without help from another person (even if you are free to move around) before needing to sit down	15
	2 (b)	Cannot sit in a chair with a high back and no arms for more than 10 minutes before needing to move from the chair because the degree of discomfort makes it impossible to continue sitting	15
	2 (c)	Cannot rise to standing from sitting in an upright chair without physical help from another person	15
	2 (d)	Cannot move between two seated positions located next to one another without physical help from another person	15
	2 (e)	Cannot stand for more than 30 minutes (even if free to move around) before needing to sit down	6
	2 (f)	Cannot sit in a chair with a high back and no arms for more than 30 minutes without needing to move from the chair because the degree of discomfort makes it impossible to continue sitting	6
	2 (g)	None of the above apply	0

Activity	Descriptors		Points
3. Bending or kneeling	3 (a)	Cannot bend to touch knees and straighten up again	15
	3 (b)	Cannot bend, kneel or squat to pick up a light object (such as a piece of paper) placed 15cm from the floor on a low shelf, then move that object and straighten up again, without the help of another person	9
	3 (c)	Cannot bend, kneel or squat to pick up a light object on the floor and straighten up again without the help of another person	6
	3 (d)	None of the above apply	0
4. Reaching	4 (a)	Cannot raise either arm to put something in the top pocket of a coat or jacket	15
	4 (b)	Cannot put either arm behind your back to put on a coat or jacket	15
	4 (c)	Cannot raise either arm to the top of your head to put on a hat	9
	4 (d)	Cannot raise either arm above your head height, as if to reach for something	6
	4 (e)	None of the above apply	0

Activity	Descriptors		Points
5. Picking things up and moving or transferring them by using your upper body and arms (excluding all other activities named in Part 1 of this Schedule)	5 (a)	Cannot pick up and move a 0.5-litre carton full of liquid with either hand	15
	5 (b)	Cannot pick up and move a one-litre carton full of liquid with either hand	9
	5 (c)	Cannot pick up and move a light but bulky object (such as an empty cardboard box) requiring the use of both hands together	6
	5 (d)	None of the above apply	0
6. Manual dexterity	6 (a)	Cannot turn a 'star-headed' sink tap with either hand	15
	6 (b)	Cannot pick up a £1 coin (or equivalent) with either hand	15
	6 (c)	Cannot turn the pages of a book with either hand.	15
	6 (d)	Cannot physically use a pen or pencil	9
	6 (e)	Cannot physically use a conventional keyboard or mouse	9

Activity	Descriptors		Points
	6 (f)	Cannot do up or undo small buttons (such as shirt or blouse buttons)	9
	6 (g)	Cannot turn a 'star-headed' sink tap with one hand, but can turn it with the other	6
	6 (h)	Cannot pick up a £1 coin (or equivalent) with one hand, but can pick it up with the other	6
	6 (i)	Cannot pour from an open 0.5-litre carton full of liquid	6
	6 (j)	None of the above apply	0
7. Speech	7 (a)	Cannot speak at all	15
	7 (b)	Speech cannot be understood by strangers	15
	7 (c)	Strangers have great difficulty understanding speech	9
	7 (d)	Strangers have some difficulty understanding speech	6
	7 (e)	None of the above apply	0

Activity	Descriptors		Points
8. Hearing with a hearing aid or other aid, if normally worn	8 (a)	Cannot hear at all	15
	8 (b)	Cannot hear someone talking in a loud voice in a quiet room well enough to distinguish the words being spoken	15
	8 (c)	Cannot hear someone talking in a normal voice in a quiet room well enough to distinguish the words being spoken	9
	8 (d)	Cannot hear someone talking in a loud voice in a busy street well enough to distinguish the words being spoken	6
	8 (e)	None of the above apply	0
9. Vision including visual acuity and visual fields, in normal daylight or bright electric light, with glasses or other aid to vision, if such aid is normally worn	9 (a)	Cannot see at all	15
	9 (b)	Cannot see well enough to read 16-point print at a distance greater than 20cm	15
	9 (c)	Have 50 per cent or greater reduction of visual fields	15
	9 (d)	Cannot see well enough to recognise a friend at a distance of a least five metres	9
	9 (e)	Have at least 25 per cent, but less than 50 per cent, reduction of visual fields	6
	9 (f)	Cannot see well enough to recognise a friend at a distance of at least 15 metres	6
	9 (g)	None of the above apply	0

Activity	Descriptors		Points
10 (a) Continence other than enuresis (bed-wetting) where the claimant does not have an artificial stoma or urinary collecting device	10 (a) (i)	Has no voluntary control over the evacuation of the bowel	15
	10 (a) (ii)	Has no voluntary control over the voiding of the bladder	15
	10 (a) (iii)	At least once a month loses control of bowels so that the claimant cannot control the full evacuation of the bowel	15
	10 (a) (iv)	At least once a week loses control of bladder so that the claimant cannot control the full voiding of the bladder	15
	10 (a) (v)	Occasionally loses control of bowels so that the claimant cannot control the full evacuation of the bowel	9
	10 (a)(vi)	At least once a month loses control of bladder so that the claimant cannot control the full voiding of the bladder	6
	10 (a) (vii)	Risks losing control of bowels or bladder so that the claimant cannot control the full evacuation of the bowel or the full voiding of the bladder if not able to reach a toilet quickly	6
	10 (a) (viii)	None of the above apply	0

Activity	Descriptors		Points
10 (b) Continence where the claimant uses a urinary collecting device, worn for the majority of the time, including an indwelling urethral or suprapubic catheter	10 (b) (i)	Is unable to affix, remove or empty the catheter bag or other collecting device without physical help from another person	15
	10 (b) (ii)	Is unable to affix, remove or empty the catheter bag or other collecting device without causing leakage of contents	15
	10 (b) (iii)	Has no voluntary control over the evacuation of the bowel	15
	10 (b) (iv)	At least once a month, loses control of bowels so that the claimant cannot control the full evacuation of the bowel	15
	10 (b) (v)	Occasionally loses control of bowels so that the claimant cannot control the full evacuation of the bowel	9
	10 (b) (vi)	Risks losing control of bowels so that the claimant cannot control the full evacuation of the bowel if not able to reach a toilet quickly	6
	10 (b) (vii)	None of the above apply	0

Activity	Descriptors		Points
10 (c) Continence other than enuresis (bed wetting) where the claimant has an artificial stoma	10 (c) (i)	Is unable to affix, remove or empty stoma appliance without physical help from another person	15
	10 (c) (ii)	Is unable to affix, remove or empty stoma appliance without causing leakage of contents	15
	10 (c) (iii)	Where the claimant's artificial stoma relates solely to the evacuation of the bowel, at least once a week loses control of bladder so that the claimant cannot control the full voiding of the bladder	15
	10 (c) (iv)	Where the claimant's artificial stoma relates solely to the evacuation of the bowel, at last once a month loses control of bladder so that the claimant cannot control the full voiding of the bladder	9
	10 (c) (v)	Where the claimant's artificial stoma relates solely to the evacuation of the bowel, risks losing control of the bladder so that the claimant cannot control the full voiding of the bladder if not able to reach a toilet quickly	6
	10 (c) (vi)	None of the above apply	0

Activity	Descriptors		Points
11. Remaining conscious during waking moments	11 (a)	At least once a week, has an involuntary episode of lost or altered consciousness, resulting in significantly disrupted awareness or concentration	15
	11 (b)	At least once a month, has an involuntary episode of lost or altered consciousness, resulting in significantly disrupted awareness or concentration	9
	11 (c)	At least twice in the six months immediately preceding the assessment, has had an involuntary episode of lost or altered consciousness, resulting in significantly disrupted awareness or concentration	6
	11 (d)	None of the above apply	0

Part Two: Mental, cognitive and intellectual function

Activity	Descriptors		Points
12. Learning or comprehension in the completion of tasks	12 (a)	Cannot learn or understand how to successfully complete a simple task (such as setting an alarm clock) at all	15
	12 (b)	Needs to witness a demonstration, given more than once on the same occasion, of how to carry out a simple task before the claimant is able to learn or understand how to complete the task successfully, and would be unable to successfully complete the task the next day without a further demonstration of how to complete it	15
	12 (c)	Needs to witness a demonstration of how to carry out a simple task, before the claimant is able to learn or understand how to complete the task successfully, and would be unable to successfully complete the task the next day without a verbal prompt from another person	9
	12 (d)	Needs to witness a demonstration of how to carry out a moderately complex task (such as the steps involved in operating a washing machine to correctly clean clothes) before the claimant is able to learn or understand how to complete the task successfully, and would be unable to successfully complete the task the next day without a verbal prompt from another person	9

Activity	Descriptors		Points
	12 (e)	Needs verbal instructions as to how to carry out a simple task before the claimant is able to learn or understand how to complete the task successfully, and would be unable, within a period of less than one week, to successfully complete the task the next day without a verbal prompt from another person	6
	12 (f)	None of the above apply	0
13. Awareness of hazard	13 (a)	Reduced awareness of the risks of everyday hazards (such as boiling water or sharp objects) would lead to daily instances of or to near-avoidance of:	15
	13 (a) (i)	injury to self or others, or	
	13 (a) (ii)	significant damage to property or possessionsto such an extent that overall day-to-day life cannot successfully be managed	
	13 (b)	Reduced awareness of the risks of everyday hazards would lead for the majority of the time to instances of, or to near-avoidance of:	9
	13 (b) (i)	injury to self or others, or	
	13 (b) (ii)	significant damage to property or possessions to such an extent that overall day-to-day life cannot successfully be managed without supervision from another person	
	13 (c)	Reduced awareness of the risks of everyday hazards has led, or would lead, to frequent instances of, or to near-avoidance of:	6

Activity	Descriptors		Points
	13 (c) (i)	injury to self or others, or	
	13 (c) (ii)	significant damage to property or possessions but not to such an extent that overall day-to-day life cannot be managed when such incidents occur	
	13 (d)	None of the above apply	0
14. Memory and concentration	14 (a)	On a daily basis, forgets or loses concentration to such an extent that overall day-to-day life cannot be successfully managed without verbal prompting from someone else in the claimant's presence	15
	14 (b)	For the majority of the time, forgets or loses concentration to such an extent that overall day-to-day life cannot be successfully managed without verbal prompting from someone else in the claimant's presence	9
	14 (c)	Frequently forgets or loses concentration to such an extent that overall day-to-day life can only be successfully managed with pre-planning, such as making a daily written list of all tasks forming part of daily life that are to be completed	6
	14 (d)	None of the above apply	0

Activity	Descriptors	Points
15. Execution of tasks	15 (a) Is unable to successfully complete any everyday task	15
	15 (b) Takes more than twice the length of time it would take a person without any form of mental disablement to successfully complete an everyday task with which the claimant is familiar	15
	15 (c) Takes more than one and a half times, but no more than twice, the length of time it would take a person without any form of mental disablement to successfully complete an everyday task with which the claimant is familiar	9
	15 (d) Takes one and a half times the length of time it would take a person without any form of mental disablement to successfully complete an everyday task with which the claimant is familiar	6
	15 (e) None of the above apply	0
16. Initiating and sustaining personal action	16 (a) Cannot, due to cognitive impairment or a severe disorder of mood or behaviour, initiate or sustain any personal action (which means planning, organisation, problem solving, prioritising or switching tasks)	15
	16 (b) Cannot, due to cognitive impairment or a severe disorder of mood or behaviour, initiate or sustain personal action without verbal prompting from another person in the claimant's presence for the majority of the time	15

Activity	Descriptors	Points
	16 (c) Cannot, due to cognitive impairment or a severe disorder of mood or behaviour, initiate or sustain personal action without verbal prompting from another person in the claimant's presence for the majority of the time	9
	16 (d) Cannot, due to cognitive impairment or a severe disorder of mood or behaviour, initiate or sustain personal action without frequent verbal prompting from another person in the claimant's presence	6
	16 (e) None of the above apply	0
17. Coping with change	17 (a) Cannot cope with very minor, expected changes in routine, to the extent that overall day-to-day life cannot be managed	15
	17 (b) Cannot cope with expected changes in routine (such as a pre-arranged permanent change to the routine time scheduled for a lunch break), to the extent that overall day-to-day life is made significantly more difficult	9
	17 (c) Cannot cope with minor, unforeseen changes in routine (such as an unexpected change of the timing of an appointment on the day it is due to occur), to the extent that overall day-to-day life is made significantly more difficult	6
	17 (d) None of the above apply	0

Activity	Descriptors	Points
18. Getting about	18 (a) Cannot get to any specified place with which the claimant is, or would be, familiar	15
	18 (b) Is unable to get to a specified place with which the claimant is familiar without being accompanied by another person on each occasion	15
	18 (c) For the majority of the time is unable to get to a specified place with which the claimant is familiar without being accompanied by another person	9
	18 (d) Is frequently unable to get to a specified place with which the claimant is familiar without being accompanied by another person	6
	18 (e) None of the above apply	0
19. Coping with social situations	19 (a) Normal activities (for example, visiting new places or engaging in social contact) are precluded because of overwhelming fear or anxiety	15
	19 (b) Normal activities (for example, visiting new places or engaging in social contact) are precluded for the majority of the time due to overwhelming fear or anxiety	
	19 (c) Normal activities (for example, visiting new places or engaging in social contact) are frequently precluded due to overwhelming fear or anxiety	6
	19 (d) None of the above apply	0

Activity	Descriptors		Points
20. Propriety of behaviour with other people	20 (a)	Has unpredictable outbursts of aggressive, disinhibited, or bizarre behaviour, being either:	15
	20 (a) (i)	sufficient to cause disruption to others on a daily basis, or	
	20 (a) (ii)	of such severity that although occurring less frequently than on a daily basis, no reasonable person would be expected to tolerate them	
	20 (b)	Has a completely disproportionate reaction to minor events or to criticism to the extent that the claimant has an extreme violent outburst leading to threatening behaviour or actual physical violence	15
	20 (c)	Has unpredictable outbursts of aggressive, disinhibited or bizarre behaviour, sufficient in severity and frequency to cause disruption for the majority of the time	9
	20 (d)	Has a strongly disproportionate reaction to minor events or to criticism, to the extent that the claimant cannot manage overall day to day life when such events or criticism occur	9
	20 (e)	Has unpredictable outbursts of aggressive, disinhibited or bizarre behaviour, sufficient to cause frequent disruption	6

Activity	Descriptors		Points
	20 (f)	Frequently demonstrates a moderately disproportionate reaction to minor events or to criticism but not to such an extent that the claimant cannot manage overall day to day life when such events or criticism occur	6
	20 (g)	None of the above apply	0
21. Dealing with other people	21 (a)	Is unaware of impact of own behaviour to the extent that:	15
	21 (a) (i)	has difficulty relating to others even for brief periods, such as a few hours, or	
	21 (a) (ii)	causes distress to others on a daily basis	
	21 (b)	The claimant misinterprets verbal or non-verbal communication to the extent of causing himself or herself significant distress on a daily basis	15
	21 (c)	Is unaware of impact of own behaviour to the extent that:	9
	21 (c) (i)	has difficulty relating to others for longer periods, such as a day or two, or	
	21 (c) (ii)	causes distress to others for the majority of the time	
	21 (d)	The claimant misinterprets verbal or non-verbal communication to the extent of causing himself or herself significant distress for the majority of the time	9
	21 (e)	Is unaware of impact of own behaviour to the extent that:	6

Activity	Descriptors		Points
	21 (e) (i)	has difficulty relating to others for prolonged periods, such as a week, or	
	21 (e) (ii)	frequently causes distress to others	
	21 (f)	The claimant misinterprets verbal or non-verbal communication to the extent of causing himself or herself significant distress on a frequent basis	6
	21 (g)	None of the above apply	0

Test for whether you have Limited Capability for Work-Related Activity

You will not have to do work-related activity if you can satisfy at least one of the following:

Activity	Descriptors	
1. Walking or moving on level ground	Cannot:	
	1 (a)	walk with a walking stick or other aid, if such aid is normally used
	1 (b)	move with the aid of crutches, if crutches are normally used, or
	1 (c)	manually propel the claimant's wheelchair more than 30 metres without repeatedly stopping, experiencing breathlessness or severe discomfort

2. Rising from sitting and transferring from one seated position to another	Cannot complete both of the following:
	2 (a) rise to standing from sitting in an upright chair without physical help from someone else, and
	2 (b) move between two seated positions next to one another without physical help from someone else
3. Picking up and moving or transferring by the use of the upper body and arms (excluding standing, sitting, bending or kneeling and all other activities specified in this Schedule)	Cannot pick up and move 0.5-litre carton full of liquid with either hand
4. Reaching	Cannot raise either arm as if to put something in the top pocket of a coat or jacket
5. Manual dexterity	Cannot:
	5 (a) turn a 'star-headed' sink tap with either hand, or
	5 (b) pick up a £1 coin or equivalent with either hand
6. Continence	6 (a) Continence other than enuresis (bed-wetting) where the claimant does not have an artificial stoma or urinary collecting device
	6 (a) (i) Has no voluntary control over the evacuation of the bowel

	6 (a) (ii)	Has no voluntary control over the voiding of the bladder
	6 (a) (iii)	At least once a week, loses control of bowels so that the claimant cannot control the full evacuation of the bowel
	6 (a) (iv)	At least once a week, loses control of bladder so that the claimant cannot control the full voiding of the bladder
	6 (a) (v)	At least once a week, fails to control full evacuation of the bowel, owing to a severe disorder of mood or behaviour, or
	6 (a) (vi)	At least once a week, fails to control full voiding of the bladder, owing to a severe disorder of mood or behaviour
	6 (b)	Continence where the claimant uses a urinary collecting device, worn for the majority of the time, including an indwelling urethral or suprapubic catheter
	6 (b) (i)	Is unable to affix, remove or empty the catheter bag or other collecting device without physical help from another person
	6 (b) (ii)	Is unable to affix, remove or empty the catheter bag or other collecting device without causing leakage of contents
	6 (b) (iii)	Has no voluntary control over the evacuation of the bowel

	6 (b) (iv)	At least once a week, loses control of bowels so that the claimant cannot control the full evacuation of the bowel, or
	6 (b) (v)	At least once a week, fails to control full evacuation of the bowel, owing to a severe disorder of mood or behaviour
	6 (c)	Continence other than enuresis (bed-wetting) where the claimant has an artificial stoma appliance
	6 (c) (i)	Is unable to affix, remove or empty stoma appliance without physical help from another person
	6 (c) (ii)	Is unable to affix, remove or empty stoma without causing leakage of contents
	6 (c) (iii)	Where the claimant's artificial stoma relates solely to the evacuation of the bowel, has no voluntary control over voiding of bladder
	6 (c) (iv)	Where the claimant's artificial stoma relates solely to the evacuation of the bowel, at least once a week, loses control of the bladder so that the claimant cannot control the full voiding of the bladder, or
	6 (c) (v)	Where the claimant's artificial stoma relates solely to the evacuation of the bowel, at least once a week, fails to control the full voiding of the bladder, owing to a severe disorder of mood or behaviour

7. Maintaining personal hygiene	7 (a)	Cannot clean own torso (excluding own back) without physical help from someone else
	7 (b)	Cannot clean own torso (excluding back) without repeatedly stopping, experiencing breathlessness or severe discomfort
	7 (c)	Cannot clean own torso (excluding back) without regular prompting from someone else in the claimant's presence, or
	7 (d)	Owing to a severe disorder of mood or behaviour, fails to clean own torso (excluding own back) without:
	7 (d) (i)	physical help from someone else, or
	7 (d) (ii)	regular prompting from someone else in the claimant's presence
8. Eating and drinking	8 (a)	Conveying food or drink to the mouth
	8 (a)	Cannot convey food or drink to the claimant's own mouth without physical help from someone else
	8 (b)	Cannot convey food or drink to the claimant's own mouth without repeatedly stopping, experiencing breathlessness or severe discomfort
	8 (c)	Cannot convey food or drink to the claimant's own mouth without regular prompting from someone else in the claimant's physical presence, or

	8 (d)	Owing to a severe disorder of mood or behaviour, fails to convey food or drink to the claimant's own mouth without:
	8 (d) (i)	physical help from someone else, or
	8 (d) (ii)	regular prompting from someone else in the claimant's presence
	8 (b)	Chewing or swallowing food or drink
	8 (a)	Cannot chew or swallow food or drink
	8 (b)	Cannot chew or swallow food or drink without repeatedly stopping, experiencing breathlessness or severe discomfort
	8 (c)	Cannot chew or swallow food or drink without repeated regular prompting from someone else in the claimant's presence, or
	8 (d)	Owing to a severe disorder of mood or behaviour, fails to:
	8 (d) (i)	chew or swallow food or drink, or
	8 (d) (ii)	chew or swallow food or drink without regular prompting given by someone else in the claimant's presence

9. Learning or comprehension in the completion of tasks	9 (a)	Cannot learn or understand how to successfully complete a simple task (such as the preparation of a hot drink) at all
	9 (b)	Needs to witness a demonstration, given more than once on the same occasion, of how to carry out a simple task before the claimant is able to learn or understand how to complete the task successfully, and would be unable to successfully complete the task the next day without further demonstration of how to complete it, or
	9 (c)	Fails to do any of the matters referred to in (a) or (b), owing to a severe disorder of mood or behaviour
10. Personal action	10 (a)	Cannot initiate or sustain any personal action (which means planning, organisation, problem solving, prioritising or switching tasks)
	10 (b)	Cannot initiate or sustain personal action without requiring daily verbal prompting from someone else in the claimant's presence, or
	10 (c)	Fails to initiate or sustain basic personal action without requiring daily verbal prompting given by some else in the claimant's presence, owing to a severe disorder of mood or behaviour

11. Communication	11 (a)	None of the following forms of communication can be achieved by the claimant:
	11 (a) (i)	speaking (to a standard that may be understood by strangers)
	11 (a) (ii)	writing (to a standard that may be understood by strangers)
	11 (a) (iii)	typing (to a standard that may be understood by strangers)
	11 (a) (iv)	sign language (to a standard equivalent to Level 3 British Sign Language)
	11 (b)	None of the forms of communication referred to in (a) are achieved by the claimant, owing to a severe disorder of mood or behaviour
	11 (c)	Misinterprets verbal or non-verbal communication to the extent of causing distress to himself or herself on a daily basis, or
	11 (d)	Effectively cannot make himself or herself understood to others because of the claimant's disassociation from reality owing to a severe disorder of mood or behaviour

13 Appendix 2

Weekly benefit rates 2010/11

These figures take effect from the week beginning 12 April 2010.

MEANS TESTED BENEFITS	
Income Support and Income-Based Jobseeker's Allowance	
Personal allowances	
Single person, under 18	51.85
Single person, aged 18–24	51.85
Single person, aged 25 +	65.45
Lone parent, under 18	51.85
Lone parent, aged 18 +	65.45
Couple, both under 18	51.85/78.30
Couple, one under 18	51.85
Couple, one under 18, one 25 and over	65.45
Couple both 18+	102.75
Premiums	
Carer	30.05
Disability, single	28.00
Disability, couple	39.85
Enhanced disability, single person/lone parent	13.65
Enhanced Disability, couple	19.65
Severe Disability, per qualifying person	53.65

Housing Benefit and Council Tax Benefit	
As for Income Support/Income-Based JSA or Pension Credit, except for:	
Personal allowances	
Single person, 16–24 (n/a for Council Tax Benefit if under 18)	51.85
	51.85
Lone parent, under 18 (n/a for CTB)	78.30
Couple, both under 18 (n/a for CTB)	102.75
Couple, one or both 18+	57.57
Child	
Premiums	
Family	17.40
Family, baby rate	10.50
Entitled to ESA components	
Work-related activity	25.95
Support	31.40
Working Tax Credit (annual rates)	
Basic element	1,920
Couple/lone parent	1,890
30 hours element	790
Disability element	2,570
Severe disability element	1,095
Childcare costs, one child (per week, 80% up to)	175
Childcare costs, two children (per week, 80% up to)	300
Child Tax Credit (annual rates)	
Family element	545
Baby addition	545
Child element	2,300
Disabled child	2,715
Severely disabled child	1,095

NON MEANS-TESTED BENEFITS

Bereavement Benefits [c2]

Bereavement Allowance	97.65
Widowed Parent's Allowance	97.65
Bereavement Payment (lump sum)	2,000

Carer's Allowance

Carer's Allowance	53.90
Adult dependant	31.70

Child Benefit

Only/eldest child	20.30
Per other child	13.40

Disability Living Allowance

Care component:	
Lowest rate	18.95
Middle rate	47.80
Highest rate	71.40
Mobility component	
Lower rate	18.95
Higher rate	49.85

Employment and Support Allowance

Personal allowances

Single person	
Under 25	51.85
25 or over	65.45
Lone parent under 18	51.85
18 or over	65.45

Couple	
Both under 18	51.85
Both under 18 with child	78.30
Both under 18 (main phase)	65.45
Both under 18 with child (main phase)	102.75
One 18 or over, one under 18	102.75
Both over 18	102.75
Claimant under 25, partner under 18	51.85
Claimant 25 or over, partner under 18	65.45
Claimant (main phase), partner under	65.45
Premiums	
Enhanced disability	
Single	13.65
Couple	19.65
Severe disability	
Single	53.65
Couple (lower rate)	53.65
Couple (higher rate)	107.30
Carer	30.05
Components	
Work-Related Activity	25.95
Support	31.40
Industrial Injuries Disablement Benefit and Analogous Industrial Injuries Scheme	
(Variable depending on % disablement)	
Under 18	17.87–89.35
Under 18 with dependants	29.16–145.80
Aged 18 +	29.16–145.80

Jobseeker's Allowance (contribution-based)	
Aged 16–24	51.85
Aged 25 +	65.45
Maternity Allowance	
Standard rate	124.88
Adult Dependant	41.35
Statutory Maternity, Paternity and Adoption Pay	
Standard rate	124.88
Earnings threshold	97.00
Statutory Sick Pay	
Statutory Sick Pay	79.15
Earnings threshold	97.00
NATIONAL MINIMUM WAGE (per hour)	
From October 2009	
Aged 22+	5.80
Aged 18–21 or in approved training	4.83
Aged 16–17	3.57

Endnotes

[c2] Widow's Pension and Widowed Mother's Allowance paid at same rates.

14 Index